Advance Praise for *Redemption: A Street Fighter's Path to Peace*

From the media

"A British 'karateka' offers a bone-crushing, lip-splitting, and often elegant memoir of a tough guy searching for higher meaning through the study of martial arts."

—Kirkus Reviews

"In this memoir describing how karate turned
displays passion and grit in spades."

—Christine Canfield, ForeWor

From readers

"Be prepared to think because as Mike once more to karate than kicking and punching.'"

—Lyn J. Jehu, martial artist; faculty member, University of South Wales, Department of Education and Social Sciences

"Clarke reflects on his journey in what's both an entertaining and meaningful look at a portion of the life of a martial artist."

—Alain Burrese, author, martial artist, safety self-defense instructor, attorney

"[*Redemption* is] what our karate is supposed to be about: taking the lessons learned in the dojo and applying them in the rest of one's life."

—Frederick W. Lohse III, A.M., Ed.M., martial artist, chief instructor, Kodokan Boston

"This is an uplifting story of one man's quest to find himself through the discipline of martial arts."

—Kris Wilder, author, martial artist

"A very interesting, fruitful, and at times testing and heartfelt story, *Redemption* charts a journey that has seen the author make the transition from unruly street fighter to disciplined budoka."

—Glyn Jones, renshi sixth dan, Ryusyokai Okinawa goju-ryu karate

"I have no hesitation in recommending this book to anyone who seeks to understand the transformative role karate can have in your life."

—John Mercer, author, martial artist, senior psychologist

"An insightful and eloquently written account of the adventure and the transformative potential of legitimate traditional karate training."

—Mark Tankosich, martial artist; assistant professor/ martial researcher and translator, Hiroshima University of Economics

"A work of hope that gives again order to the practice of martial arts, a work that gives an accent on the health of the human spirit, which will always be superior to physical force . . ."

—Jean-Michel Serra, seventh-dan martial artist

"*Redemption* opens a door for us all to inner peace."

—Charlotte Kirchgaesser, author, martial artist

"[*Redemption*] belongs in every serious karate student's library."

—Chuck Merriman, martial artist, former senior security officer at United Nations, personal bodyguard to many Hollywood stars (Michael Jackson, Diana Ross, Kiss)

"This is an inspirational story of a young man rescued from the brink of self-destruction by karate and how he never gave up hope, channeling his natural fighting instincts to create a life of value and great achievement."

—Garry Lever, author; martial artist; police officer, London Metropolitan Police

"The perfect tale of how the martial arts can transform us into human beings of great compassion, and hard-won wisdom."

—Matthew Gouig, author, martial artist

"An engaging and insightful account of a student's journey along the path."

—Daniel Kogan, author, martial artist

"I recommend this book to all those interested in karate, as this story tells us how budo can be a catalyst in changing our lives."

—Richard Barrett, author, martial artist

"Mike is treading the right path, a path worth following—no matter what martial art it is you train."

—John Rockstom, sixth-dan martial artist

"An intensely personal yet instantly accessible autobiography . . . A must-read for the serious martial artist of all levels."

—Thomas B. Shea, sixth-dan martial artist, author, professor at University of Massachusetts

"To my mind, Mike is just about the best martial arts writer around."

—Tony Smibert, seventh-dan martial artist; president of Aiki-Kai Australia; senior councilor, International Aikido Federation

REDEMPTION

A STREET FIGHTER'S PATH TO PEACE

By

Michael Clarke

YMAA Publication Center, Inc.
Wolfeboro, NH USA

YMAA Publication Center, Inc.
Main Office:
PO Box 480
Wolfeboro, New Hampshire, 03894
1-800-669-8892 • info@ymaa.com • www.ymaa.com

ISBN: 9781594393785 (print) • ISBN: 9781594393792 (ebook)

Edited by Dolores Sparrow
Editorial assistance by T. G. LaFredo
Cover design by Axie Breen

20220714

Publisher's Cataloging in Publication

Names: Clarke, Michael, 1955– author.

Title: Redemption : a street fighter's path to peace / by Michael Clarke.

Description: Wolfeboro, NH : YMAA Publication Center, [2016] | Includes bibliography.

Identifiers: ISBN: 978-1-59439-378-5 (print) | 978-1-59439-379-2 (ebook) | LCCN: 2016933955

Subjects: LCSH: Clarke, Michael, 1955– | Martial artists—Great Britain—Biography. | Karate—Psychological aspects—Personal narratives. | Martial arts—Personal narratives. | Boxers (Sports)—Great Britain—Biography. | Juvenile delinquents—Great Britain—Biography. | Self-realization. | Self-actualization (Psychology) | Peace of mind. | Conduct of life. | BISAC: SPORTS & RECREATION / Martial Arts & Self-Defense.

Classification: LCC: GV1113.C58 A3 2016 | DDC: 796.815/3092—dc23

Everything here is true, but it may not be entirely factual. In some cases the author has compressed events; some identifying details have been changed to protect the privacy of the people involved. The events are portrayed to the best of the author's memory.

Printed in USA.

CONTENTS

DEDICATION

THIS BOOK is dedicated to the memory of my parents, Katherine and Thomas Clarke. Sadly, their lessons of love, respect for others, and having a sense of balance in life took far longer for their youngest son to understand than they would have wished. My deep sense of regret for the shame I visited upon them during the turbulent years of my youth will remain with me forever. In return for my stupidity and utter disregard for their feelings, I received from my parents nothing but unconditional love. I now understand that loving another person, even your children, is an extraordinary act of generosity. I also recognize that it takes a particular level of maturity to accept the love of another. During my transitional years, as I was busy roaring my way through adolescence, silence would have served me better. I once thought anger to be the strongest human emotion; I now realize its influence is insignificant in comparison to the eternal force that love creates. Like many young men growing up in difficult circumstances, I wasn't up to the task of loving and chose instead the easier option: hate. As I grew older I learnt from my mistakes, and eventually the example and advice of my parents began to gain purchase in my life. Although I struggled at times, I left my world of violence behind and made my peace with society: I also spent decades thanking my parents for their gift of unwavering love and generosity.

ACKNOWLEDGMENTS

BOOKS ARE seldom written alone. Even when written in isolation there are others, waiting, ready in the wings. I would like to acknowledge my wife Kathy for her help preparing the original edition of this book and for allowing people into our private life, at least a little. Her support in the writing of this story has always been greatly appreciated, and although her arrival occurs toward the end of the book, her presence and influence in my life is all-pervasive; without Kathy, I would be a very different man and would have experienced a very different life. There are no words I know that are adequate to thank her for sharing her life with me . . . of all people.

Sincere thanks must go to my seniors and contemporaries in karate for the examples they have provided. It is the result of our experiences, or so I believe, that makes us who we are, and that being the case, I have needed everyone I have ever met or interacted with in order to be where I am now. For good or bad, without the involvement of others in my life I would have had little opportunity to discover where my personal boundaries lie. Now living the life I truly wanted, I realize my success was less about what I was prepared to do to get it and more about what I was prepared to let go so that I could find it. Letting go is perhaps man's true final frontier, for without the capacity to keep life simple, a deep and lasting contentment will remain forever beyond the horizon. Stillness, in body and mind, remains outside the experience of many, until illness or death imposes it. I have learnt not to wait for either, but to balance the chaotic nature of life with the tranquility of being still. To the men and women who, by their example, allowed me to discover this most valuable tool for living, I offer my sincere thanks and gratitude.

Finally, you would not be holding this book, or tablet, in your hand if it were not for the ongoing support of my publisher David Ripianzi and the dedicated folk at YMAA Publication Center: Thank you! But as all writers know, it is the relationship between them and their editor that really matters; it is entirely due to the tireless effort of my editor Dolores Sparrow that the jumble of awkward words that fell upon the page in front of her were transformed into something approaching literature. Given my rough skill with the pen, it was no mean task, and my appreciation runs especially deep.

PREFACE

IN 1985, in front of a borrowed typewriter, I sat down to write my first book. I had written very little since leaving school at the age of fifteen; even so, at the age of thirty, the opportunity to write a book arrived and I did what I could to take advantage of it. My journey to Okinawa a year earlier to study karate was rare. Few British karateka had reached the island before me, and upon my return to England, the interest in my experience soon led to the publication of my first magazine article. From that article, published in Terry O'Neill's *Fighting Arts International*, a book deal quickly followed. I am not Japanese, nor did my involvement with the sporting side of karate ever amount to much, so with the exception of *Moving Zen*, detailing the exploits in Tokyo of the Welshman, C. W. Nicol, there were few karate memoirs available from the hand of a Western karateka.

All that was a long time ago. Although the book, *Roaring Silence*, became something of a landmark publication in the karate literature at the time, it was not well supported by the publisher, and within a few years it fell out of production. Writing, however, like karate, has become an important part of my life, and in the years since 1985, I have written and published over five hundred articles and interviews in martial arts magazines around the world, as well as going on to write four more books. In October 2003, I finished writing a sequel to my first book, *Small Steps Forward*, publishing the book myself and limiting the print run to just five hundred copies. It sold out in six months. I've been asked many times since then if either book would ever be published again, and I'm happy to say that I am now in a position to make that happen. It has taken some time, but I'm very pleased to have made good on the promise to make my first book available once again, and here it is. It has a different title today and is twice the length of the original book, but at its core is the same message: take control of your life by taking responsibility for your actions, and reap the benefits of living a good life.

The manuscript for *Small Steps Forward* is back on my desk. Revisiting some of the moments that created the narrative found in both this book and *Small Steps Forward* has given me an opportunity to research the timeline more accurately than before and to re-examine the events shaping my karate training and personal life at that time. However, I have to say it has not always been a joyful experience. Looking back over my life often revealed events and people I would sooner forget. Nevertheless, the whole point of this book and *Small Steps Forward* is to relate something of my early and middle years walking . . . no, stumbling along the middle path that is budo karate.

The mistakes and pitfalls you will discover in the following pages will, perhaps, serve as a warning not to repeat them yourself. Neither this book nor its sequel was written to provide a detailed description of the physical training I was doing at the time, so anybody looking for such information will be sorely disappointed. The book works best if it is read with an open heart and a mind that isn't searching for a catalogue of physical techniques and a series of "Ah-ha!" moments. From the vantage point of age, it is possible to look back and connect the dots that chart one's life. Once you read this book, you may find it useful to chart your own course through life and the learning of karate. Living well and karate training share a number of common traits, the first of which is learning through experience; who among us has lived a life without errors being made and disappointments being felt?

And who, at times, has not been the beneficiary of extraordinary good luck? An important life lesson my study of karate has taught me is this: you not only have to walk your own path through life, you have to build the path as you go!

For the most part, I have kept the introductory sections of this book very similar to the earlier edition, with only a few minor changes to indicate the way I was thinking when the book was first written. Many of my thoughts back then (1985) now seem as naïve as the writing style I employed at the time. Although in fairness to myself, I can admit to receiving a great many gracious comments from a wide variety of people across the martial arts landscape. That said, I have also been on the receiving end of comments made by people who were anything but complimentary. Some of the letters I received were wrapped in threats of violence. I was never in the slightest bit concerned for my safety though, as anyone cowardly enough to issue threats anonymously was no threat to me at all. I always thought it odd that people with such a spineless disposition could, at the same time, think of themselves as karateka. I've since come to understand that the capacity for dualistic thinking is perhaps one of the stronger characteristics of human nature.

The fact that one angry young man (me) was able to find something of value in his study of karatedo gives rise to the hope that many more can do the same. The paradox of authentic karate training is not an easy one to put into plain words. Becoming nonaggressive through the study of fighting remains too unlikely a scenario in the minds of the general public. Nevertheless, in my case, spending the past four decades fighting the negative aspects of my character in the dojo has proven to be a far healthier alternative for me and society than fighting others on the street. Authentic training in karatedo, the way of karate, remains for the youth of today an underrated and underused alternative to incarceration and a life wasted behind bars.

INTRODUCTION

BECOMING A karateka, a person who pursues karate with a sincere heart and open mind, is no easy task. In this book, I am telling the story of my experiences, both good and bad, during the first ten years of studying karate: my beginning. For the first time, I am also going to look back, in more detail, at my behavior in the years leading up to entering a dojo. I'm doing so in an attempt to shed light on the choices I was making in life back then, choices that saw me languishing in a prison cell on my eighteenth birthday, instead of going out on the town with my friends to celebrate the arrival of my transition into adulthood. I think it will become evident early on that the grip I had on life as an adolescent emerging into manhood was slipping away, lost as I was in a downward spiral of frustration and violence. Had I not stumbled upon karate when I did, there is no doubt in my mind that I would have continued to live my life drifting from one drama to the next, out of control, a life that would sooner or later lead to my inevitable self-destruction. That didn't happen, and so I want to address the paradox of karate in this book, and how, with the correct guidance, it is possible to achieve a sense of balance and control in life.

When this story was first written, during the spring and summer months of 1985, I wanted to relate my limited progress in karate at the time and bring to light the mistakes I had made along the way. By doing so, my hope for the book was that readers might be saved from living through similar mistakes. I now understand that we have to learn by experience: life is an exercise in existentialism. Still, I thought an awareness of my teenage years and my early training in karate might help others avoid the same pitfalls and make their life a little bit easier to navigate. Throughout the original text, I tried my best to describe events as they actually happened, or at least, as I perceived them happening; but if, with the passage of time, I now know differently, I'll mention it. I have also tried to avoid embarrassing or offending individuals who find themselves implicated, either directly or indirectly, in the story being told. For those who come after me on the difficult but exciting path of karate, I hope this book will entertain and enlighten. I once saw a black belt as the symbol of mastery only to discover some years later that it held no such power.

There are many things capable of halting progress in karate: pride, greed, laziness, impatience, and a lack of moral courage. These are among the character traits that will bring to an end any progress made. Because of this, there is an unrelenting need to be vigilant and to guard against such things, never assuming they have been assigned to the past simply because of efforts you may have made long ago. Eastern wisdom tells us there are many different paths to the top of a mountain, but from the summit, the view is the same for all. In my experience, nothing will serve you better as you head toward the top of your own mountain than a genuine, sometimes brutal, sense of truth. Being true to yourself from the beginning will ensure any change in direction is short lived. Our ego, that false friend to us all, will do its best to persuade you that shortcuts are achievable, but believe me, there are none. It would be impossible to relate everything I experienced during the first decade of my training in karate, but I hope I have included all the major landmarks from those early years.

Back in January 1974, I was young, headstrong, impulsive, extremely violent, and very often on the edge of self-destruction.

But somehow, in that same year, I also turned a corner that would take my life in a new and very different direction, along a path I would follow for the rest of my life. Coming to grips with karate was, during my early years, an enormous burden, something I often imagined I could do without. Like a second conscience, I was confronted with the things I learnt about myself, and they plagued me with doubt as well as providing moments of clarity when I thought to myself, "I can do better than this." When a sense of consideration toward others began to surface within me, it became clear that karate was challenging me to change, and just like my transition from adolescence to adulthood, it was often a painful process. As I approached middle age and karate had been a part of my life for more years than it had not, it demonstrated its capacity to be of tremendous support, providing consistency and simplicity, and clearing my mind of so many unnecessary distractions.

Now, in my sixties, karate is like an old and trusted friend and, like all good friends, reminds me to remain true to myself. Regardless of how I have perceived karate over the years, my commitment to it has been constant, and because of that I have managed to absorb its core message—at least a little. I am by no means alone in having achieved this; indeed, there are a great many individuals around the world who have made far more progress than I have. But it is with the understanding that the study of authentic karate can, literally, change lives that I invite you to read on.

This is the story of my beginning in karate and where I was coming from on the night I walked into a dojo for the first time.

CHAPTER ONE

"A hasty temper can be provoked by insults.
Then recklessness leads to destruction."
–Sun Tzu, The Art of War

Being born the fifth child into a working-class family of six children guaranteed I had a fight on my hands from the very beginning. That my siblings and I grew to be productive members of society suggests that my childhood, although often chaotic, served me well. Dublin, Ireland, was not the attractive city in 1955 that it is today, so my birth on the fourteenth of May that year, in the upstairs front bedroom at 88 Kylemore Drive, rekindled thoughts in my father's head of returning to England. As a young man, he lived and worked in London. Throughout World War II, the long hours he toiled in an engineering plant were counter-balanced by his volunteer work as an Air Raid Warden. "Turn that light out!" was, he once told me, a common order barked at the top of his voice. After the war, he returned home to Dublin to marry his childhood sweetheart, my mother. The small end-terrace house my family occupied in the Ballyfermont district of Dublin was, by the time I arrived, already well past its capacity to provide adequate accommodation, and so in 1958, when I was three years old, the family moved to Manchester in the heart of England's industrial northwest. Employment was abundant in England after the war, and for the next two decades, the country witnessed unprecedented growth as Britain emerged from the wreckage visited upon it by the conflict. This was to be the first of a number of migrations for me, although the others that followed wouldn't come about until much later, in my adult years.

In his younger days, my father had been a keen amateur boxer and had taken part in many tournaments, winning trophies and medals that I now hold onto with quiet pride. His exploits on the football (soccer) field did not go unnoticed either, and as a young man he took to the field a number of times with the Bohemians, one of Ireland's top amateur football clubs. He was offered 'papers' (a contract) on a number of occasions from professional clubs in the Irish league, but turned the offers down. Back then, what few professional sportsmen there were, were paid a normal wage; a far cry from the obscene amounts of money they attract today. Fearful of losing his steady wage as an engineering apprentice with the government-owned Irish Rail, he continued with the amateur game. A good friend of his did the opposite, choosing instead to play football full time. In his second season, he broke his leg during a game and was carried from the field. He never played football professionally again. Unfortunately, his position as an apprentice was lost also. The saying "Fortune favors the brave" is true enough, for where would the world be without individuals who are prepared to accept the risk and move forward into unknown territory? I asked my father if he ever regretted not turning professional when he had the chance. "Not at all," he told me. "I've played the game all my life, and I kept my job."

My father died in 2009 at the age of eighty-nine; his love of football stayed with him until the end. Although he stopped playing the game in his early fifties, as Britain's oldest football referee, he took control of as many as three amateur games each week until well into his eighty-fifth year, a feat of fitness and longevity that saw him featured many times on local and national television, as well as in numerous British and Irish newspapers. As engrossed in football as my father was in his middle and later years, it was his accounts of fighting in the ring and the training he did to prepare for it that captured my imagination. Once, in an effort to make the weight for an upcoming fight, he went to work and dressed himself in two pairs of overalls, a large sweater, and a balaclava; then he climbed into the boiler of a steam locomotive and cleaned it out by hand. The plan worked perfectly. He lost the required weight and made the weigh-in for his next fight. How he fared on that occasion I don't recall, although as I said, it was never the fighting that gripped my imagination; it was the training.

The things he did to get ready for a fight fascinated me, chasing chickens around a friend's backyard, drinking raw eggs, and even using his own urine to toughen the skin on his knuckles. To me, such stories were mind-blowing, otherworldly; I was amazed that ordinary people, like my dad, would apply themselves to 'the fight' like this. Long before I heard the word 'karate', or became aware of Okinawa and the fighting art that evolved there, I knew there were men, other than the military, who trained themselves for combat. He told me, too, of the fights he had growing up on some of the poorer streets of Dublin back in the 1930s.

The reckless abandon and excessive living of the Roaring Twenties never made it to Dublin's working-class areas with quite the same heady rush they had in the city's more respectable quarters. The Great Depression that followed a few years later, however, arrived, took up residence, and flat-out refused to leave. According to my father, there was no such thing as the 'good old days': only hungry ones. When my father was a small child, his father died, so my dad grew up working odd jobs before and after school to help support his family. Shoes, he told me, were saved for church on Sundays and going to school. Other than that, it was bare feet and "Watch out for nails in the road!" He took a job delivering milk in the mornings and working after school for a butcher. Back then, animals like sheep, pigs, and chickens were commonly slaughtered in the backyard of the butcher's shop. As a small boy it was my father's job to hold on to the pig's back legs once the butcher had tethered the beast's head to a post; a special iron bar, a poleaxe, was then placed on the pig's skull, between its eyes, before being struck one mighty blow by the butcher's hammer. Death came quickly to the animal, and for his role in its demise my father was allowed to take home some of the offal, a valuable supplement to the family table.

Given the childhood my father endured, I always appreciated his reluctance to take risks later on in life when the promise of an easy living playing football was stacked up against a steady weekly wage. Settling the family in a new country was not easy for my parents. Although my father had secured work before leaving Ireland, his income provided barely enough to keep the family housed and fed. I was much too young to understand what was happening around me, but my parents had a struggle on their hands that would continue long after our life in England settled down. Decisions were made and options taken that would haunt both my parents for the rest of their lives. Families, so often the seat of great comfort and support, can sometimes become an arena of deceit and treachery, places where promises are made and broken, and help extended with hidden motives in mind. Although I knew little of such things at the time, the grown-up world swirled around me like an emotional tornado; it was a storm that would eventually weaken my mother's spirit and harden my father's.

While my mother suffered bouts of depression later in life, my father's coping methods were less internal, and I have vivid memories of his frustration spilling over into acts of destruction. I never once saw my father hit another person, but to my recollection, at least two internal doors in the house died at his hands. In spite of witnessing the occasional outbursts of anger and frustration from my father, and seeing my mother crying for no apparent reason, my childhood was a happy one. By today's standards, I grew up in abject poverty, but I never grew up unhappy or under the threat of abuse. My home was a safe place. I have never lived a day of my life without the knowledge that I am loved: I'm not sure how many people can say the same.

It must seem strange that my early childhood is remembered with such fondness. I was just three years old in 1958 when my family left Dublin to live in Manchester. As an adult myself, decades later, I would personally experience the emotional and financial difficulties that accompany the upheaval of migration when my wife and I left England to begin a new life in Australia. As a child, I knew nothing of the strain my parents were under throughout the late 1950s and into the 1960s. Because of the stress of establishing themselves in a new country, the inevitable cracks appeared and just like fissures in a volcano, they led to eruptions that rivaled anything Mother Nature had to offer. Listening to the rows going on downstairs from the safety of my bed, the cursing, the crashing, and the slamming of doors, was muted only by my head being buried deep in my pillow and my fingers pushed even harder into my ears.

The following morning it was never certain how many cups the family still had to drink from, or plates to eat off of, for they would regularly fall victim to the rage that swept through the house like a tornado on such occasions. Coming down the narrow staircase the next morning I often didn't know what would greet me when I opened the door. My parents fought over few things: one being a lack of money, the other being family interference that reached out from Dublin, across the Irish Sea, into the heart of my otherwise happy world. My dad worked as a fitter for British Rail, responsible along with others for the maintenance of rolling stock and locomotives. This was the age of steam and it was dirty, heavy, and sometimes dangerous work. He worked a three-shift rotation of lates, earlies, and nights, over three weeks, and never failed to take advantage of any available overtime; to say he worked hard scarcely does justice to his efforts during those years.

Although due to the size of my family and the mortgage on our tiny home, money was always in short supply. Fun usually came with few overheads, like visiting the local 'Sunblest' bakery to solicit 'stale cakes' or 'yesterday's biscuits' from the van drivers, or raiding the 'posh people's' gardens in Victoria Park to help ourselves to apples and pears from their fruit trees. These annual events, although falling into the realm of petty crime, were conducted without malice on our part. Nothing was ever damaged. In fact, 'scrumping' for apples was conducted more like a commando raid than a break-in. Getting in and out without being noticed only endorsed my prowess and that of my fellow street urchins as expert hunter gatherers; we were capable, too, of manufacturing our own transport from nothing more than a few discarded wheels and a length of timber. We were a pretty self-reliant bunch, as were most kids back then.

We had little expectation for shop-bought toys, and even if we did, the likelihood of getting our hands on them was slim. With the exception of Christmas and birthdays, my friends and I either found or made the things we played with. It's no wonder that my childhood memories are, at least in part, of a time when the world was a trouble-free place to be. As I recall, the only serious threat to the stability of my world was the trouble that blew regularly across the sea from Ireland. For most of my childhood, the word 'Dublin' was a dirty word, synonymous with the friction it visited upon my otherwise happy life.

In spite of the adversity experienced by my parents as they struggled to raise their family in less than ideal circumstances, my siblings and I were never under threat from the kind of child abuse seen with such regularity in the media today. Yes, my childhood situation was impoverished, but there was no sense of that in mind at the time: everyone I knew lived as we did. My parents were imbued with the natural quick wit of the Irish and the blarney flowed through our home like the soundtrack of a movie. When neighbors gathered together the 'craic'[1] was something fierce. My siblings and I grew up in a harsh world for sure, but it was an existence protected by a doting mother and a loving father.

I have fond memories of growing up on the inner-city streets of Chorlton-on-Medlock in spite of its unsavory reputation. Not exactly one of Manchester's most salubrious districts, it was a neighborhood where prostitutes worked the pavement opposite my home, illegal bookmakers took bets in back-alley cellars, and street brawls were commonplace. It was a place where Irish laborers (navvies) gave way to their liking for 'the drink' and Caribbean revelers gave in to their dislike of drunken Irishmen trying to gain access to their late night drinking clubs and shebeens.[2] As a schoolboy, I was rarely involved in fighting past being a witness, but this changed soon after I left school in 1970, at the age of fifteen. That's when my pugilistic activities began and grew rapidly, becoming a major part of who I was, or at least who I saw myself as at the time. Over the months following my departure from the world of formal education, I enrolled in a different kind of school: the classroom was the street and the lessons were provided by exchanging 'ideas' with my fellow pupils. I happily attended class as often as I could, becoming involved in violent altercations with those who sought to inflict their will over mine.

During my first year attending 'fight-school', I initiated few, if any, of the conflicts that came my way, but a teenager's life in a city like Manchester always had its problems. In the summer of 1969, the skinhead cult found its way from America to England, and all over the country, young working-class men and women were embracing it with fervor. Unlike their American counterparts, however, British skinheads had little to do with Adolf Hitler or a love of the Nazi Party. Skinheads in England were racists, for sure, but the attraction of the cult in the UK had more to do with music, fashion, and fighting, rather than establishing a new world order.

The year after I left school, in 1970, I was ready to become a skinhead. It didn't happen straightaway, as the look wasn't thought well of by prospective employers and the media were doing their best to blame everything from school truancy to the state of the national debt on the out-of-control youth who were now terrorizing the country. The idea, as far as I understood the role of a skinhead, was to look as tough and menacing as possible; so to this end I bleached Levi denim jeans, wore high-laced Doc Martin boots, and had my head completely shaved. Though such a look would cause hardly a glance these days, back in the early 1970s it was enough to make people cross the street to avoid me. Of course, looking tough didn't necessarily mean that you were, and so for most skinheads it was important to belong to a gang. From a gang you could gather the courage to front up to almost anybody or anything. The two most dominant gangs in Manchester at the time were the 'Hulme Team' and the 'Wythenshawe Crew'. Both had hundreds of members, many of whom had fearsome reputations, and though there were other gangs in other districts of the city, none came close in size or reputation.

An older brother of mine was associated with leading members of the Hulme Team, and this in turn gave me a certain amount of standing on the street by virtue of the family connection. Not that I was ever a member of the Hulme Team, or any other gang for that matter. Still, I did enjoy some fringe benefits due to the reputation held by my brother and his 'friends'. But this notoriety was not always welcome, and on a few occasions proved positively dangerous. It was not unusual to confront people who wanted to fight with me just because I was the brother of someone they didn't like. Fortunately for me, I learnt I could fight and fight well. These engagements often served as an invitation to others to try their luck, and like moths to a flame, they did just that. Frequently resembling a scene from a Wild West movie where two gunslingers would step outside to settle their differences, I'd be called out to fight in front of an expectant crowd who stood just far enough back to dodge the blood, but close enough to witness the gore.

Strange as it might seem, I began to enjoy these fights and the adulation that followed them when I emerged victorious; had I lost as often as I triumphed I may well have held a different point of view. Still, I was now averaging two fights a week, almost always on a Friday or Saturday night. Fueled by alcohol—yes, I was an underage drinker too—and a simmering anger, I began to look for conflict with people from the very crowd I'd been fascinated by: skinheads. Looking back, I simply grew tired of people who couldn't live up to their image, tough guys who weren't tough unless they were in a gang, villains who never got arrested because, in reality, they never did anything illegal. For many, being a skinhead was more about image than anything else.

A veteran of conflict on the streets and only seventeen years old, I let my hair grow again and stopped listening to reggae and ska, the music skinheads had claimed as their own. Even that irony was not lost on me: a racist group of white people had adopted the black music of the Caribbean! My attraction to fighting, however, far from diminishing, grew ever more intense. Almost every weekend saw me fighting in dance clubs, pubs, at football games, or in the street, as I made my way from one drinking establishment to another. It wasn't difficult to find a fight in Manchester's Piccadilly bus station in the 1970s or in the park that once stood alongside it. Though not exactly a killing field, Piccadilly Gardens was not the kind of place you entered after dark, unless you were confident of your pugilistic skills. Unsure of where my life was heading, I made a number of attempts to legitimize my aggression. My entry into Her Majesty's Armed Forces was denied due to poor vision in my damaged right eye, so I approached the French Foreign Legion as well as the

US Marine Corps, but again, failed to gain entry. Meanwhile, back on the street, I continued to spend my weekends searching for an opportunity to trade blows with anyone willing to stand before me.

Inevitably, my antisocial ways led to problems with my parents, and of course, the police. A trail of particularly nasty clashes led to a number of arrests throughout the latter months of 1972 and into the following year, but the arrests only added to my already growing reputation as someone to be wary of. On Friday, May 11, 1973, I found myself standing in the dock in the Manchester Crown court. As I sat on the bench waiting for the judge to enter, I knew I was facing the very real prospect of a custodial sentence. Up to then I had managed to avoid time behind bars due in part to my age and the gullibility of a judicial system that looked upon out-of-control adolescents like me as lost souls in need of nurturing, instead of the selfish, uncaring, and malicious individuals we truly were. My parents who, with all the love they could muster for their wayward son, had paid all my previous fines while clinging to the remote hope I would start behaving myself. They had, in reality, enabled my bad conduct. It is with no small amount of shame that I look back on the love of my parents and their deeply felt fear for my future well-being, and how that love was met with sullen indifference on my part. At the time, I simply didn't comprehend the additional pressure I was placing on the two people who loved me the most. It was an attitude I grew out of in the years that followed, but I have never truly forgiven myself for the trouble I brought to their door and the shame I put them through.

The incident bringing me before a judge on this occasion had its origin in my dealings with three young men that I now stood accused of beating so badly they all required hospitalization. In the weeks and months prior to our meeting, they, along with others in their gang, had taken it upon themselves to regularly and systematically beat the retarded brother of an old school friend. Not content with giving their victim a regular kicking, on one

EMBASSY OF THE
UNITED STATES OF AMERICA

DEFENSE ATTACHE OFFICE
London, England

Grosvenor Square
London W1A 1AE
13 February 1973

Dear Mr Clarke:

Reference is made to your recent letter concerning enlistment in one of the United States Armed Forces.

The sending of recruiting information within a foreign country is prohibited. However, for your guidance in this matter, an applicant for enlistment in the United States Armed Forces must be a citizen of the United States or an alien who has lawfully entered the United States for permanent residence under a normal immigrant visa.

Before an applicant for enlistment can be considered, he must meet one of the above requirements. Applications for enlistment can only be processed in the United States through a recruiting office. Additionally, you would have to take the necessary physical and mental examinations to determine your qualifications for possible enlistment. We regret that no application for enlistment can be processed until such time as you are in the United States. Even then, we cannot foretell whether you would, in fact, be enlisted since such enlistment is dependent upon qualifications and the needs of the Services at such time as an individual applies. Further, an individual must become a US citizen before he or she could be selected for Officer Training for the purpose of being commissioned in any of the US Armed Forces.

Information concerning immigration procedures may be obtained by visiting or writing to the Visa Section, United States Embassy, Grosvenor Square, London W1A 1AE, or to the US Consular Office nearest you. An immigrant visa cannot be granted for the specific purpose of enlisting in the United States Armed Forces.

Your interest in the Armed Forces of the United States is greatly appreciated.

Sincerely,

G.D. RYAN
LTJG, US Navy
Operations Coordinator

occasion they decided to add to his humiliation by stealing his belongings and leaving him stripped to his underwear in the middle of the street. When I heard this story, I was outraged, and as fate would have it, the paths of three of the gang members involved crossed mine later that very same night.

The judge said it was a case of "misplaced loyalty" toward my friend and his brother, adding that the world would descend into chaos if individuals took it upon themselves to settle matters in this way. He continued, "The charges you are facing, and of which you have been found guilty, have to be dealt with harshly. Grievous bodily harm, actual bodily harm, and assault and battery are serious assaults against the person, and while I understand what motivated you in this instance, your record before the court leads me to believe a significant custodial sentence is necessary." The judge went on to say that he hoped the two-year prison term he was about to impose would give me time to ponder my life to date, as well as the destructive direction it was headed.

I can look back now with a sense of gratitude for the 'time out' the judge provided. It allowed me to take a long, hard look at myself and to conclude that I had indeed been wasting my life for quite some time. Sitting in the holding cell below the court, I looked around at the others in the room: misfits, all of them. I knew right there and then that I'd made a major mistake. Time slowed to a standstill that day. It was difficult to collect my thoughts and get my head around what had just happened: I was going to prison! Sitting handcuffed in a prison van, as it made its way through evening traffic to one of Britain's harshest jails, brought my life into sharp focus; just two days before my eighteenth birthday I was on my way to Strangeways Prison. Renamed later as Her Majesty's Prison Manchester, it had always enjoyed a fearsome reputation. Opened in the summer of 1868 to hold a thousand prisoners, Strangeways Prison remains to this day a notable landmark on the Manchester skyline. Nicknamed 'Psychopath Central' it was, just nine years before my arrival there, the site of Britain's last execution, that of John Walby (aka Gwynne Evens), who was hung for the murder of John West, on August 13, 1964.

The Victorian prison, with its haunted-house Gothic architecture, did little to put my mind at ease. Even now, over forty years later, I can still call to mind the sound of the gates crashing closed behind me and can connect to the feeling of sickness in the pit of my stomach. The uncertainty of what the next two years might bring my way was overwhelming. It's interesting to note that Strangeways Prison has the highest number of suicides of any correctional institution in Britain; having come of age behind its walls, I am not at all surprised by this statistic.

The first month of my sentence was served in a place I knew well from the outside, but never in my wildest imagination thought that one day I would call it home. My silent vow to keep my head down, do my 'bird' (time), and get out as soon as I possibly could was already made before the gates closed. I learnt within hours of my arrival that life on the inside bore no resemblance at all to the life I lived on the outside. What counts for normal behavior among people depends entirely on which side of the wall you are talking about. On the inside, the rules were basic but clear, and life was at times brutally simplistic. Being stabbed with a 'shiv' (homemade knife, made from almost anything, also known as a 'shank') just because you picked up the piece of toast someone else had his eye on, was not such a strange event; and though I shake my head in disbelief now, I can remember the day I almost suffered the same fate all because of a roast potato! Fortunately, I was able to face down my would-be attacker that day, and convince him he would either have to kill me and face the rest of his life behind bars, or I would eventually get out of the prison hospital and kill him. Inside, life was often that simple, and often that ludicrous.

Discipline was strict, and I learnt too that the screws (prison officers) were not there to help. As much as I could tell, they were there to have a quiet life and heaven help anybody who disturbed their peace. To underscore this idea of 'peace and quiet' firmly in the minds of those new to life on the 'in', each new intake of prisoners was provided with a practical demonstration of the consequences awaiting anybody who deviated from the established order. As fate would have it, I was chosen to be the recipient of the demonstration for this particular intake. In the center of the cellblock, at the spot where the four wings came together in a hub, was a large octagonal iron grill set into the floor, in the middle of which stood a large octagonal table made of wood. On the table lived the register of inmates and a second book containing both the standing orders as well as the orders of the day. A small group of inmates fresh from the induction center, myself included, had been left by the grill by two screws with an order to stand still and be quiet, which we dutifully did.

We looked like contestants in a bizarre game show in which we had all won the same set of prizes: a bunch of ill-fitting clothes, one blanket, two sheets, a pillowcase, and a piss-pot. Within moments of being left alone, another screw walked toward us, a man so impeccably turned out it was easy to imagine that a quick turn of his head might just see him cut his throat on the blade-like edge of his shirt collar. This man was no stranger to an iron, as the razor-sharp line of his shirt collar was repeated on the trousers and sleeves of his uniform. That he was a drill sergeant, in his own head at least, was immediately obvious and something I could have accommodated had the dream stopped there; but this man was intoxicated by the power he had over others and took every opportunity to indulge his fantasy at the expense of those entrusted to his care.

He was looking for someone to participate in his next demonstration and I had the misfortune of being the one he chose. Fixing his gaze on me, he made quite a show of placing his clipboard on the table, and then, with a great deal more deliberation than necessary, he placed his pen upon the clipboard: he then turned his full attention my way. The insults he began hurling made little impact, as I was feeling as low as I had ever felt in my life and was already lost in a crippling sense of captivity. I could barely hear a word he was saying, so it wasn't until his second or third scream for me to “Come here!” that his command finally registered. As I began to move toward him, my arms still loaded with my newly acquired belongings, he stepped forward and caught me with a punch square on my jaw. It was a blow that sent me sprawling, along with my bedding, clothes, and piss-pot, back across the iron grill. It was then explained to everybody present that the grill was out of bounds to inmates, and infringements of the slightest kind would be dealt with harshly. No one in the group, least of all me, was left unconvinced as to the sanctity of that grill. So another demonstration had been conducted and another group of young men had been put on notice. As for my jaw, well, the bruising which I was later asked to explain and which I chose to lie about, settled down after a few days.

In truth, I had been hit much harder on the street. Still, I wasn’t sure how much I would be able to take before hitting back, and that worried me. Not hitting back was a new concept for me, one that along with my new reality I was going to have to learn to deal with. Left alone for the most part after the demonstration, I was slowly beset by a feeling of dread. I made a terrible mistake, choosing a way of life that focused on fighting, drinking, and having a bad attitude. In prison, such fame, or infamy, that I had enjoyed on the street counted for nothing. I am not ashamed to say that for a lot of the time I was in Strangeways I was fearful, although I would have died a hundred times over before showing it. My apprehension stemmed from the continual uncertainty of what could happen once my cell door was opened, and whether or not I had it in me to walk away from trouble. From day one of my life behind bars, I was meeting people whose sentence had been lengthened due to fighting and causing havoc, and I knew that I too could easily go the same way. I had little confidence that I could control my rage once it was ignited, and in this place, there was no shortage of people willing to introduce a spark to an already short fuse.

Between the idiots I mingled with and the strict discipline imposed by the screws, it was often a struggle to get through each day. My only relief came when I was 'banged-up', the term used for being locked in your cell. Because I was serving time for crimes of violence, I had a cell to myself; the solitude came as a great relief from the day-to-day contact with my fellow inmates. The residents on each of the four landings in K-wing took turns to 'enjoy' an evening's recreation before being returned to their cells at 8:30 p.m. Every fourth night, prisoners were allowed to spend time on the wing outside their cell, watch TV, play table tennis, or listen to music. I often chose to forgo spending time with my neighbors, preferring instead to find distraction in the pages of a book. Besides, recreation was often used as an opportunity to settle old scores, and I had no desire to get caught up in any peripheral fallout from the outbreaks of violence that kicked-off at least once a week.

I was learning to live life by the bell. I was awakened from sleep by a bell, forewarned that the cells were being opened by a bell, ordered to 'slop-out'[3] by a bell, go down to the landing to collect my meals by a bell, and get back to my cell by a bell. Perhaps the most difficult thing about prison life in 1973 was the imposed decision making; my day was planned for me down to the minute, and I had no say at all. I simply did what was expected of me when the bell rang. A half-hour passed between the first bell of the day to the second, and in that time I had to be out of bed and dressed, ready to slop-out when the doors were opened immediately following the second bell. Fifteen minutes later a third bell signaled the call for breakfast, and I made the long walk to the ground floor of the wing to collect my food on a tin tray, before making the long walk back up to my cell: I never ate a hot meal in Strangeways.

The bells that followed throughout the day saw inmates return their breakfast trays and set out their beds, ready for cell inspection.

The top and bottom sheets were taken off the bed and folded lengthways into long strips about a foot wide. The blanket was spread over the mattress and the corners tucked neatly under in a precise way, once referred to as 'hospital corners'. The two sheets were then laid on top, along the length of the bed at either side, and again, tucked in at both ends to make a crisp, straight, line. Between the two broad white strips made by the sheets every item of issued kit—soap, toothbrush, and spare clothing—was laid out in a particular way, beginning from the top of the bed and working down to the bottom. My bed had to be neat, clean, and have nothing missing from the range of kit that had been issued; if even a single item was absent or in the wrong place on the bed, I would be placed on report,[4] an act that always resulted in a loss of privileges. The laying out of kit each day was all about the prison system exercising discipline, of course, but it had for the screws, a secondary significance: personal control.

The daily inspection of cells may have been routine, but it wasn't the only time the screws would visit. Random inspections were common, as were searches. One day, about an hour after the usual inspection had taken place, the door to my cell swung open unexpectedly and three screws entered. I was ordered to stand with my hands behind my back and my face up against the wall. With my legs spread and my feet about a yard back from the wall, I was now leaning forward against the wall, my bodyweight resting on my forehead; it was a difficult position to hold, and the immediate vulnerability of the position was exactly what the screws wanted. As I maintained the required position, dealing with the growing discomfort of my situation, the bed was tipped over, sending my kit sprawling to every corner of the cell. Neatly folded clothing was shaken and thrown about and the toothpaste squeezed from its tube to fall in a sticky mess on the floor. The visit lasted no more than a few minutes, after which I was told to clean my cell ready for a governor's inspection in half an hour. What pleasure grown men derived from such acts of bastardy I'll leave for others to decide. Perhaps they thought it enhanced their manhood. Who knows? It didn't break my spirit though; if anything it only made me appreciate my own stupidity, for I alone, by virtue of my poor choices, had put myself in the cell, in the prison, and in the hands of the screws and their childish dreams of being tough guys.

In April 1990, seventeen years after my time on K-wing, Strangeways Prison exploded into anarchy. For twenty-five days, hundreds of prisoners destroyed large sections of the jail in a riot that led to the death of one prisoner, forty-seven prisoners being hurt, and one hundred and forty-seven prison officers being injured. For decades, prison officers had controlled inmates with intimidation, violence, and the misuse of sedatives, in particular, the drug Largactil, also known as the 'liquid straight-jacket'. In a world within walls, closed off from the rest of humanity, prisoners lived a Dickensian existence at the mercy of prison officers who were charged with their welfare. That spring, the oppression had become too much for some, and following a series of beatings, a group of prisoners decided to take retribution. The riot began in the chapel before spreading quickly to other parts of the prison.

The one fatality of an inmate came about not at the hands of the authorities but from his fellow prisoners. Derek White was an alleged sex offender remanded into custody while awaiting trial on charges of indecent assault and buggery. Under the protection of 'rule 43', a designation applied to inmates who needed protection from the general prison population, White, along with others, was attacked and beaten by the mob when it burst into the segregated part of the prison. He suffered several head wounds, a dislocated shoulder, and internal chest injuries, no doubt the result of being stomped on; but he didn't die from the beating immediately. Instead, White passed away in the North Manchester General Hospital to where he had been evacuated. The screws may not have dealt the blows that killed White, but their cowardice, in my opinion, contributed to his death.

While I have little sympathy for prison inmates, I recognize how grievances surface, and how in this case, given the behavior of some officers in Strangeways, those grievances gave way to aggression. I believe prison should be a place of punishment, and it should discourage a return visit; it should be a harsh environment loaded heavily with discipline and toil: but it should never be brutal. In the brief time I spent in Strangeways during the spring of 1973, I was allowed outside for one hour a day to exercise: walking the line. I was allowed one communal shower a week, issued a single sheet of paper to write a letter once a week, and allowed a one-hour visit every second weekend. During the visits, no physical contact was allowed; there was no chance to feel the warmth of another person who was dear to you, not your girlfriend, nor your mother, or even your child if you had one. The Strangeways riot, described by the Greater Manchester Police Commissioner as "the most savage incident of its kind ever experienced within the British prison service," was a turning point in the treatment of prisoners in Britain.

In the weeks and months following the riot it was noted in an official report that the confrontation may well have been contained within the chapel had the prison officers who were first called to the original disturbance not abandoned the gate to the chapel block and run for safety. When I read that, I smiled to myself, remembering my own encounters with several officers and the lack of moral fiber that shone from their eyes, eclipsed only by the brightness of the shiny silver buttons on their tunics. That they abandoned their post and ran, allowing the riot to escalate out of control, came as no surprise to me. A great many reforms were instigated following the government-sponsored "Woolf Report," in which twelve recommendations and two-hundred and four accompanying proposals were put before Parliament by Lord Woolf.

Personally, I think, at least in Great Britain, the pendulum has now swung from one extreme to the other. These days, prison inmates are allowed to wear their own clothes, have a TV and radio in their cells, and play computer games; they have access to public phones, allowing them to call home whenever they feel like it. Ironic clichés abound as a result of successive governments' inability to grasp the equilibrium of crime and punishment. Examples of psychopaths gaining a tertiary education in psychology and fraudsters who graduate with a degree in accounting point to a system that remains out of whack.

When I think of the situation as it stands in Britain today, I am reminded of an old adage: the road to hell is paved with good intentions. I'm also left wondering where the sense of punishment is in all this 'humane' treatment of offenders. Where is their sense of loss to come from if they stand to lose very little by their imprisonment? When the time came, I was relieved to leave the walls of Strangeways behind, even though my relocation to another tight-security prison was not much better. My five weeks within Strangeways' walls had made a lasting impression; the jail had seen the last of me and would claim no more of my life. As I was bussed across the country to be incarcerated elsewhere, I silently confirmed my intention to stay out of trouble, but it was a promise that would prove easier to make than to keep. Both of my brothers served in the British Army, and each can remember their army number. Looking back to the beginning of my nineteenth year on earth, I can only boast a prison number, 900822, and a Strangeways' cellblock address, K.4.10. (K-wing, landing number 4, cell number 10). Unlike my brothers, my numbers evoke no sense of satisfaction.

Life in Hindley Closed Borstal[5] was only marginally better than at my previous address. After a month of evaluation and psychological testing in Strangeways, it was decided my sentence needed to be served under continuing tight security; I was considered too volatile and violent for anything other than the strictest regime, so there would be no open fields on a prison farm for me. Although I thought of myself at the time as no great threat to anybody who was no threat to me, society was looking at me through a different lens. To the rest of the world I was a strong young man who was prone to extraordinary outbursts of violence and rage. Looking back now, it would be a difficult assessment to disagree with.

Since leaving school at the age of fifteen, I had failed to develop a vision for how my life might unfold. I had no sense of direction, and almost immediately, my lack of education led to frustration that in turn boiled over into violent conduct. I had demonstrated time and time again that my hair-trigger temper was uncontrollable, and how, once my anger was ignited, there was no stopping me. All but the most determined and able combatants who stood against me had suffered badly for it. Since being incarcerated, I had tried my best to stay out of trouble because it became clear to me very early on that I could not beat the system: no one could. The screws had the world inside the walls exactly as they wanted it. At times, the frustration I felt from holding my tongue and keeping my fists in my pockets brought me to tears when I was alone in my cell. I hated being locked up, I hated the screws, and I hated my fellow inmates; but most of all, I hated myself for putting me there.

At least in Hindley there were no hardened old lags on the lookout for a chance to get their hands on and into the tender flesh of teenage boys. Still seared into my memory was an episode that took place during my very first week in Strangeways when I witnessed an attack on 'fresh meat', as we were known. It happened when a small group of us were being escorted from one part of the prison to another: the speed and nature of the assault left me staggered. Pinned against a locked gate by older inmates on the other side, several pairs of hands reached through the bars like some kind of vengeful octopus and violated the boy being held fast in their grip; the attack lasted less than half a minute, but in that time the boy had his trousers pulled open and had been entered from the rear by grubby fingers belonging to who knows who. And all the while, another pair of hands covered the young boy's eyes, and held his mouth firmly shut. When the screw returned, he found us on the opposite side of the corridor to where he left us and a sobbing teenager slumped in a pile of tears by the gate to the adults' workshop. His clothes were disheveled, his dignity had been stolen, and his spirit was now broken beyond repair.

It was a salutary lesson for everybody who witnessed the attack. We were now living on another planet, a world where there were predators and prey, and we were the latter. I never saw that boy again after he was taken away to the hospital wing, but I heard later that he had tried to commit suicide. He was only serving a six-month sentence for being in a stolen car; he wasn't the driver, just a passenger. He had now paid a very high price for his sin. My time in Strangeways Prison was sufficient to convince me to change my ways. I had seen enough during my stay there to assure me that life behind bars was in fact no life at all. Had I been allowed, I would have returned home a changed person even then, but by the time I left the walls of Strangeways behind, I was still looking at another twenty-three months of incarceration ahead of me: ample time to ponder the choices I'd been making in life up to that point.

Hindley has, since my time there, become a young offenders prison, but back in 1973 it was used to house the very worst of Britain's underage criminals. Normally, young delinquents served their time in the facility closest to their home, but if they proved to be particularly problematic, then they were shipped off to Hindley; as a result, this particular Borstal was like no other in the country, for it was home to troublemakers from all over the UK. Each of the four cellblocks (wings) in Hindley had a 'daddy', a tough guy who the screws tolerated because it helped make their lives easier. Acting as an unofficial 'godfather', daddies ran things like the black market in tobacco and protection rackets. They influenced who got what to eat and controlled the supply of hot water in the communal bathrooms. Along with the help of a few heavies, new inmates were made aware of the pecking order by the daddy soon after their arrival, via threats of unspeakable acts of violence against those who didn't accept their authority.

In West Wing, my new home, the release of the incumbent daddy, just the week before my arrival, had left a power vacuum that was in the process of being filled by a group from Newcastle, in England's northeast. Their ambition to take control of the wing was unorganized and, frankly, lacked the cruelty and sadistic approach that was necessary to bring people into line. As a result, some capitulated while others like myself chose not to; this led to a few interesting 'conversations' with various members of the group. With the absence of a clear pecking order among the inmates, a great deal of tension was in the air, and the prospect of a fight erupting once the cell doors were opened was never far away. I was not the only new arrival refusing to fall into line. There were others too, but due to my small stature, at just five and a half feet tall, I guess I was considered an easy target by the Newcastle gang. As far as I was concerned, that was their first mistake.

I had been counseled by a screw in Strangeways to take each day as it came, not to think about my release date, but to live in the moment instead. Although I didn't recognize it at the time, it was a pearl of wisdom worthy of a Zen master. I was trying very hard to stay in control but it wasn't easy; back then, I solved most of my problems with my fists. It was a strategy that had served me well for the most part, but had ultimately let me down. I was aware of that and aware also of the consequences in prison if I let my fists do the talking. So even though the candidates for the daddy position did their best to intimidate me, I managed to avoid a physical confrontation. Everything was going fine, and perhaps because of that I let my guard down. Over a week had passed without incident. I was beginning to settle into a routine and even, dare I say it, make friends. The friendships made inside are not like those made in the outside world. They are more like a cluster of alliances against a threat from greater numbers than you can deal with on your own. Favors are exchanged and bonds made between 'friends', but no one ever really trusts each other. Alliances can, and do, change and when that happens, an individual's situation can change dramatically overnight. From a position of relative safety, it was possible to find yourself exposed to any number of threats due to a shift in alliances. The people I became 'friendly' with I already knew from Strangeways; they too were handy with their fists, which meant the boys from Newcastle would have to work hard to get me on my own if they were planning to 'make an example' of me. I had no fear of a confrontation. I just didn't want the fallout that would come as a result, or any extra time being added on to my sentence.

Induction into the general population of Hindley took planning, young men under pressure can be volatile, and so for a short time there were few demands made upon a new arrival. But all that changed when individuals were assigned work details and expected to fit in with their fellow inmates. Over three weeks a new arrival's introduction to work consisted of a number of different jobs, with everybody beginning in the garment shed. Learning to use a sewing machine and mastering a straight line of stitching proved beyond the ability of many. So the second week often brought great relief when new inmates moved next door to the metal recycling shed, a smelly, noisy, and dirty environment, where lengths of old lead-coated copper cable were hacked at for eight hours a day in order to retrieve the precious metal. Week three saw work move to the electrical shed, where mind-numbing days were spent assembling electrical plugs. To ensure an industrious output, a quota of four hundred plugs per inmate per day was in place, with the loss of privileges in store for any inmate who failed to reach his daily quota.

After three weeks, the job situation changed. Depending on suitability, and to a lesser degree, choice, inmates were moved into jobs that the Borstal's management hoped would keep them gainfully occupied for the length of their stay. The three-week assessment, coupled with a formal interview that took place during the second week, dictated each inmate's work detail for the immediate future, at least. Movement between jobs was permitted, but it was rare, given that most inmates used their position in the 'good' jobs as leverage to improve their supply of tobacco and other sundries. A kitchen hand, for example, could solicit a few extra cigarettes by slipping extra food onto the right tray, or making sure someone received a larger piece of 'duff' (cake) for supper. They could also dish out punishment on behalf of others, for a price, by spitting on an inmate's food, urinating in their tea, or worse, ejaculating in the soup that was sometimes served for supper during the colder months. I never drank soup in Hindley: not once! I only ever drank tea I saw poured directly from the urn, and watched carefully as my food was dished out at every mealtime. Once, when I suspected my duff had been contaminated, I threw it out the window for the birds to eat. The following morning, smiling faces confirmed I was right to give the birds a feed. I left it a while, and then took my revenge with great satisfaction.

It took a little while, but eventually I secured a job as one of the 'off-wing' cleaners. Each morning I left the cellblock and spent my time cleaning and polishing places like the chapel, offices, and the visitors block. For the most part, I spent the day alone and was happy to be in my own company. I usually arrived back on the wing an hour before the others, and so had the luxury of having the communal shower room to myself most days. For the final month at Hindley, I worked on the prison farm. This allowed me a significant level of liberty as it meant going outside the walls and spending my days one step closer to freedom. On the farm, I helped to raise Hereford calves and get them ready for market; but it was only during my final week that I realized exactly what that meant. Unlike the calves that left the farm for the final time to meet their appointment with the slaughter man, I left the farm on my final day heading toward a far brighter future. But all that was some way off, for I had yet to navigate my immediate future.

During my second week at Hindley, I found myself with a group of other new arrivals waiting to be assessed for future work details. It was a slow process and the morning was dragging on. Sitting in a room with nothing to do became too much for some; so once the usual topics of adolescent conversation were exhausted, a spitting competition got underway to see who could propel their saliva the farthest. It wasn't long before the game deteriorated into a free-for-all, with morons spitting at each other from all directions. Until that point three of my new-found friends and I had been sitting to one side of the growing excitement; when one of the idiots doing the spitting was hit on the side of the face by a huge green gob of phlegm, he turned on me, convinced I had spat on him. Unhappy with the sticky mess he was trying to remove from the back of his ear, his threats turned personal and specific.

A detailed description of what he and his friends were going to do to me spewed from his mouth, but the real mistake he made was in calling me a bastard. Back then, that one word was guaranteed to bring me to the boil and set in motion a cascade of events that had only two possible outcomes, both of which involved serious injury and an ambulance. His right hand was resting on the edge of a desk, so I raised my knee and stamped my foot down as hard as I could on his fingers. His screams echoed through the corridors of the education wing and brought the screws running. They arrived just in time to save the young man from serious injury, but too late to stop me from following through with my kick. By the time I was dragged off him, he already had three broken fingers, a broken nose, a split lip, and was suffering from hair loss due to the huge clump I was holding in my hand. Had I not been stopped by the screws when I was, I would have gone on to do a lot more to him, for once my temper was aroused it abated only when either I or my adversary lay motionless.

The injured inmate was taken to the hospital while I, having been at Hindley for a mere ten days, was now on my way to the 'block' for ten days' punishment. In the block, a strict regime of discipline was enforced with a rigidity that bordered on mental abuse. I have no doubt today's liberal attitudes toward punishment would see my treatment in the block as unacceptable, but as someone who has experienced it, I would argue otherwise: punishment should be punishing. Silence was the golden rule in the block, as I and the other residents, whom I was never allowed to see, lived out our days in isolation. The cells were not as big as a regular cell, and once inside I spent twenty-three hours out of every twenty-four, locked in it. With only a small container to use as a toilet, a wooden chair to sit on, and a wooden table to house a jug of water and a book, the cell was completely empty. An orange light in the middle of the ceiling burned twenty-four hours a day; the only natural light entered through a tiny square window set high up on the back wall.

The walls in the block were thick enough to dull the screams of my co-inhabitants when they cracked under the strain of the harsh discipline and the relentless silence, but not thick enough to drown them out altogether. I never saw any of the other inmates, although I sometimes heard them crying for their mothers at night. Each day in the block began with a loud bell at five-thirty in the morning. The main light in the ceiling came on and that was the signal for me to get ready for 'opening up'. Each of the ten cells opened onto a central open space, a large rectangular hall that was kept immaculately clean. When the door was unlocked, I was told to

"Step out!" Once outside the cell I was ordered to remove the long, one-piece, cotton nightshirt I had climbed into at eight o'clock the previous evening. Now fully naked, I put my underwear and trousers on before being escorted by two grim-faced screws to the small sink and mirror at one end of the central hall. Here I slopped-out, and washed my face and under my arms; I took a shave each morning too, but with a safety razor that left my jaw looking like it had seen a broken bottle rather than a shaving device.

The area was then cleaned and left spotless before I was escorted back across the hall to my cell to complete getting dressed. Once that was done, I entered the cell and removed the plank of wood that served as my bed, folded the two sheets into neat piles, and took all three items to a room at the far end of the hall. I then returned to the cell and brought inside the small table and chair I'd placed outside the previous evening. Along with a jug of water, a book, and my makeshift toilet, there would be nothing else in the cell with me for the rest of the day. The two meals I received each day were served through a hatch in the door. There was a time limit on how long I had to eat my meals; anything that wasn't consumed by the end of it I had to pass back through the hatch when the trays were collected. At the discretion of the screws, prisoners on the block were allowed to exercise, alone, in a large cage for one hour each day. I remember this 'privilege' was not extended to me on two occasions during my tenure, why I am not sure. On the block, it was forbidden to speak unless asked a direct question, so on each occasion I let the moment pass and continued to count the days until my return to the regular prison population.

At eight o'clock each evening, following the sound of the bell, the cell door opened and I was ordered once again to step out. I removed the table, the chair, the book, and the water jug, and placed them neatly next to the doorway; if necessary, I also slopped-out. I then collected my plank (bed), the two sheets, and my nightshirt from the room at the end of the hall. Putting the plank and the sheets inside my cell, I stepped outside the door to undress and once again climb into the nightshirt. My clothes were then folded neatly and placed on the chair before I stepped back into the cell and the door closed and locked behind me. With one thin sheet over the hard wooden 'bed' and one sheet to act as a cover, I became adept at switching arms to act as a pillow whenever I turned over. Sleep never came easily while I was in the block. The long hours of inactivity throughout the day did little to make my body tired, and the orange light that was never turned off made it difficult to drift off in the darkness once the sun had gone down. Oddly, I became accustomed fairly quickly to the plank of wood that was my bed. I never found it comfortable, but it was better than lying on the cold floor and that was the thought I held onto each evening. Life in the block was harsh, but in another way it was also simple. I could at least read a book during the day, and in doing so, remove myself from my surroundings by losing myself in the story. The twice daily undressing in front of the screws, the plank of wood that passed for a bed, the absence of darkness when it came time to sleep, and the burden of strict silence produced the mental beating that awaited those who found themselves taking the lonely walk to the northwestern corner of Hindley where the punishment block stood.

By today's standards, I dare say many would consider the regime excessive, perhaps cruel; but as someone who has been on the receiving end of it, I see little wrong with discipline or the premise that punishment should be just that: punishing. In 1973 I had, and still have today, no problem with the notion of being punished by society for my antisocial behavior. As a number of people within the prison service were quick to point out, if I couldn't do the time, then I shouldn't have done the crime: a view that for me, remains difficult to argue with. I had no problem taking whatever punishment the system placed in front of me, but I had no time at all for individuals who sought to capitalize further on my situation. As much as I enjoyed a fight, I have always detested bullies. My time in the block so soon after my arrival had served to give notice to all those who might have thought to make a move on me; I wasn't shy about fighting, or slow about it either.

My repatriation to the normal prison community brought with it a certain level of respect from the other inmates; they knew how tough conditions were in the block, where the usual placement lasted just two or three days. Returning unbroken, having endured ten days, was a powerful statement. I could not only give a beating, but I could take one too! Over the next few days the inmates jostling for the new position of 'daddy' made their approaches and offered me their gifts and promises, but I was having none of it. I took their roll-ups[6] and their chewing gum, their toothpaste and their shampoo, but I declined every invitation to align myself with anybody. My aim was to get through the next two years with as little drama as possible and return to the real world as soon as I could. There was a chance of going before a parole panel after just six months, if my record stayed clean, but I had already shown that my aggressive nature was still smoldering below the surface. It's tough to stay away from trouble when trouble comes looking for you, yet for a while I managed to do just that.

You may remember earlier I mentioned an incident where I faced the prospect of being stabbed, and maybe even being killed, over nothing more than a roast potato. Well, that was about to happen, and it all began innocently enough one evening after work. In Hindley, apart from supper, which consisted of tea and cake or sometimes a cup of soup and was consumed in your cell after lock-up, all meals were taken communally in a large room set aside for the purpose, called the canteen. Within the canteen, there was an unwritten, but strict, rule about who sat where. Place yourself on the wrong chair or at the wrong table and your life and immediate health were likely to change in an instant. Although the screws called up each table to the counter to be served their meal one at a time, the inmates who served the meals were often under the control of the daddy. They might be in debt to him, or be victims of a protection racket, so they sometimes skimped on the portions of inmates who would not complain and gave the extra food to the daddy, or those in his favor.

Due to my reputation, I never failed to receive my due plateful but others at my table were not always so fortunate. It was a scam that always appeared cowardly to me. The food was dreadful and never plentiful. Still, mealtimes were a highlight of the day, so it just seemed wrong to me that certain people would exploit the situation for their own benefit. As I said, I never did like bullies, so one evening when the tablemate in front of me was denied a roast potato and told to move on, I reached over and grabbed the largest potato on the tray and dropped it on his plate. My face must have said it all because the server didn't say a word and dished up my potato as if nothing had happened. The incident caused a hushed rumble of disbelief to ripple around the canteen. I'd made a call on a racket others had put in place. They would have to do something about that or risk losing their ability to continue running it. They made their move that evening on the second-floor landing.

'Bang up', the term used for being locked in your cell, was at nine o'clock each evening, and one hour later, it was lights out. As I made my way, alone, to the top landing where my cell was located, I was met by the gang running the food scam. I was halfway up a flight of stairs when they stepped out from the shadows: so I stopped. The staircase was much narrower than the landing so if a fight kicked off, as I expected it to, they would have to come at me one at a time. Aware of the situation themselves, they called me up "for a word" but I was not about to have this fight on their terms. Besides, walking farther up the stairs would have momentarily put my head level with their feet, and that would have given them too much of an advantage. No, if they wanted to get their hands on me they were going to have to do it one at a time: on the stairs. A shank, a kind of homemade knife, was brandished and passed from one pair of hands to another in a way reminiscent of the queen card in a game of find-the-lady.

The implication was clear, I was going to be hurt, and I would never know for sure by whom: at least that was their plan. But I knew from experience that the longer their leader talked the less likely it was he would do anything. Truly dangerous people offered no preamble and they gave no warning; they just did whatever it was they had in mind to do. With each passing moment, I became more and more confident that none of the people in front of me was really dangerous. Oh sure, they were capable of giving me a beating if the circumstances were just right, but my sense of insecurity was quickly diminishing. At some point, my would-be attackers began to realize this impasse was going nowhere, and as a couple of inmates passed me on their way up to their cells, I seized the opportunity to move onto the landing with them. I immediately stood toe-to-toe with the leader. The only thing stopping him from going over the rail to the floor below was my desire to avoid more trouble, which would result in more punishment.

Although the punishment block held no fear for me, life was a lot easier here on the wing. So I made it clear to him that we needed to move on from this or he would have to kill me there and then. If he didn't, if he and his cronies only gave me a beating, then I would get out of the prison hospital at some point in the future, and I would kill him! I'm not sure if I actually meant it, but my tone of voice and posture was enough to convince him I did, and that was good enough. By now, there were a great many eyes around the landing and stairwell to witness what was happening. From that day on, my time at Hindley passed without incident. My willingness to take situations like this to the ultimate conclusion straightaway stemmed from two motivating factors. The first was I have always despised overbearing cowards, and the second was my feelings back then that I had nothing to lose. My life was heading nowhere, fast. I knew it; I just didn't know how to stop it. A couple of months later, changes were made to the intake of prisoners, and Hindley became the exclusive home of local delinquents. It was perhaps a good thing, as much of the tension in the jail was caused by the rivalry between regional football clubs. Footage of rioting fans shown on Saturday evening's six o'clock news often led to outbreaks of violence somewhere within the walls of Hindley. Under the new system, the residual problems didn't stop, but they diminished, as there were now fewer football clubs represented among the general population.

With the exception of an addiction, where your life is dictated by the tether of your craving and the cruelty with which it pulls on you, prison is without doubt the greatest waste of a life one can imagine. Like everybody else I met inside, I vowed never to return, but for that to happen it was going to take a major change in the choices I made. I was released early from Hindley in December 1973, having served eight months behind bars; the remainder of my sentence was to be served under license, with strict parole conditions that would see me returned to prison should I break them. For the next sixteen months, I reported to a probation officer who kept a close eye on me. My return home was a mix of joy and sadness for my parents; although happy to welcome me back into their home, they remained fearful that I would slip back into my old ways. Convincing them that I had changed would take time. Words alone wouldn't be enough. I had to grow up, and I had to do it soon. My conduct had visited enough heartache and humiliation on them to last a lifetime; I had no desire to continue bringing any more their way. My father managed to secure a job for me at the foundry where he worked.

Having left the railway, he was now running the internal store and spare parts department for a nationwide leaf spring company.

Leaf springs form part of the suspension system on off-road vehicles and trucks. The bigger the vehicle, the bigger the springs. My new job was in the foundry where the springs were made and repaired. It was hot and heavy work, and dangerous too. Burns were commonplace and sometimes severe, although I was fortunate in that I never suffered as badly as others did. This was not the kind of work you did for the love of it, but I needed to build a record of employment and develop a sense for earning a living. As the months passed, I was given more and more responsibility and eventually I operated my own gas-fired furnace. This occupation was not for me, and I knew I would leave it behind as soon as an opportunity presented itself. I continued at the foundry for a little over a year, but eventually left when I found work with a furniture company. My life was only somewhat calmer now; I drank less on the weekends and fought with others only if they were determined to fight with me. I had no desire to return to a cell and tried very seriously to live a life that did not include brawling, but it wasn't easy because my anger was still quick to emerge on a number of occasions.

My freedom was jeopardized by a lack of control that was aided and abetted by alcohol-induced poor choices. That I managed to avoid the police was due more to good luck than good judgment, and this caused me to think again about some of the choices I was continuing to make. In the first few months after returning home, I had broken the conditions of my parole a number of times without being caught. One fight resulted in my being stabbed in the abdomen and losing a good amount of blood. I should have gone to the hospital. Instead, I went to a friend's house and cleaned up in his kitchen. And then, as I sat in his car, pinching the open wound in my side together with my fingers, we made the seventy-five-mile drive to the coastal resort of Ryle in North Wales. I couldn't risk going to the emergency department at a local hospital. Had a cop been there and begun asking questions, I would have found myself heading back to prison once the stitches were in place. Besides, I had no idea which hospital my challenger had been taken to; soon after he stabbed me I left him lying in a pool of his own blood on the ground, and he wasn't moving. I heard later that he had suffered no long-term damage, but I greeted the news with indifference. He had made his move and then 'cheated' by using a weapon. In my mind, he deserved all he got. This was the last serious fight I had on the street, but it wasn't the last time I lost my temper.

Although I didn't recognize it immediately, the night I entered a karate dojo[7] for the first time proved to be the conduit to a new way of living. In my ignorance I went along to see just how good the so-called karate expert teaching there really was. While my friends were raving about everything karate, Bruce Lee, and the almost mystical powers their karate teacher possessed, I held thoughts of maybe taking him on and giving him a good slapping! That I was still thinking in this way is a good indication of just how difficult it was proving to be for me to make the transition from a violent, antisocial young man to the calmer and more social adult I wanted to be. The night I began training in karate, January 29, 1974, is the landmark in my life that changed everything. At last, I had made a choice that would shape the rest of my life for the better. As the next few years unfolded I would make progress and falter in almost equal measure, at times achieving glimpses of clarity and calm, only to suffer periods of blinding self-doubt and sickening rage. Any dreams I entertained of dueling with my friend's karate teacher soon vanished when I saw him sparring with a senior student. I was many things back then: young, arrogant, aggressive, and generally unhappy—but I was never suicidal!

CHAPTER TWO

"Teachers open the door. You enter by yourself."
–Chinese proverb

THERE ARE moments in life that stay with us forever, remaining vivid in our minds long after other memories have faded. One such moment for me is of returning home from my first karate training session exhausted, and because karate dojo back then rarely had access to showers, I was still wet with sweat; but more than anything else, I was excited and eager to return for more. That night I hardly slept a wink. A lot of people around the world were investigating the Asian martial arts back then. Bruce Lee movies were playing to full houses, and up and down the country karate clubs were bursting at the seams with new and prospective members. As a guest of Her Majesty the Queen, my isolation meant the kung fu phenomenon that was sweeping the world had passed me by. The excitement my friends displayed about martial arts often left me feeling disconnected. I just could not understand what all the fuss was about. Interest in the Asian martial arts grew to epidemic proportions in the Western world at this time. Naïveté had a part to play in this for sure. Nevertheless, the youth of the day, as well as many adults too, became intoxicated by the possibility of becoming a master of the martial arts.

In Britain, at least, kung fu and karate shared the lead in the charge to accommodate the growing hunger for instruction, but jujitsu and taekwondo ran a close second in the number of new students who were stepping onto the mat for the first time. Other martial arts, such as judo, kendo, and aikido,[8] brought up the rear. For many, judo proved too real and kendo too expensive; as for aikido, well that never took off until another nudge from Hollywood came along in the person of Steven Segal some years later. Since Segal's movies hit the screen, it has become as easy to find a master of aikido living in your neighborhood as it is to find someone who has invented his own style of karate. Once a martial art becomes popular, it seems there is no shortage of individuals ready to attach themselves to it and then engage each other in a race to the bottom. Dismantling the essence of the art, they eliminate the remarkable and replace it with mediocrity. While good for profiteering by some, the art itself suffers a lingering decline into irrelevance.

I began training in karate for a number of reasons. I was attracted to fighting and karate seemed like a good way to do it without getting into trouble. I also wanted to maintain the high level of physical fitness I attained from the mandatory circuit training I had been doing at Hindley, and I wanted to prove to my friends that I was, for all their karate skill, still someone to be reckoned with. But, as I mentioned earlier, perhaps the most bizarre reason for going along to the dojo on that cold, wet night in January 1974 was to see if I could take on the instructor and give him a bit of a slap! My outlook on life back then was very different; it was in many ways childishly simplistic. There were no shades of gray; everything was either black or white. In a cognitive sense, I was struggling to grasp a clear picture of where I stood in the world, and from that lack of clarity emerged my frustration and frequent violent outbursts. I saw myself as a no-nonsense tough guy, a hard man who had just been released from serving time behind bars.

The word karate meant nothing to me. Although I had heard a lot about it, I had never seen anybody doing it, so I was keen to see what all the fuss was about. Within minutes of watching Mr. David Vickers sparring with his senior student, thoughts of emulating Julius Caesar's arrival in Britain ("I came, I saw, I conquered") evaporated like the mist on a river when the sun comes up. I watched both men move in ways I had never seen anybody move before, but it was the kicking that grabbed my attention the most. In all my time fighting on the streets I never imagined such kicks were possible. I understood intrinsically that there would be value in learning karate. As you might guess, my challenge to Mr. Vickers never happened. I began training in karate that night and have continued training—forty-two years and counting!

Just six weeks after my first training session, I stood in front of Roy Stanhope, 4th *dan,*[9] the chief instructor for the Shukokai Karate Union in England. With little fanfare, I passed my first grading test in karate and returned home that Saturday afternoon with the lofty rank of 8th *kyu.*[10] Although in truth, the 8th kyu rank in karate is little to brag about, I felt a real sense of achievement; no longer a raw beginner, I started to believe it was only a matter of time before I would become a force to be reckoned with in the dojo. From the vantage point of time, it is easy to see that I had yet to grasp even the most basic tenets of *budo,*[11] but like many in the West, my instructor included, I was being spoon-fed a kind of karate that was big on show and small on substance. I was aware of none of that back then; I knew only that my climb on the ladder of colored belts had begun and that the climb would lead me to the prize I and every other red-blooded young man at the time wanted: a black belt! To be awarded a black belt in karate was the Holy Grail, the peak of Everest, and the winner of the Derby all rolled into one. It was something everybody was trying to attain, but few were achieving. Getting my hands on a black belt was going to take time and effort, and what we in Manchester called 'bottle' (guts!).

For many, their quest led to injury and disappointment, and countless numbers abandoned karate long before claiming their prize, exhausted from their efforts. I think many in the Western world, instructors and students alike, had the wrong idea of what karate was all about back then, but we did what we could and we did it with passion. To think of missing a training session because of a cold or a headache was unheard of in the dojo I belonged to, as it was in almost every other dojo in the country in the early 1970s. With an attitude reminiscent of a scene from the movie, *Monty Python and the Holy Grail,* if you lost an arm, you fought with one hand; if you lost a leg, you hopped; and if there was nothing left of you but your head, then you learned to bite! Karate training forty years ago may well have lacked the insight and refinement it enjoys at present, but the passion of that time is now rarely seen.

The summer of 1974 brought many new experiences my way, in and out of the dojo. I had not yet managed to give up street fighting completely. That is to say, I was still inclined to lose my temper with people if they annoyed me too much. My problem was I had a boiling point set closer to dry ice than to water, and so it still took very little to get me to stop talking and start fighting. Clearly, I was going to have to become less irascible and learn to control myself; the question was could I do it before being re-arrested and returned to Hindley. Worse still, was I going to do something incredibly reckless and end up killing someone? In 1974, the prospect of that happening was all too real, but as the year rolled on I continued to work hard at controlling my temper. I had the chance to observe my instructor in action against his peers for the very first time. Along with other members of the dojo, I traveled over the Pennine hills from Manchester to the Yorkshire town of Rotherham. The 1974 Shukokai Karate Union's northern championships had a gladiatorial reputation: an annual event with a fearsome status that was entered into only by the very brave, the very skilled, or the very stupid! Terms like 'bloodbath' and 'abattoir' were used to describe the scene that spectators flocked to in droves.

The similarities between the crowd's thirst for blood and the antics of the mob that surrounded me when I fought on the streets were not lost on me. I smiled to myself as I recognized familiar ground. How far, I wondered, had we come from the days of ancient Rome when the crowd roared for the blood of another to be spilt for the sake of entertainment. Karate is no stranger to the shifting qualities of human nature. I simply was not educated enough in the ways of people or karate back then, but I recognized certain traits and took note of my observation. 'Rotherham', as the annual tournament was referred to, was quite simply a very tough event fought by hard-hitting men looking to prove a point. Women in karate competitions in the 1970s were rare, and if they did make an appearance then it was only in the *kata*[12] division, never *kumite.*[13] In spite of Rotherham's gruesome reputation, there was no shortage of people willing to subject themselves to the risks inherent in their participation.

I remain uncertain about the percentage of those I watched that day who were brave, skilled, or just plain foolish , but I have a vivid recollection of admiration being felt for all the participants I saw, as they bowed to their opponent and then engaged each other with jaw-dropping ferocity. The spectacle of so many strong karate men fighting, bout after bout, was a little overwhelming at times; until then, I had seen few better at karate than my own instructor. The bouts were hard and fast and full of techniques I had before then seen only on the big screen. Blood flowed freely for much of the time, and the nurse manning the first-aid station was certainly earning her wages. At one point in the day, I ambled over to the area where the injured were taken to have their wounds attended to and watched as the nurse stitched gashes above eyes and splits in lips. I watched her manipulate several fingers back into their normal position and reset a dislocated shoulder, but I never once saw her use any kind of sedative or anesthetic!

I remember the wonderful demonstrations by senior members of the association: Stan Knighton, Eddie Daniels, and Butch White, and for the first time, watching a Japanese *karateka*[14] take to the floor and give a display of kata. Keiji Tomiyama was a twenty-four-year-old 4th dan fresh from Japan and as sharp as a razor. As the guest of honor, he brought the auditorium to complete silence when he walked into the middle of the floor. With the audience hushed in anticipation, he knelt to remove the belt and jacket from his *dogi*[15] before rising to his feet again. I had seen nothing like this before and can remember the hairs on the back of my neck stood up and there were goose bumps on my arms. Tomiyama sensei returned to his feet slowly, and in doing so, took command of all present, me included. The kata he demonstrated that day was *sanchin*,[16] and it triggered in me a glimpse of what was possible, with time and a relentless dedication. I knew little then of the impact the young Japanese man in front of me was going to have on my life, but all that was waiting for me in the future; the only thing I knew for sure was I wanted to be that good myself one day.

The fight I remember most vividly from Rotherham was the team match between Manchester and Sheffield. I was, of course, supporting the men from Manchester though I knew only one of them, my instructor, Mr. Vickers. This was the first time I was able to watch him pit his skills against opponents at his own level, contemporaries who were fighting just as hard to finish him off as he was to dominate them. When the two teams lined up and bowed to the judges, the atmosphere was electric. There is a sense of rivalry between the counties of Lancashire and Yorkshire that stretches back five hundred years to the fifteenth century. In 1455 a series of battles erupted across England as two powerful families laid claim to the throne. The final clash came in 1485 when the last of the armies defending the house of York were defeated by forces from the house of Lancaster, an event that gave rise to the Tudor dynasty. Known as the Wars of the Roses, each side had as its emblem a rose, red for Lancashire and white for Yorkshire. When the Tudors began their rule of England, they changed their emblem to incorporate both roses: the white of Yorkshire was now held fast in the center of the larger and all-encompassing red rose of Lancashire—the Tudor rose! I have my doubts as to how many others present that day would have understood the source of the rivalry between the two counties. Still, over the years, many 'grudge' matches have developed across a wide range of sporting contests, and karate was no different. The assembled spectators knew that this event, above all others that day, was going to be a spectacle not to be missed.

Each of the team's five members took his turn to step into the center of the square and engage his opponent in fast and furious combat. No quarter was asked and none was given. There was a lot of pride at stake here, and even though such things as pride should have played no part in the events of the day, karate as a sport is embedded in the same unhealthy ground as every other sport: to acquire success from the failure of others. The techniques on display were often wild and the fighting spirit of those men left nothing to the imagination. Following a particularly savage display of pugilistic talent from both sides, the win that year went to Sheffield—by default. Four of the five members from the Manchester team lost their bout due to the use of excessive contact in a contest that had witnessed blood, and even teeth, fly across the competition floor. Yes, indeed, Rotherham was not for the fainthearted. I returned home with a new level of respect for what it was going to take to wear a black belt. I had no fear of fighting, none at all, but I harbored doubts that I would ever develop and refine my karate skills to the level I had seen that day. The learning of karate is by no means straightforward; yes, it requires long hours of physical exertion, it takes no small amount of courage and a commitment to memory of many intricate details, but above all, it takes 'feeling'. I was sure I had what it would take to develop a good feeling for karate.

I trained at the Ming Chaun Karate Dojo. Its headquarters was in Ashton-under-Lyne on the eastern edge of the Greater Manchester conurbation. The name of the dojo was the result of a conversation between Mr. Vickers and *sifu*[17] Danny Connor, a pioneer of the Oriental fighting arts in England. The name fuses the Chinese 'Ming' dynasty, a time when the fighting arts flourished, with *chaun*, the Chinese word for fist. As karate was sweeping around the world like a shockwave, few who flocked to training knew that many of the techniques in karate could trace their geneses beyond Japan, beyond Okinawa, and even beyond China, all the way back to India and the Buddhist monk Bodhidharma (Da Mo), who early in the sixth century made an epic journey from the subcontinent to what was then the eastern edge of the known world: China. From China, where the physical exercises and fighting techniques Da Mo introduced developed over time into Shaolin Temple Boxing, it spread to the island of Okinawa to become the indigenous fighting methods known as 'ti'.

With successive generations, the name Okinawans used for their martial art changed; 'ti' became 'toudi', and later 'te', simply meaning 'hand'. Finally, around the early years of the twentieth century, 'te' changed its name again, becoming 'karate': 'empty hand'. But regardless of the name used, the unarmed fighting arts we think of today as karate flourished in Okinawa for centuries before being introduced to Japan, and from there, to the rest of the world. The name of the dojo paid homage to the long and ancient history of fighting techniques that we practiced and aspired to understand.

For the most part, I trained about ten miles away from the main dojo, at the Didsbury branch of the Ming Chaun, where, along with about fifty others, I tried my best to come to grips with karate. The dojo consisted mostly of low-ranking students. There were a few higher-level kyu grade members, but not many. I recall two *sempai*[18] in particular, students who held the rank of 1st kyu, the grade just below black belt. One sempai, Mike, had an easy-going nature, and although I never got to know him all that well, I knew he was a family man. He was in his early thirties and rarely missed a training session. Most evenings it was Mike who led the warming-up exercises before the students were split into smaller groups according to their rank and ability. Mike's approach to dojo etiquette left a lasting impression on me; he was strict with new students and keen to leave them with no misunderstandings as to the role and importance of etiquette in the learning of karate. Any slip-ups were dealt with quickly and decisively, and new students soon learnt to behave appropriately in order to avoid his attention. Mike taught all new students for the first month or so of their training, a system that proved to be an effective method of culling individuals who were not willing to accept the discipline of karate. While I found Mike's instruction easy to follow, I soon discovered the physical postures he was teaching me were a lot harder to master than I imagined they would be. As time passed, I moved on from his direct instruction, but I never failed to refer to Mike's knowledge whenever I became confused.

The second 1st kyu at the dojo in Didsbury also impressed me, but for very different reasons. I've long since forgotten the man's name, an indication perhaps of my dislike for him; I do remember, however, that he was a very different character altogether from Mike. On the occasional evenings when Mr. Vickers and Mike were both away from the dojo, the 1st kyu allowed his true nature to shine: he was an ugly man. Not long after I had successfully passed the test for 7th kyu, Mr. Vickers put the Tuesday evening class in the hands of this unpleasant sempai. In those days, it was not uncommon for karate instructors like Mr. Vickers to spend each evening teaching in different locations across the city. The demand for karate was greater than those in a position to instruct could handle, and so in many dojo, instruction was given by the student holding the most senior grade. I didn't like my sempai but with my reliance on public transport I was restricted to the Didsbury dojo.

One Tuesday evening I witnessed first-hand the bizarre nature of individuals who come to believe that karate has imbued them with an authority they simply don't have. The class had been called into line and knelt in *seiza*.[19] Everyone was expecting to perform *mokuso*,[20] the short period of quiet reflection before launching into our usual warm-up routine. But that night, our 1st kyu instructor had other plans. Instead of mokuso, he sat for a moment, as if gathering his thoughts. Then he drew a letter from the inside of his jacket. It was said to have been written and sent to him by Roy Stanhope, the 4th dan chief instructor for Shukokai karate in England. The exact wording of the correspondence escapes me now, but at its heart, the message directed us to stop training with our instructor Mr. Vickers, and from that night onward train only with the 1st kyu who was reading the letter.

I remember feeling momentarily confused, then angry. Afterward, my friends and I walked home through the rain together, discussing the letter and trying to make sense of what was going on. I had my doubts that the letter was genuine: it simply didn't make sense to me. As far as I was aware, my instructor had done nothing wrong, he had broken no rules, and even if he had, what would it have to do with the 1st kyu? I smelt a rat. My friend, John Carey, and I decided to approach our instructor even though the letter had warned against taking such action; any further contact with Mr. Vickers, the letter said, would lead to expulsion from the association. But, as Shakespeare might have said it, there was "something rotten in the state of Denmark." John and I were determined to find out what it was. Once the letter had been brought to our instructor's attention, the matter was resolved within days. The happy ending, as far as I was concerned, resulted in the 1st kyu and his fraudulent letter being sent packing from our dojo and the association. Mr. Stanhope's signature was forged; the letter was a fake, just like its author. The affair was not over yet. However, it would take a little longer for the final chapter of this sorry saga to play out, but play out it would, and though I didn't know it at the time, I would be there to witness it.

With the 1st kyu gone, training settled back to normal, and his presence in the dojo faded from the collective memory of the students sweating it out in the heady atmosphere of flailing limbs and loud *kiai*.[21] Several months passed and I began to look for ways to test my skills in the arena of competition. Sparring in the dojo was still very challenging for me, but over time the students grew to know each other's fighting style; a pecking order was established, with a few at the top who seemed to triumph no matter how hard the rest of us tried. From memory, I was somewhere in the middle, although that all depended on who was present in the dojo on any given evening. Still, I was itching to try my luck with others from outside my usual circle of opponents. My first opportunity came with word of a 'friendly' competition between a few other Shukokai dojo in the area. Our dojo agreed to take part, and duly arrived at the Colliehurst Karate Club ready to do battle. In truth, none of us had a clue what the day would bring; we spent a fair amount of time sparring during our normal training, but competition sparring was a little different. For a start, it had rules!

So not fully understanding what to expect, we changed into our *keiko-gi*[22] and made our way to the side of the fighting area that was marked out in white tape on a hard, wooden floor in the center of the hall. The number of spectators gathered to view the afternoon's proceedings came as a surprise; none of us had fought in front of an audience before. Our collective apprehension grew as we continually looked to each other for moral support. I can't be sure about the rest of the team, but I was feeling sick. Curiously, I noticed a young woman take her place on one of the teams, and as fate would have it, I was drawn against her in my first fight. I could not believe my luck. This was going to be a walk in the park as far as I was concerned. In my mind, it was as good as getting a free pass to the next round in the competition. With my first-round opponent now firmly in my sights, my growing apprehension began to subside.

The four teams lined up in front of the judges' table to bow and begin the afternoon's activities. With the draw already made to see which teams would fight first, we were up first, facing off against the team made up of four young men and a 'girl'. My friend John stood up to fight first, and during his bout scored twice on his opponent; it was enough to win when the final "Yame!" ("Stop!") was called. I was up next and felt supremely confident about how easy this was going to be. I was going to dispatch the young lady standing in front of me before she knew what was happening. It would have served me better to remember the advice my parents often gave me about pride coming before a fall, but as usual back then, I chose instead to listen to another voice, my ego, which was about to take a hammering, and rightly so, now that I think about it.

Giving my opponent nothing for the courage she was showing that day as the only female in a contest, we faced each other and bowed. The referee yelled "Hajime!" (Begin!). I shot forward and kicked her with a *maegeri* (front kick) in the stomach. She immediately bent doubled in pain and dropped to the floor holding her arms around her body. My kick could have resulted in a badly bruised body, or a more serious internal injury, but in that moment I appreciated none of that. There was no cheering from the crowd, none of the wild applause that had greeted the points scored in the first bout. Instead, my kick was met with a stony silence. The officials crowded around the young lady, and slowly, she was brought back to her feet. No point was awarded by the referee; instead, I received a warning for making excessive contact. In truth, I was unaware of exactly what it was I had to do to score a point in a competition. I knew I had to hit my opponent, and I knew there were some parts of the body that were off limits, but how cleanly my technique had to be delivered or how decisive the strike had to be was still a bit of a mystery.

When the fight continued it was clear that my opponent was now scared; she backed away from every movement I made toward her. Stepping out of the designated arena twice invited a warning from the referee. A penalty would result if it were done a third time. Eventually, I managed to trap her in a corner from where there was little room for escape. I had to be careful here I told myself; one false move and I could hit her too hard, and then I would find myself disqualified. No points had been scored by either party and time was running out; my team was urging me to hit her. We needed the win even if it was only by a *wazari* (half a point). Supporters from both sides began yelling as the clock clicked down to the final seconds of the fight. That's when it happened. I glanced across to my team, taking my eyes off my opponent for just a fraction of a second, and bang! She hit me full in the guts with a strong *gyakuzuki* (reverse punch), and it was all over. The referee's arm shot straight in the air as he yelled "Yame!" ("Stop!") and then ordered us back to our starting positions in the center of the arena. He then awarded my opponent *ippon* (one full point), before restarting the contest. Only a few seconds later the timekeeper raised his flag, bringing the fight to a close.

The crowd erupted, and I returned to my teammates looking and feeling like a stunned fish! Even before my backside had touched the floor, I was already thinking of quitting karate when I sat back down with my friends. After all, this wasn't real fighting. It was just playing at it. I was a good fighter and I had a criminal record to prove it. As soon as rules and regulations are introduced, well, look what happens. The thought of being beaten in my first karate competition by a girl was a very bitter pill to swallow, and try as I might to write it off, my ego was already screaming at me to quit karate. At the end of the first round, my team had won by four fights to one, with me the only one to lose! We then faced off against the winners of the other match, the team from Ardwick Sports Centre. Students of Mr. Stanhope, they all wore a green belt, which made them the highest-ranked karateka fighting that day. I won my next fight and felt much better as a result; each team member on both sides fought with a great deal of spirit, but at end of the contest my team lost by just one-half of a point.

Feeling a good deal happier with my performance the second time around, and with my third fight of the day also resulting in a win, earlier thoughts of quitting karate left me as quickly as they had arrived. My first karate competition had been an education in more ways than one, and a lesson I have never forgotten. The young lady recovered completely from my kick. I saw her afterward at a grading test, where we talked and joked about the day she beat me in a fight; she held no ill feelings toward me, although I never got the same impression from her boyfriend. My teammates, as all good friends do, never let me forget that I had been beaten in a fight by a girl, and once again I was forced to admit, at least to myself, that my parents knew what they were talking about.

A few weeks after the competition, I was asked to take part in a demonstration with members of the main dojo in Ashton-under-Lyne. The part I was asked to play was simple enough; all I had to do was run through some *ippon kumite* (one-step sparring) exercises with a fellow 7th kyu. Together, we trained over and over in order to get our display just right, but on the day of the demonstration the huge audience seemed to spook my sparring partner. He grew more and more nervous as our part in the demonstration came closer, so by the time we stood up to take to the stage, my partner was completely overwhelmed. He had the look of a cat being placed in a bath of water to be washed: wide-eyed and ready to go ballistic. His usual skill and control left him, and as a result, on the very first exchange of techniques I took an elbow strike in my back: delivered with full power. It was such a strong technique that he tore the right trapezius muscle in my upper back. At the time I felt no great discomfort although I was instantly aware of the damage when the blow landed; we continued with the display, the pain only setting in afterward, after my body cooled down. The injury put me out of action for the next three weeks, during which time I could only sit to one side in the dojo and observe the training rather than participate.

As strange as it might seem these days, the thought of missing a training session just because I had an injury was something that never entered my head. I didn't want to miss anything that was being taught, so even if I could not physically train I continued to go to the dojo to watch and learn; I was by no means alone in doing this either. Everybody else in the dojo did it too. Sickness, a condition that confined you to bed, was a different matter, but if all you had was an injury then your attendance in the dojo was expected. I resented my enforced lay-off from training and returned to the dojo floor with renewed vigor as soon as I could.

Just two months later, a second chance to try my luck in competition came along. With the rather grandiose title of The Manchester Inter-Club Challenge, the tournament was open to kyu grade students only and attracted entries from all over the Greater Manchester area. I'm not sure how many teams participated in the contest, but I do remember that our team was disqualified for being overly aggressive. In truth, the problem was down to me again; I was the one disqualified, and because it was a team event, my dismissal resulted in the whole team being forced to withdraw from the competition. Although I was trying very intensely to curb my natural aggression, I sometimes had 'bad days'. Unfortunately, I was experiencing such a phase on the day of the competition. Having fought well in the first round match, winning without any great drama, team morale was high. So in the second round we decided to reverse the order each team member fought. I would now be fighting last. By the time it was my turn to step up, the other teams had two wins to their credit, so the decider was down to me.

Our opposition had come a long way to be there, and they each wore a brown belt, making them senior in grade to my teammates and me. But I was not overly concerned by this, as I had just passed my 6th kyu test the day before and received high praise from Mr. Stanhope for my spirited performance during the exam. So with one win already to our credit, things were looking good for us. I stepped out to face my opponent as he stepped out to face me from the opposite side of the fighting area. At the command of the referee, we bowed to him, and then to each other. The fight was started with a loud shout of "Hajime!" ("Begin!") and my opponent leapt forward immediately, punching at me with a powerful *oizuki* (stepping punch) to my face. He was clearly out to intimidate me from the start, and had his sudden attack not caught me off guard, he may well have succeeded. But in my effort to block his assault, I stumbled backward out of his way, and the big toe on my right foot was bent backward, under my foot. The toe took the full weight of my body as I reversed over it, and the pain shot through me like a bolt of lightning. As the pain surged through my body, it tripped my anger switch, triggering my rage. The internal fuse had blown, and I was now ready for a real fight.

My opponent had committed himself completely to his attack, and though I managed to block it, his body had continued forward collecting me and carrying both of us out of the fighting area: I was furious. My toe was throbbing wildly and swelling in size with each passing moment. Someone was going to pay for the nausea rising in my gut, and as teammates helped us both back to our feet I knew exactly who that someone was going to be. When the fighting resumed, I was the one who leapt forward yelling like a madman. A front kick landed heavily into my opponent's bladder, and as he doubled over, I brought my fist down hard onto the side of his head. It was clear to everybody watching that I had lost control. The referee pulled me off and threw me back to my starting position; my opponent was brought back to his feet and helped to recover his composure. He was shaken and dazed but elected to carry on. Before the fight continued, I was issued an official warning, *hansoku chui*, and a full point was now awarded to my opponent. I was told to calm down. But I was having none of it. In my mind, this jerk had hurt me and he was going to pay for it; to me it was as clear and simple as that.

The call to begin fighting was given and I repeated the same attack as before only this time catching my opponent with a powerful punch that landed square on his nose. With no gloves or sparring mitts to offer protection, his snout took the full impact and burst like a ripe tomato: his blood and snot exploded everywhere. At that point, the entire place burst into an uproar as the referee dragged me away from my opponent who was lying on the ground holding his face in his hands. For a brief moment, complete pandemonium broke out, but calmness was restored soon after my friends and I were ejected from the competition—and the building. I cared little for the resulting chaos my behavior had caused at the time. As far as I was concerned, I felt vindicated. This was the closest I had come to having a real fight in quite some time and though I shouldn't have, I felt bloody marvelous! My brother who had been sitting in the audience and had witnessed the event was looking puzzled. "I thought you had to show control?" he asked. "I did," I said. "He's still breathing, isn't he?" As you can see from my comment and behavior, I still had a lot of growing up to do. The tenets of budo were all around me, yet I was having a tough time absorbing them. I shudder to think how my life would have evolved had I not continued to turn up at the dojo each week. In hindsight I can see my life hung very much in the balance for a few years back then, and my future could have gone either way; I'm grateful therefore to be writing this from the comfort of my home and not a prison cell.

Because of the quick turnover of students at the dojo, I found myself somewhere in the middle as far as rank was concerned. Occasionally, I was asked to take charge of the new students, introducing them, just as Mike had introduced me, to the basic exercises and etiquette of karate. I was hardly the best candidate for the job, but Mr. Vickers knew nothing of the struggle for calm going on inside me. In front of him, I did as I was asked and made every effort to do the job correctly. I did want to live a calmer life, but I often found it difficult to hold my tongue and keep my opinions to myself. Although being assertive is not a bad thing, it isn't helpful when coupled with ignorance; and back then, my knowledge of life and karate was tenuous to say the least. With the passing of time and a good deal of effort on my part, the rage that once had so much control over me would subside: thankfully, it now lies dormant. Yet I remain conscious of my nature and stay mindful of the consequences should I make the choice to revert to my former ways. The likelihood of that happening is not great, but I cannot in all honesty say it is impossible. I am a human being, with all the imperfections that entails. I believe the life I am living now has been shaped to a large degree by the choices I have made and the experiences I have had as a result of those choices; because of that, understanding my true nature has been vital. Although I was introduced to that nature as an adolescent, it took me some time to truly get acquainted; my parents would have said, too long.

Karate had quickly become an important part of my life and I was now training hard and often. Each Sunday morning my friend, John Carey, and I headed for the Ardwick Sports Centre, located a few miles southeast of Manchester's CBD.[23] In those days, sifu Danny Connor held a very popular kung fu class in the upstairs gymnasium at the center; John and I would sit quietly peeking through holes in the large curtain that ran the length of one side of the gym. While the kung fu students were being put through their paces, John and I made notes of the advice being given and the postures being performed. When the kung fu class was over, the floor was opened up to anyone who, for a small fee, wanted to use it. As it was such a big space, many karate instructors used it to hold private lessons for karateka who wanted to train outside the usual confines of their dojo. They paid their instructors extra for this, of course, though what they received in return for their money was debatable. They practiced little that my friend and I didn't also practice, and for a fraction of the cost. John and I stood within earshot of many a private lesson taking place on the other side of the curtain and followed the instructions the private students were receiving.

Spending up to six hours each Sunday at the sports center over the next two years led to many great experiences; as a result, I believe John and I progressed quicker than we would have by simply attending the two classes a week being offered at the Didsbury dojo. Along with my Sundays at the sports center and my weekly trips to the main dojo in Ashton-under-Lyne, karate was taking up most of my life outside working hours. I still found time to party, but the angry young man inside me who solved his problems by fighting was slipping away. That young man who needed to feel the rush of adrenaline through his veins brought on by the 'fight' was not exactly dead: but he was terminally ill. I knew the thoughts and dreams that were replacing my frustration were a much healthier option for me, easing as they did the burden I frequently felt my life to be. Even so, I had a long way to go to reach a place where the rewards of committing myself to karate would outweigh the struggles of coming to grips with it. By the end of my first year of training, I held the rank of 6th kyu. I was extremely fit and strong, and the heavy work at the foundry and my karate training kept me in peak condition. That's when life stepped in to apply the brakes: I developed an inguinal hernia. My father had also suffered from the same medical condition as a young man, and so it seems I had inherited at least a propensity for the condition.

The hernia began to show itself as a small lump at the base of my torso, and eventually grew so large that I could push my gut and four of my fingers through the hole in my abdomen. With some reluctance I visited a doctor who grew immediately concerned that my gut might twist and become blocked. If that happened, I was in danger of developing septicemia, blood poisoning. Left unchecked, septicemia quickly leads to death. Speedy arrangements for my admittance into the hospital were made, and the surgery followed soon after that. Before the operation, the surgeon explained the hole was too big to simply stitch my muscle together, so a patch was placed over the gap to repair the damaged muscle. In later years, that patch would fail and I would face the same operation to fix two more tears in my abdominal wall; but all that would happen many years from now. For now, I was keen to get fixed and get back to training. My time in the hospital was not completely wasted as far as karate goes. John gave me a copy of *Karate's History and Traditions*, by Bruce A. Haines,[24] and for the first time I began reading in detail about many different forms of empty hand fighting and their migration across Asia.

I was surprised to learn that karate originated on the island of Okinawa and not on mainland Japan as I, and just about everyone else back then, had been led to believe. The content of the book was a revelation to me, and set me on an ever-deepening path of study and learning. On his daily ward rounds, the surgeon spotted the book on the bedside table and inquired about my interest in the martial arts. I told him of my training in karate over the past year, as well as my keenness to resume once I was healed. He was horrified and absolutely adamant that my association with karate should stop. Leaving me in no doubt of his opinion that any continuing involvement in such a sport would be madness, I thanked him for his advice, but kept my real feelings to myself. Although I had entered an occasional competition, I never thought of karate as a sport. Far from it. 'Sport' sold karate short in my mind. My intention was to continue with karate training and just as soon as I could. I have forgotten who it was, my mother probably, who noted that in the space of just one short year, I had suffered a badly torn muscle in my back and a hernia, not to mention countless cuts, black eyes, and an assortment of bruises, strains, pains, and all manner of knocks and bumps, and for what? What indeed! All I knew for sure was that I had stumbled upon something I instinctively believed would help me. Although never sure how, where, or when karate's purpose would reveal itself to me, I knew only that without it I would be on the road to perdition.

Leaving the hospital and having to rest from strenuous activity for several weeks, I began to read more and more about karate, not that I could find much written material of any great quality to read back then. There were a few 'style' specific titles on the shelf, but I didn't want to learn karate techniques from a book; so I took to reading whatever karate magazines I could get my hands on. Becoming fit again was my first aim; once I had achieved that, I was ready to continue to battle my many insecurities. The Bruce Haines book captured my imagination and opened many avenues of thought previously unexplored by me. That I had actually read a book at all back then was a feat in itself, and I began to wonder if I would ever master karate. By investing most of my free time and energy into training, would I ever get to wrap a black belt around my waist? As a nineteen-year-old growing up with an uncertain future in front of him, such thoughts were at once daunting and powerfully attractive. Five weeks after leaving the hospital, I lined up for my first karate lesson since the surgery. I knew I had to take it easy, but I was desperate to get back into my keiko-gi and feel the sweat running down my back again. Such is the intensity of youth that I put myself in danger of undoing all the work the surgeon had done to repair my body.

At the time, all I could see was my limited abilities in karate were slipping away due to a lack of practice. More by providence than anything else, I managed to negotiate my way through a second year in the dojo with few problems, at least of a physical kind. The usual fat lips, split eyelids, the almost-broken fingers, and the badly bruised arms and legs were always close by; yet I managed to avoid most of them over the next twelve months. Perhaps with more insightful instruction and smarter training, injuries would have been less common, but karate dojo in the early and mid-seventies were populated, for the most part, by young men who didn't mind the consequences of trading blows that were generated more by spirit than technique. In retrospect, it is easy to point the finger and recognize the huge errors everyone was making; nevertheless, I think the spirit that existed in karateka from that time would put to shame many modern-day practitioners.

In October 1975, I attended my first karate *gasshuku*.[25] Held at the National Recreation Centre (Lillieshall) deep in the English countryside, the former stately manor house was transformed to provide a world-class training venue for Britain's elite athletes. When not in use by Britain's best, other sporting bodies hired the facilities. My fellow karateka and I were by no means the best that Britain had to offer, but two of the gasshuku instructors, Stan Knighton and Eddie Daniels, were past members of the British All-Styles Squad that had beaten the Japanese National Karate Team, the first ever to achieve such a feat. The training promised to be intense, and I was looking forward to it immensely. Traveling from Manchester to the Staffordshire countryside with Frank, a clubmate and fellow 4th kyu, Mr. Vickers had given us permission to attempt our 3rd kyu promotion test. We both harbored dreams of returning in triumph, each of us wearing a brand-new brown belt. It was obvious, at least to us, that everybody would soon appreciate how good we were. We didn't know it at the time, but we were in for one hell of a shock! The gasshuku ran from Monday to Friday with training divided into four separate sessions every day; each session was led by one of the four senior instructors from the Shukokai Karate Union.

From the very first warming-up exercises, I knew it was going to be a difficult week. Nevertheless, I was in my element, and though the training was more intense than I was used to, I was enjoying myself immensely. It became apparent early on that there was diversity across the group now training together. The way each kata was performed, for example, depended on which part of the country a karateka came from. Some kata differed quite markedly from its counterpart in a different city. The kata *bassai dai,* in particular, stood out as an example of the inconsistency that existed. I remember wondering how this could be. How could the kata be different, given we all belonged to the same organization and trained in the same style of karate? England is not that big a country so how these differences had evolved was a puzzle to me. I was reminded of the Galapagos Islands, where every island has its own unique variation of each species. The anomaly in the kata was all very confusing and not at all what I expected to find. How was I going to pass a grading test performing a kata from Manchester when the judging panel was made up of instructors from the cities of Sheffield, Stoke, and Birmingham? Never mind, my karate was so good I was bound to gain promotion regardless of the differences. My confidence was not universal, however, as the clubmate I'd driven with to the gasshuku had slipped away in the night, ninja style, and gone home. When dawn broke on Wednesday morning, I discovered I was alone!

The week passed, and I grew a few more bumps on top of the bruises from previous days. I was enjoying training with new people, and now that my clubmate had gone home, everyone I trained with was new. Rather than feeling intimidated, I welcomed it. I discovered that many of my techniques worked well on some people but then hardly at all on others. Why this happened made me look deeper into what I was doing. The notion of having to make adjustments to my techniques entered my thinking for the first time. Until then, I believed every technique would work as long as I executed it with as much speed and strength as I could manage. The idea that I needed to adjust my karate to suit a particular opponent's attack had never occurred to me. I had little real understanding of how to make angles or set up the appropriate distance between my opponent and me. As a result I went about trying to make karate an exercise in 'one-size-fits-all'. The gasshuku highlighted a need to adapt what I was doing according to who I was trying to do it to.

I didn't master every new idea that came my way during that week, but I did manage to open a few doors in my mind and slowly develop a new way of thinking. In later years, I would experience an ever-greater shift in my approach to karate, but right now, I was hungry for promotion. Toward the end of the gasshuku, an 'open-draw' kumite competition was arranged. With no regard to rank, size, or weight, names were simply put into a hat and drawn at random. My name went into the hat straightaway. Only twenty-five or so of the hundred and twenty attending the gasshuku took part in the kumite, and all but four of those who did wore a black belt. The kumite came and went and to be honest it was no big deal at all; even so, a surprising number of people avoided it. I found myself standing before Mickey Horsburgh, a 3rd dan karateka from Birmingham and a member of the Shukokai National English Squad; he beat me with very little trouble, but I took some satisfaction from my eagerness to face him. Later that night the gasshuku instructors stood a round of drinks for all those who had participated in the contest, a small prize maybe, but recognition nonetheless of a challenge issued and a challenge met.

The next day I lined up with the other 4th kyu students, all of us hyped up and ready to go. As the grading progressed, I grew more and more confident of success. The *kihon* (basic) section had gone well, as had my performances of kata. With no errors so far and only two rounds of fighting, I left the dojo after the test convinced I had not only passed but passed with distinction. I can actually remember thinking it was one of the easier grading tests I had taken part in. There was always a slim chance I might be unsuccessful, I suppose, but such an outcome never crossed my mind. My skill was obvious, my fighting spirit clear and in truth, not far short of awesome. How could the grading panel not pass me? Later, in the lecture theater where the results were to be announced, I settled into my seat confident of receiving the applause of my fellow karateka. The senior instructors entered the room and silence fell over the gathering. In order of the grade being issued and within that in alphabetical order, each candidate's name was called out in turn and their success or failure proclaimed for all to hear. Eventually the announcements reached 3rd kyu and the names began to be read. "Anderson, pass. Arkwright, pass. Ashton, pass." On down through the A's and the B's the proclamations came until finally they reached the C's. This was it. My moment of glorious recognition had arrived at last and I could hardly contain my excitement. "Clarke," I was on my feet before my name had left the instructors lips, "Sorry you've failed. Please try again."

What! What did he just say? I could not believe my ears. What just happened? They must have made a mistake, mixed me up with someone else. Yes, that's it. I felt sick! A feeling of utter devastation washed over me, flooding into every part of my body; so total was the shock I could hardly breathe, let alone speak. Sinking back into my chair, the announcements continued, although I never heard them. What on earth had gone wrong? How could such a thing happen? Sitting in my chair, my world came crashing down around me. It was years later that I discovered the lesson in the events of that day. Immediately afterward, and for quite some time, I was raw from the experience. Although I never thought of quitting as I had after losing my first competition fight to a young woman, my ego was badly shaken by my first genuine encounter with failure. The expression on my face during my first night back in the dojo following the gasshuku must have been a clue to the other students. Even before I changed into my keiko-gi, my failure to gain promotion was abundantly clear to everyone. No one said much in the changing room, but the purple belt I wrapped around my middle said it all. Still, none of this stopped Mr. Vickers from picking his moment to ask. Lining everyone up in preparation for the evening's training, he asked the question he had no need to ask: "So . . . how did you get on?"

The inquiry was not a request for information but an opportunity for me to face the truth and to give that truth a voice, so I threw it out there for all to hear: "I failed." What followed was a training session I have never forgotten, a session that turned out to be the toughest since walking into the dojo for the first time just a few short years ago. Pushing me to the point of exhaustion, only to pull back before pressing hard once again, Mr. Vickers' tactic of filling my head with other thoughts—like survival—stopped me from dwelling on the events of the previous week. His strategy worked, of course, for I had no time to feel sorry for myself or bask in the combined condolences of the dojo members. For the two hours that followed the initial bow, it was all I could do to stay upright and breathe. Many years later, I realized the true lesson I had been taught that night, and when the penny finally dropped, I became overwhelmed with a feeling of gratitude toward my instructor.

While I believed that he was probably punishing me in front of the other students for not passing the test, he was in fact going about the business of teaching me a very important lesson. In Japanese, the slogan most often used in a situation like this is "Nana korobi ya oki"—"Seven falls, eight rises." Perseverance was the lesson here, perseverance and resilience; both were virtues I needed to cultivate if I hoped to make any sort of progress in karate. Failures and setbacks had to be taken ownership of, pondered, and learnt from. I came to understand that it is through our failures that we learn our most profound lessons, but only if we have the strength of character to accept our failings, and then enact changes. An ability to recognize our failures is of little use if we lack the moral fortitude to correct them.

The following weekend Mr. Vickers took me to Sheffield to train at the dojo of Stan Knighton, one of the instructors from the gasshuku in Lillieshall. Although the training was for instructors from the Shukokai Karate Union my name had somehow, and quite miraculously, been listed as an assistant instructor. It was a great honor for me to line up with many of the senior people in our organization, albeit at the far end of the back row. The pace of training was daunting, and it wasn't too long before I began to struggle. Frankly, some of the technical details were beyond me; nevertheless, I was aware of just how special an opportunity this was and tried my best to grasp it with both hands. Once a month for the following six months, I trained at the Yorkshire Karate Centre, and in that time partnered up with many of the Shukokai top fighters of the day, men like Terry Pottage, Ossie Rowe, Les Carr, and Alan Balmforth, and on occasion, visiting guests from other schools of karate like Eugene Codrington. These were heady days for me and due to this kind of extra support from my teacher I was more than ready when the next opportunity for promotion came along. On December 14, 1975, I traveled to the city of Stoke in the English midlands. Standing in line, I was no longer suffering from delusions of grandeur; I was simply there to do the best karate I could. My promotion to 3rd kyu that day was the best Christmas present I could have wished for.

Shortly after my promotion, I had my first karate lesson with a Japanese instructor. Until then I had only ever seen one Japanese karateka in person: Mr. Tomiyama. From that experience, and the limited exposure I had to Japanese karateka on film and in photographs, I assumed all Japanese were on the small side. Arriving in Bolton with my teacher, Mr. Vickers, to train with Shigeru Kimura sensei shattered all my preconceptions on that score, for he turned out to be a giant of a man. Kimura sensei was built like a bull, close to six feet and broad shouldered; his reputation among karate men was legend. He looked a little scary to me, although he had a very relaxed manner about him; it became clear as the training progressed that he possessed a massive amount of power and wasn't shy about demonstrating it. The training was everything I hoped it would be. It was special, containing ideas and concepts unlike any I had come across before. The entire lesson concentrated on a few basic kicking and punching techniques, but it was the delivery of them that formed the focus of our efforts.

Balance and bodyweight distribution came under the microscope, as well as how these details were relevant to the smooth transmission of power. Kimura sensei was a hard taskmaster and seemed to have little patience with those failing to grasp his ideas. I did enjoy the challenge of the training, though I found much of it tough going. As far as I could tell, the training was geared to get people thinking, in great detail, about the things they were doing. Kimura sensei could be a bit sarcastic at times, but I never saw him bully anybody, as I have since seen other Japanese instructors do. After training, he was very approachable and pleased to answer the questions that were put to him; I had hundreds to ask, but didn't have the nerve to ask them! On that occasion, I gave in to my sense of indecision, and as the moment passed so too did my opportunity to speak with Kimura sensei, a potential conversation slipping into history and lost forever, or so I thought.

As 1976 passed from one month to the next, my feelings for karate deepened. I was working a great deal on flexibility and kicking techniques in an effort to mitigate my physical flaws. My kicking techniques were improving noticeably and because of that, I was feeling more comfortable with my body; during training, I was able to turn my mind to things other than merely surviving the lesson. This was also the year when, along with the rest of the Ming Chuan Dojo, I parted company with the Shukokai Karate Union and became affiliated with the Shukokai World Karate Union. Not much of a change in the name, but a world (no pun intended) of difference in the direction each group was heading. It was also my first real introduction to karate politics and how the desires of men often conflict with the ethics of budo. For those not privy to how two separate groups existed side by side in a small country like England, perhaps a brief history lesson is in order.

In 1973, Master Chojiro Tani, the Japanese founder of the Shukokai organization, came to Britain to teach and hold friendly competitions. The Shukokai Karate Union (SKU) was asked to host the Japanese visitors but their executive committee declined, and because of this, the SKU's secretary, Mr. Bob Aikman, resigned. He wanted more interaction with the Japanese, not less, and believed ties between England and Japan should be strengthened. Along with five other dojo, Mr. Aikman established the English branch of the Shukokai World Karate Union (SWKU) and became a part of a larger group affiliated directly with Tani sensei's organization in Japan, through the already existing Shukokai World Karate Union in Europe (SWKUE). Although the SKU retained the services of Kimura sensei, who operated independently of Japan and was based in America, the SWKUE came under the direction of Yasuhiro Suzuki sensei and was based in Brussels, Belgium. As well as Suzuki sensei, having a small team of Japanese instructors already living in Europe, including Mr. Tomiyama, was a huge attraction for me. Rather bizarrely, the SKU was recognized by the governing body for karate in England as the official group for Tani-ha Shito-ryu, while the SWKUE was not.

Regardless of the politics involved, the SWKUE continued to grow and prosper and in 1974 was in a position to invite Master Tani and a team of university students to England. In spite of repeated efforts by the SWKUE to have a Japanese instructor live in England, it proved impossible to implement due to objections lodged with the Immigration Department by the SKU executive for the required visa. Thus, for many years the two karate groups existed in an uneasy truce, sharing the same history and the same techniques, but not, it would seem, the same ideals. Forty years ago it was uncommon to have more than one organization per country representing a single school of karate, but as the number of students increased and the potential for huge incomes became apparent to a larger number of would-be instructors, the urge to break away and establish new groups became too much. For many, standing on the top of their own small hill was preferable to being halfway up a mountain. Unfortunately, it's a trend that not only increased over the following decades, but also gained in popularity, and has now become an acceptable part of the karate experience for the majority of karateka in the world today. Association hopping is, for some, the only way they can acquire a promotion.

On September 19, 1976, as the last days of summer were giving way to the cooler winds of autumn, I made the long drive south from Manchester to Peterborough with Mr. Vickers. The English branch of the SWKUE, under the direction of Aikman sensei, was holding its national championships, and we had been invited along to watch the tournament and discuss the possibility of affiliating. Walking into the sports hall, we found the activities of the day already well underway. From what I could see of the karate on display, I wanted to join straightaway, but it wasn't my decision to make, and as a relatively unimportant member of the dojo, it was not my place to voice an opinion unless asked. The tournament was extremely well organized, with three different areas functioning at the same time, each one housing kumite, kata, or *kobudo*[26] competitions. The fighting was fast and furious, and the kata looked sharp, but it was the weapons that caught my imagination. I had not seen this kind of competition before; I knew the weapons existed, but I had no idea who was teaching them and how I could learn. I was quietly praying my sensei would decide to affiliate so I could gain access to everything I witnessed that day. Fortunately, he did.

On the drive home, I remember having a big smile on my face, for I believed my karate training had turned a corner and the future was looking good. Over the next year and a half, I spent three out of every four Sundays traveling the eighty miles to either Nottingham or Derby with my teacher and a fellow student, Dave Millard. Together we attended the SWKUE *yudansha*[27] training and tried our best to bring our kata and technique into line with the standard set by Mr. Aikman. As the months passed, all three of us were invited to take part in the tournament squad training, held once a month. These training sessions had a more sinister tone to them. I'm using the word sinister here because team selection training was taken very seriously; the fighting was demanding, the kata exact, mistakes were frowned upon, and a poor display of spirit during kumite would see you treated very harshly. There was a discipline to the danger each karateka was walking into on these Sunday training sessions. Although safe in terms of intent, as no one was out to deliberately hurt another karateka, still, accidents were frequent in the highly charged atmosphere. Broken fingers, noses, and ample amounts of blood from the many split lips and cut eyes were not uncommon, and neither were cracked ribs. Even though this was a long way from fighting on the street, it was sufficiently close to summon a number of familiar feelings in me.

Knowing how I was about to spend the next four hours, I often had to visit the toilet to be physically sick before I was ready to take part in the training. Once the training got underway, my anxiety soon faded, giving way to an urge to prove myself. I am quietly proud to say I made the team every time selection was on the table, and for two years represented England in tournaments across Britain and Europe. The team selection sessions were so difficult to get through that, for me at least, the competitions often felt less demanding. I never confused, as some karateka did and still do, tournament fighting for the kind of battle that takes place on the pavement or parking lot; sport karate was all a big game to me, exciting and fun, challenging and hard work, but that's all. Tournaments have a lot to offer the young who want a challenge, but they are no closer to real fighting than a flight simulator is to landing a real jumbo jet in a lightning storm—at night! No one should confuse competition sparring, even with its potential for injury, with the dangers associated when fighting on the street.

My biggest disappointment during my involvement with sport karate came after I was selected to fight against a visiting Japanese team. Just a few weeks before the competition was set to take place, it was canceled due to Tani sensei becoming ill. Oh well, I had at least made the team, and for me that was always a huge hurdle to overcome. The tournament was rescheduled to meet a team of Shotokan karateka, but I remember little from the day's fighting except that we won the competition rather convincingly. It was nice to win, it always was, but in truth I would have sooner faced a Japanese opponent and lost; for me, the attraction of tournaments was to face the ordeal of the fight. The obsession with winning and success at all cost on display in karate competitions today bears no resemblance to the struggles faced by karateka in former times. With little or no padding, karateka faced each other knowing they were likely to be hit, even if they eventually won the contest. Displays of courage and 'spirit' were commonplace once upon a time; but so uncomfortable is the modern sport of karate with injury and failure that the kumite participants wrap themselves in gloves, guards, and masks, while kata competitors are allowed to 'interpret' a kata as they see fit, thus removing the fear of making a mistake. Any deviation from the usual performance of a kata is now simply explained away as a 'personal interpretation': how convenient. Today's sporting karateka have made it easy for my generation to say, "Things were 'different' in my day," and truly mean it!

The sporting complex attached to the Anderlecht football stadium in the Belgian capital, Brussels, was the location of the SWKU European championships. In those days, contestants entered both the kata and kumite competitions; the notion of specializing in one or the other had yet to emerge. My performance in the kata competition wasn't helped by the choice of kata I made. Free to perform the kata of my choice, I should have picked one that played to my strengths, but I was nervous, so I settled on doing sanchin kata. It was slow and repetitive, so less chance of making a mistake . . . at least that was the plan. What actually happened was I fell into the trap of doing the kata too slowly, and I put way too much effort into breathing like a bear about to pounce. I lost my concentration and lost count of the number of punches I had done: this wasn't how things were supposed to have unfolded.

In an effort to bring the kata to a close properly, I had to improvise so I added an extra *mawashi uke* (double-handed block), but even as I did it I knew my plan had gone terribly wrong. I now had to step back to the *yoi* position (found at the start and finish of a kata) with my left foot instead of my right. This was decades before the rules were changed to accommodate mistakes, and with thousands of eyes looking at me, I would have dug a hole and crawled in if I could have. Instead, all I could do was stand there and face the judges. Thankfully, they didn't keep me waiting long and I was dismissed from the kata competition with the lowest average score they could award. I wanted to do better, and in subsequent tournaments I did, but not before I learnt to control my nerves. Friends rallied around and offered reassurance, but I knew I had blown a chance to push my mental faculties further and take one more step closer to achieving a better level of self-control. Ignorance can be bliss, according to some, and in this case it might bear some truth, for had I known how long it was going to take to acquire the meager amount of control I possess today, I may well have set my sights a little lower.

I fared much better in the kumite division. Of the two teams representing England, 'A' and 'B', I was a member of the 'B' team. Also, I entered the individual open competition, a division open to all ranks. So my busy day of fighting and running around to a different area after each fight left me little time to ponder the kata fiasco of that morning: I had fights to win, and so far I was doing quite well. The first ten times I stood to face my opponent I sat back down the winner. After a good start, the 'B' team was knocked out of the competition, but my progress in the individual competition was going well; my confidence was high, and looking at the others who were left, I knew I could go further. All I had to do was avoid some of the bigger guys like England's own Bob Lord, 3rd dan. Standing well over six feet tall, Bob was making easy work of his opponents. As I was a lowly 3rd kyu, our paths rarely crossed during squad training, but unfortunately for me, today was going to be one of those rare occasions when they did.

Tomiyama sensei called Bob and me to the center of the mat where we bowed and made ready to fight. I wasn't sure what Bob had in mind with regard to tactics but they were almost made redundant within seconds of the call to begin: "Hajime!" ("Begin!") Rushing toward me with a lunging punch to my head, Bob closed the gap between us in a fraction of a second. Unaware of his punch—I simply didn't see it—I dropped onto one knee and landed a solid reverse punch squarely into his body; Bob flew back several feet before landing on his backside. A mighty roar rose from the crowed; everyone was amazed by my apparent speed and sense of timing. But I confess, there was no one in the arena that day more surprised than I was. Where the punch came from was beyond me; yes, I had been trying to fight like that, but I wasn't having much luck until today. So there I was, only seconds into a three-minute fight with 'Big Bob' and I was already winning. Had the combat stopped there and then, I would have returned home from Belgium a very happy man. Unfortunately, it didn't.

Bob went on to win the match, when, as soon as the last 'thirty seconds' call was given, the fight suddenly became more 'real'. I could see the change in his eyes; I knew the look well. If I were going to win this contest, I was going to have to avoid his techniques for the next half minute or take the fight to him and make him deal with my attacks. Either way, it was clear I was no longer engaged in an exchange of point scoring. Bob threw a front kick, which I dropped both hands to deal with; it was a stupid thing to do, I know, but Bob was a big guy, an angry guy, and a guy out to prove a point rather than score one. His kick was powerful and I knew it would hurt if it landed; no sooner had my arms dropped to defend myself when his fist shot forward and found its target on the part of my face where my teeth lived. I remember the blinding blue flash and a strange ringing in my ears that changed to a hissing noise; my blood was splattered everywhere, and one of my front teeth was protruding through a hole under my bottom lip. But I had not gone down; I was on my feet: still standing. Even though I was having a problem knowing what day it was, let alone what had just happened, I reverted to 'street-mode': hands up, chin in, and fists tight! Tomiyama sensei was yelling at me, "Are you okay?" "Yes sensei, I'm fine, I'm fine," was the only reply I knew to give.

The world had gone quiet, my eyes were wide and scanning for the next attack; for a moment I was no longer in a competition. That punch was too 'real'. Incredibly, Bob was awarded ippon—a full point—and the fight restarted. Now I was just trying to keep out of his way, Bob had just landed a blow as hard as I had ever been hit by anyone, and I was in no hurry to take another. As he moved toward me through a fog of blurred vision, a bell rang to signal the end of the contest: a win for Bob by half a point. The crowd booed and whistled and Bob got angry. I was just happy for a chance to let the medics look at my mouth, and then drown my sorrows in a few cold Belgian beers. No real harm was done in the long run. Although it had been a while, taking a hit like that was nothing new to me. The scar where the tooth punctured my lip remains, just one of the many 'medals' I collected over the years. My father used the term when talking about the injuries he received in the ring as a boxer. The tough looking guy with the 'medals', that is, the broken nose and eyelids heavy from frequent impact, wasn't the man to watch out for. Instead, my father always counseled me to pay more attention to the person 'awarding' the medals.

For the next year and a half, I continued to train hard and often. Traveling to different parts of the country on the weekends had become a way of life by now and my enthusiasm for karate was still very much on an upward curve. Two more promotion tests were taken and passed, and by the end of 1977, I was doing what I could to fine-tune my techniques ready for the *shodan*[28] test. Shodan, the first level of black belt, is in truth no great achievement; it is merely a first step, a place for beginners. But I, like many others back then, held on to the falsehood that it implied mastery. It's a myth among karateka and the general public that has endured, although for the life of me I cannot understand why. In a world where children as young as six years old are given a black belt to wear, it begs belief that anyone who would do that could also consider himself a karateka. On Sunday, January 15, 1978, when I walked into a small church hall in Nottingham along with fifteen other hopefuls ready to be tested, I believed a successful test would somehow endow me with skills and understanding beyond the reach of other mortals.

We entered the hall at 1:30 p.m. and emerged nine and a half hours later at ten o'clock. A written exam lasting half an hour preceded the eight hours it took to complete the physical part of the test. It was promotion by ordeal, as was so often the case during my early days; candidates had been put through the wringer, emerging absolutely exhausted. The elation at being successful was tempered by empathy for those who had endured the test only to be deemed wanting, and as a result, faced failure. As I recall, less than half who took the test were promoted. Although several who failed the test that day walked away from karate, others continued on to succeed at a later date and in doing so learned the value of perseverance. I knew what it was like to fail a grading test, but I also knew what it was like to carry on, regardless. Learning to invest in failure is perhaps one of the most difficult lessons a karateka can learn.

When relying on my memories to recount past events, a bias for the good over the bad and the positive over the negative can dominate a particular recollection. I have tried to avoid exaggeration in either direction in order to tell the story as I truly remember it. Generally speaking, I believe that karate training was more fierce in times past, although karateka were not necessarily better people because of that. Unfortunately, there have always been individuals drawn to karate for reasons that are less than honorable, but I have learnt to divorce myself from such folk, leaving them to their own devices and stomping on their heads—metaphorically speaking—only if they intruded into my life. I have no interest in changing the world; I just try to live well in the world that I inhabit. It is not how you do karate that is important, but what you do with it. This 'truth' has endured throughout the ages and was as pertinent forty years ago as it is today. Attitudes toward kumite have changed somewhat since karate arrived in the

West. In the past, karateka would have displayed a kind of ferocity seldom witnessed today, and I think it is fair to say those who face each other across the mat these days are less likely to see the inside of a hospital emergency room as a result. Now, whether or not this is good for karate depends entirely on your understanding of what you are involved in.

These days, I think it would be difficult to find an example of the kind of kumite I am about to relate to you, difficult, but perhaps not impossible. The occasion was a return contest between the SWKU England and the SWKU Scotland. As far as friendly competitions go, the first meeting in Scotland had been an utter disaster. Nationalistic pride on both sides had boiled over and sportsmanship and good manners were trampled underfoot in a stampede to inflict real damage on the opposing side. The competition was subsequently abandoned due to the intensity of the brawling. I wasn't able to make the journey north to Scotland and so missed the furor that took place. I was, however, available for the return contest and keen to play my part in the subjugation of the clans. Gathering in Nottingham was a large crowd made up mostly of spectators eager to witness a repeat of the near-riot in Scotland. I am glad to say the day failed to descend into the chaos of the first meeting; even so, for a number of fighters it resulted in that all too familiar—back then—ride in an ambulance.

In a small gymnasium just off to the side of the main hall at the Rushcliffe Leisure Centre where the contest was about to take place, fighters from both sides gathered to warm up. I never understood why anybody thought it was a good idea to have both teams warm up in the same room. Whoever it was may have been trying to stir the pot a little before the 'kick-off' or maybe it was a complete oversight on behalf of the organizers; either way, it set the scene for some cold-blooded looks as well as some hot-blooded banter. Everything had been going well until the double doors were flung open and in strode a hairy-legged Scotsman clad in full national costume. With his kilt swinging and his sporran gleaming, I was keeping an eye on his *sgian dubh* (ski en du), the little dagger he had tucked neatly into the top of one of his stockings. Stomping around the gym singing a song from long ago, when Scotland was at war with England, his singing paused only so he could utter an insult to the nearest Englishman. I thought it funny at first, until I noticed the effect it was having on some of the newer members of our team. At the same time, the morale of the Scots was growing with each verse of his ancient refrain.

Walking out into the main hall a short while later, I was surprised to see our visitor had changed into a dogi and was now standing on the opposite side of the mat with the rest of the Scottish contingent. If the audience had come to witness a quick descent into mayhem, they were disappointed. The fighting was forceful on both sides, tough but fair; gradually, however, tempers frayed and the referees had to work harder to stop the temperature in the room from rising and the blood from flowing. The first major incident occurred about halfway through the first round of the contest. The fight was going England's way as the Scottish fighter was continually pushed back to the edge of the mat. When the call was given to indicate the fight would end in thirty seconds, the Englishman pressed home his attack. His kicks had a little more vigor than before, and the last of them, a *chudan mawashi geri* (swinging kick to the midsection) sunk deep into the Scotsman's side. He fell to the ground, his body recoiling in pain.

It took a little help from the corner judge to get the Scotsman back to his feet, but he eventually managed to stand and take his place at the side of the mat. The fight was over; the English team had secured one more win. Both fighters bowed and took a couple of steps backward out of the area, and then knelt beside their teammates. I remember clearly watching the Scotsman keel over, as he was obviously in great distress; the first aid people examined him and immediately called for an ambulance. Later that day I learned his spleen had been ruptured by the final kick delivered by his opponent. It had been a very hard kick, and the technique had done the job it was meant for in real life. It started me thinking about the fundamental error upon which sport karate is built: 'success' and how that idea depends entirely upon defining what it is to be successful.

The second major incident/accident of the day, as if to maintain a sense of karmic balance, involved an Englishman. Both fighters had given and received many heavy blows throughout their bout. Then, for no apparent reason, the Englishman dropped to his knees and held his left arm aloft, stopping his opponent in his tracks. Perhaps this was a ploy by the English fighter to lure the Scotsman into reach of some deadly new technique; whatever the reason, the move baffled not only the audience but everyone on the English team as well. Then, as if by some pre-arranged signal, everybody in the room focused their eyes on the Englishman's left hand. There, held up for the world to see, was an injury so bizarre it took a while to realize what we were looking at. The bones of his ring finger were protruding through skin in the palm of his hand, having been pushed backward from the knuckle joint.

Given the amount of blood that was streaming down his arm, he must have been bleeding all the time he was on his knees, and yet no one seemed to notice; it was the site of the bone jutting out of his hand had stolen everyone's gaze. The injury must have been incredibly painful, yet I have no memory of my teammate showing any obvious sign of pain or discomfort. No doubt he was suffering from shock as well as the dislocation. Years later, I asked him to show me his hand; his finger was still slightly deformed, and apparently it would remain so for the rest of his life. I often wonder what the litigation-happy society we live in today would make of such events. I guess it's only a matter of time before we find ambulance-chasing lawyers sitting next to the first aid stations at karate competitions: and why not? As a footnote to this story, my first fight that day was against none other than the hairy-legged Scotsman who had made his presence felt so stridently before the competition commenced. I was pleased to learn that his bark was far worse than his bite and I held the wild Jock to a draw.

CHAPTER THREE

"It's not the mountain we conquer, it's ourselves."
–Sir Edmond Hilary

As 1978 unfolded, my enthusiasm for karate continued to grow, and as winter gave way to spring followed by the longer days of summer, I was spending more and more of my free time in my dogi: training. As well as the regular training with Mr. Vickers, I was also training with friends in other schools of karate. Practicing with karateka from different schools opened my mind to possibilities I was never exposed to when training solely in the Tani-ha Shito-ryu system. From karateka like Steve O'Driscoll and Tommy Rowe from Shotokan karate, I discovered new ideas about fighting, and from John Boyle of Okinawan Goju-ryu, my karate was exposed, for the first time, to the concept of understanding kata through the practice of *bunkai*.[29] Perhaps inevitably, due to such exposure and to the depth of research and learning I was slowly waking up to, I started to become less dependent on my teacher for information and direction; my 'drift' away from him didn't happen overnight, and it certainly wasn't planned. It was an exit that was inevitable, given my desire to understand the essence of karate. My focus now had turned away from climbing the ladder of rank advancement that karate organizations construct around their members. I was looking for more from karate than belts and techniques backed by often spurious scientific explanations, and though I continued to enjoy participating in sporting competitions for a while, I was quickly growing less accepting of them as the benchmark of a karateka's fighting ability or capacity to demonstrate good kata.

It seemed to me, even back then, that 'theater' was taking precedence over substance, and as a result, karate competitions were moving inextricably away from the exchange of technique they were originally meant to be. Today, demonstrations of karate include kata set to music or singing, while displays of bunkai are little more than choreographed 'set pieces' more at home in drama school than the dojo. With participants now specializing in either kumite or kata, even their clothing has developed to suit a specific 'look'. A cursory glance at a national or international karate competition today will often allow you to pick the event a particular participant has entered simply by the cut of his or her dogi. Frankly, karate competitions have become little more than fashion shows where individuals compete with each other to 'look' the part and exhibit their acting and choreographic skills. By all means, let the children play, but please, be under no illusion: karate competitions, from local competitions to the World Karate Federation Championships, are little more than a gathering of extroverts, hell bent on showing everybody else just how good they are.

Before moving on, I want to take time to write a little about my first karate teacher, the man who helped to turn me, an undisciplined youth with an uncertain future, into a young man who was, albeit very slowly, starting to wake up to the world and his place in it. Mr. Vickers was my instructor for five years. When I began training with him, he held the rank of *nidan*, 2nd dan, and ran his karate classes with an air of discipline where etiquette was strictly enforced. My initial contact with him was scarce, due to the great number of karateka training at the dojo when I joined; new arrivals fell under the tutelage of senior students, while Mr. Vickers taught those seniors who were not engaged in helping others. The students who stayed would eventually work their way up through the ranks and at some point find themselves standing in front of Mr. Vickers. For me, graduation from the 'beginners' class was at once a pleasure and a problem: a pleasure because the training became much more interesting, but a problem because training was now with people who were a lot better than I was. Along with the increased skill of my training partners came an increase in the number of bruises I collected.

It took about two years from my entering the dojo for the first time before I could say that Mr. Vickers and I had a relationship resembling that of sensei and student. But once he began to think of me as a serious student, my training became that wonderful mix of pleasure and pain that marks the passage of a karateka. Many times, he pushed me to my limits only to ask me to go further and stretch the boundaries of my 'normal' understanding. At times, I felt he was conducting some kind of personal vendetta against me; only now, with the benefit of hindsight, am I able to appreciate just how fortunate I was to have found a teacher gifted enough to give me the lessons he did. For a time, the other students noticed the way I was singled out for 'special' attention and would jokingly ask what I had done wrong so that they could avoid getting the same treatment. It took me a long time to realize how fortunate I was, in the midst of the 'special treatment'. I could have happily left the dojo any number of times and never returned; these days I am thankful I saw that period through to the end.

One evening, after the regular training was over, I asked Mr. Vickers to teach me a kata I had seen him do with *nunchaku*.[30] I had been asking him the same question for a few months, but until tonight, his answer had always been the same: "No!" In addition, he would remind me that I had enough to do learning karate. My polite requests continued, and on this particular evening he agreed to teach me the kata after my regular training the following night. At home in my bedroom I stayed up until the early hours of the morning going over and over every move with the nunchaku I was familiar with. Not that I knew much, you understand, but I thought I could handle the weapon well enough to learn the kata my teacher had now agreed to teach me. The next evening I was at the dojo early, and I am not sure why. It's not like I could practice with the weapon, for in truth I knew just enough to look silly, a pale imitation of the scene from the movie *Enter the Dragon*, where Lee is confronted by guards as he sets about releasing the slaves being held captive by the evil Han. More often than not, I managed to hit myself with greater ease than I could hit anything else, so it was perhaps just as well the opportunity to rehearse my moves in the dojo never came about before the regular class began.

When the moment finally arrived, I stood silently to the side and slightly behind my teacher, more than ready to commit the kata to memory. He made a move and I copied him. Step by step we worked our way through the kata until it was complete. The kata was repeated this way at least ten times with me following my teacher's every move. Then he said, "Okay, this time we'll move a little faster." I was ready, certain I could keep up. Mr. Vickers did a combination of blocks, strikes, and parries, and I repeated them a few seconds later. Halfway through the kata, a diagonal strike to an opponent's head is thrown in a large arching motion. The strike swings the nunchaku behind the back of the karateka holding the weapon, before being caught by the left hand on top of the right shoulder. As my teacher went through the technique, he turned his head to see if I was following. In doing so, he missed the nunchaku as it swung up toward his face. It hit him hard in the mouth. Without saying a word, he simply spat out a broken tooth and carried on. I looked on in horror as I watched the tooth and blood spin across the dojo floor. It was one of those rare moments that allowed me a glimpse of just how dangerous this man was, and I often wondered what would happen if his single-minded attitude were ever brought to bear on another person. I committed the kata to memory that night but never asked my teacher to check it in the weeks and months that followed. In fact, I never asked him to teach me anything 'extra' again. I was too embarrassed, to be honest, and too ashamed that my childish pestering had led to such a painful and expensive event.

The price paid by Mr. Vickers was not only in the physical discomfort he felt at the time, but also in the cost of the dental treatment that followed. In karate terms, I was a child, and like all children, the demands I sometimes made carried a price tag that others were left to pick up. From that moment on, I made a concerted effort to control my desire to know everything, and as a result, I have learnt to be more patient and a lot less demanding. By the time I was getting to know Mr. Vickers as an individual, his personal life was descending into turmoil, and without going into too much detail it would be true to say that events were taking their toll. Although he kept his problems to himself, a few of us knew of his internal struggle. During the five years I was learning karate from him, we became good friends outside the dojo, but I never forgot that he was my karate teacher first and my friend second. A man steeped in karate, his library of books and publications on karate and all manner of martial arts was extensive; he also had a fine collection of Japanese swords, some of which were several hundred years old.

Karate training for Mr. Vickers began in the mid-1960s when the Wado-ryu school of karate was the most established system in the country. He never told me much about his early days of training, only an occasional remark on how tough it was; and though it is often argued by earlier generations of karateka that everything they did was harder, I never heard my teacher express such an opinion. It may be that each generation of karateka does indeed grow a little less lean, standing as they do on the shoulders of others who have gone before them, but I believe every generation of karateka produces individuals who accept the challenges of budo, as well as those who merely pay lip service to it. When you look back over time, you need to keep in mind just what it is you are looking back on. Mr. Vickers' early promotion tests were taken under Tatsuo Suzuki sensei, a legendary figure in British karate and throughout the world of Wado-ryu. Later, he tested under Masafumi Shiomitsu sensei. When the dojo he was training at abandoned Wado-ryu in favor of Shito-ryu, Mr. Vickers was left with little choice but to follow. The change did not slow his progress, however, and within two years of the switch, he passed the examination for shodan. I learnt a lot from my first teacher of karate and have always felt fortunate that it was his dojo I walked into on that winter's evening in January 1974.

For those past couple of years, my life had not been devoted to karate alone. During that period, I met a young woman, Stephanie, and as time passed, we grew close. In September 1978, after a two-year courtship and intense period of hard work and saving, we married. The wedding was a simple affair, a civil ceremony void of the fuss associated with the fairy-tale production others opt for. It made no sense to us to spend a huge amount of money for a spectacle that so many rush to go into debt for. Instead, our money was put to better use as a deposit on our new home. Built only ten years earlier, the house we bought was a neat semi-detached[31] residence in the Reddish district of Stockport, Cheshire, where we settled into domesticity and enjoyed the lifestyle we soon became accustomed to as DINKS (double income, no kids). Fairly soon my life began to take on a familiar pattern of work, training, and domestic obligations. I didn't know it at the time, but as far as stability and happiness go, I had already planted the seed of my own destruction. Outside the home, my life was evenly divided between work and training; if I wasn't doing one, then I was more than likely doing the other.

I requested permission from the chief instructor for the SWKU in England, Mr. Aikman, to open a dojo, and after a brief period of deliberation, permission was granted. The dojo was established in a rented public room just a short walk away from my new home, and within a few months I was teaching a core group of sixteen students. I now appreciate the difference that exists between a karate dojo and a karate club, and can say with some authority that back then I was running a karate club. Although I didn't appreciate the disparity at the time and would have argued strongly in defense of my dojo, nevertheless, four decades later, I have a better understanding of what I'm looking at when I observe karate training. Regardless of what my feelings were back in the day, I know better now. My early days teaching karate to others were marked by my overzealous approach to training. I remember clearly wanting everyone to be as keen as I was, as dedicated to 'the way' as I perceived myself to be, and as prepared as I was to forgo almost all other considerations just to gain an inch of ground in the pursuit of mastery.

Like a great many others, then and now, my little bit of knowledge was proving to be a dangerous thing. My annoyance at the apparent lack of enthusiasm in those who came for training was not kept hidden. I often used the mantra 'work hard or go home'. Of course, the students were no doubt doing their best. I just couldn't see it. In hindsight, I recognize I was teaching more for myself than for the benefit of the students. I was living the dream, the dream of being erudite and important, of having mastered skills and gathered knowledge that others wanted: these people needed me! Almost half a century later, the mistakes I was making and the misunderstandings I labored under have become commonplace among karate instructors. Rather than becoming extinct due to better standards of education, better leadership, and an overall maturing of the karate population, the commercialization of karate and sport are now the first points of contact with karate for most members of the public. Consequently, the karate encountered by the overwhelming majority of those looking for instruction is, I believe, diluted to the point of irrelevance.

Within twelve months of establishing the club in Reddish, I was invited to teach a karate class at the local night school. I was now teaching karate four evenings a week and revelling in it. Walking into the gymnasium of the local high school for the first time, I was amazed by the number of people who turned up to learn karate. Their reasons for doing so varied wildly. Some wanted to be fighters while others simply wanted to lose weight. No one in the gym that evening expressed a desire to connect to a different culture through the study of that culture's martial arts, which was just as well, for if they had, I was in no position to introduce them. The majority had come to learn karate to help themselves feel safe walking the streets after dark, a sad indictment on a society that back then often placed concern for the victim second to the rights of the offender. I taught at the night school for three years and during that time became aware that karate was, in the mind of the public, all things to all people. This misconception has opened a panacea of marketing possibilities. But by spreading karate's appeal over as wide a demographic as possible, karate as a martial art has lost much of its moral and physical potency.

In spite of the relentless request to teach 'self-defense', I always declined. In truth, I didn't have a clue about what self-defense techniques were anyway. If a fight were about to kick off, my 'technique' was to smash the guy to the ground and stand on his head. When I fought on the streets, I threw people through shop windows and hauled them out into oncoming traffic: I became a berserker! I knew nothing of the "If someone grabs you *here*, you need to do *this* to make him *let go*" method of self-defense, a method that was, and still is, being sold to an unsuspecting public. It's all very well to put your hand out and shout "No!" while you search your pockets for keys that might be used as a knuckle-duster, but my experience of violence on the street had taught me that self-defense came from the attitude you adopt when danger stands before you. There is a time to be submissive and a time to be aggressive, and you choose the wrong attitude at your peril. Personal conflict is no different from two great armies fighting on the battlefield: success or failure is dictated by the awareness you have for the problem before you. I have never been able to teach people to fight beyond the physical movements, and I remain at a loss to understand how others can claim that they can. Fighters, individuals who already have the ability to be vicious, can swap information and learn from each other, but without the character trait allowing you to inflict serious damage on another human being with impunity, the physical moves of a fight are of little value.

A letter requesting assistance was handed to me by Terry Murthwaite, the general secretary of the SWKUE. It was written by a man who was leading a small group of others after their previous instructor had simply walked away, citing the club as no longer profitable. Ian Standing, the letter's author, asked if a new instructor could be sent so they could continue their training. It was all a bit of a mystery really; there was no record of a club or instructor, other than me, in this area . . . so who had they been training with? A short telephone conversation between Ian and me resulted in my making a trip to Cheadle the following Saturday. With no car, the seven-mile journey involved two buses and a number of wrong turns. Still, I arrived at the club only three minutes late. Six students had turned up, and over the next two hours, we trained together, and afterward got to know each other. The story of their previous instructor's behavior was shocking, and to my surprise, he turned out to be none other than the same 1st kyu who was kicked out of the Ming Chuan Dojo and the Shukokai Karate Union for forging letters and causing mischief. Still playing out his fantasy of being a karate sensei his lack of morals allowed him to open karate clubs all around the Stockport area, accepting membership and training fees, and then simply walking away from his obligations when the income dropped too low for him to make a sufficient profit.

An insight into the odious nature of this man can be gained from the tale of my last meeting with him. It's a story that requires going back in time to the summer of 1977 when I accompanied Mr. Vickers to a dan promotion test in the city of Derby. As a 1st kyu student, I was allowed to witness a dan test prior to attempting my own, an event that was for me, at that time, only six months away. With no idea of who the candidates would be, you can imagine our surprise when we saw among them none other than our old mischief-making friend. He had applied to Mr. Aikman to take a test, citing his imminent departure to Australia as the reason. Apparently, he didn't want to leave the country as a member of his current karate association, as they were, in his words, "too commercial and only interested in making money": hence, his application to have his karate skills assessed by the SWKUE. The Shukokai organization was already well established in Australia at this time so his explanation didn't make sense. Nevertheless, he was given permission to try. Taking his place in the lineup, he saw Mr. Vickers for the first time. Clearly shocked by this, his eyes fell to the floor and remained there for the entire time he stood before the grading panel. Before the test began, Mr. Vickers asked for a brief word with the grading panel, informing them of the history he had with this particular candidate. Fully informed, the panel returned to their seats and the test began.

The shodan examination put in place by Aikman sensei involved a question and answer session, with each candidate in turn coming before the panel to answer the questions put to them. Candidates typically used this as an opportunity to declare their sincerity to the tenets of *karatedo*[32], to budo, and to just about anything good and wholesome they could think of. Reminiscent of contestants in a beauty contest wishing for world peace and an end to poverty, each candidate for shodan stood before the panel and declared his willingness to live by the code of budo, to train for life, and never to bring the great art of karate into disrepute. And so it was with great interest that I paid particular attention when my old dojo sempai stepped forward. Mr. Aikman asked him if he thought he was of good character, not prone to telling lies or generally being dishonest, and I have to say, I thought my former senior's reply was surprisingly eloquent. It was, however, a calculated response designed to leave exactly the kind of impression the panel was looking for.

Mr. Aikman continued, "And do you think it's important to show respect and even loyalty to your instructor?" Again, the answer given was just right, ticking all the boxes for honesty, integrity, and propriety. "So why then did you once fabricate a letter condemning your instructor?" asked Mr. Aikman. The candidate nearly choked, his eyes darted about from left to right in a nervous dance while he stuttered and mumbled. For the first time that day his gift for imaginative articulation deserted him. No matter how he tried, and believe me he did try, he could not come up with an answer to adequately explain himself. He failed the test that day, left the building, and was never heard of again, at least not until my first visit to Cheadle, when the man's true nature was once again highlighted by his treatment of the Cheadle students. The dojo began to falter within weeks of my teaching there. For the majority of the students, the contrast between their former instructor and me was just too much. Ian Standing, the man who had written asking for instruction, actually became my last student, and for some considerable time, the recipient of one-on-one instruction. It never dawned on me to close down the dojo simply because most of the students had left, for as long as there was genuine interest in learning karate I was happy to teach it. Slowly, new people came looking for instruction and within months the dojo was once again bubbling away to the pulse of young people engaged in karate training. The student body grew, and eventually leveled out at fourteen.

Nineteen seventy-eight was also the year Keiji Tomiyama sensei, the young man I first saw when he was demonstrating sanchin kata in Rotherham, relocated from Belgium to England and settled in the city of Leicester with his new English wife, Sally. Just before arriving, Mr. Aikman moved to Norway, leaving Tomiyama sensei to pick up the reins of leadership for the SWKU in England. Choosing not to open a dojo of his own, but instead to travel around the country visiting every dojo in the association in rotation, it was during this period I got to know Tomiyama sensei better. We got on well. I admired his karate and as our friendship grew, I began to regard myself less as a member of the SWKU association and more a student of one man: Keiji Tomiyama. By this time, karate associations had already established their stranglehold on the spread of karate to the general public, and the kind of independent thinking I was engaged in was not only rare, it was also frowned on. I am the first to admit it; appreciating karate in this way has often been the cause of problems between me and others, particularly people who saw themselves as having some kind of authority over me. But the group mentality, a hallmark of the Japanese psyche and almost every karate organization they ever established, has never held my attention for more than a moment. I can relate to an individual on any number of levels, but I have always found it difficult toeing the line or following the directives of a committee that is, more often than not, made up of insufferable people with an over-developed and always misplaced sense of self-importance. Just as there are people who are always willing to put on their dogi and sweat, there will always be people who would sooner sit around a table and talk rather than practice.

In the same year, while engaged in an English squad training session, I suffered my first serious injury. Not since I had a muscle torn from my shoulder blade during a demonstration a few years earlier had I been hit such a damaging blow; and though I didn't know it at the time, a life-threatening situation was now developing inside my body. It was nothing unusual during squad training to get hit: hard. Each of us dished it out, and no one ever complained about being on the receiving end of it either. On this particular Sunday, over the course of the training, I took any number of blows from punches and kicks. This was all part and parcel for such training, and so I gave little thought to the discomfort I was feeling at the time. Over a number of exchanges two kicks, in particular, found their target, my lower abdomen, and a third hit me with some considerable force in the groin. Because of the kicks, this squad training had been even harder than usual to get through, and afterward, when I made the seventy-mile trip home to Manchester, I crawled into my bed, exhausted, and feeling just a little sorry for myself. The pain in my body intensified, but my dislike for doctors coupled with my immature desire to tough it out kept my wife from seeking help.

Eventually, I could take the pain no longer and a doctor was sent for. He was pleasant enough until discovering how I acquired my injury. From that point on, his attitude changed to one of 'serves you right for being silly enough to do karate.' The internal bruising, as he described my condition, would soon heal he said. In the meantime, the painkillers he gave me should do the trick: but they did absolutely nothing! Three hours later, the pain in my abdomen was so intense, I knew something was seriously wrong: but what? The doctor had said it was just internal bruising, so why was I feeling so sick, and why was the pain increasing? A second doctor was called but his attitude was little better than his predecessor's. His treatment differed only in the method and strength of the painkiller he administered. This time, it was a needle jabbed unceremoniously into my rump that pushed the drug directly into my bloodstream. The rapid absorption of a stronger pain suppressant brought with it a relatively quick release from my immediate distress. The doctor left as soon as the needle had been disposed of, and soon afterward, I fell into a much needed but fitful sleep. My sanctuary did not last long, however, and I woke a few hours later wracked with pain. The lower part of my body was now bloated as was the top of my legs and my scrotum. It was as if someone had taken the middle of a sumo wrestlers' body and transplanted it onto mine.

I was very weak and began to lapse in and out of consciousness; whatever was going on inside me, it was obviously more than just internal bruising. The ambulance arrived at my home soon after the call was made and after a quick examination by the paramedics, they rushed me to the hospital. I was growing weaker by the minute and the triage doctor in the emergency department wasted no time calling for a surgeon. It was clear something had to be done and done quickly. I was, in fact, suffering from serious internal bleeding, and had by this time lost so much blood from my system that my vital organs were in danger of shutting down. If that happened, I was a dead man! As well as the internal repairs to my body, and the transfusion of blood pumped into me, the surgeon discovered one of my testicles had been ruptured and might have to be removed. I wasn't aware of any of this at the time. My wife signed the consent form allowing the surgeons to do their work, and they got on with saving me from death.

When I awoke the following day, I was relieved on a number of counts, the first being that I was still around to wake up, the second, that the damage had been fixed and the bleeding stopped, and the third, to learn that my manhood was intact. Still, I was a long way from being well. Suction tubes protruded from my body, running into bottles that collected the internal residue left behind by the trauma of the injury and the surgery done to arrest the loss of blood. Ten days after being admitted, I left the hospital feeling decidedly pleased to be alive and in full possession of all my vital apparatus. No doubt, had I been wearing some kind of protective gear I may not have suffered as I did, but such was the macho mentality within the squad that wearing groin protection was as good as hanging a sign around your neck saying, "Please Kick Here!" At my dojo, the students continued to train with Steve O'Driscoll and Tommy Rowe, my friends from Shotokan. The kind of training the students engaged in didn't matter much to me; it was only for a few months, and anyway, it was more important they continued to train with good people. Although it didn't register at the time, perhaps this is when I first began to see the redundancy in using 'styles' to package karate training. That aside, I was lucky to have friends willing to help me out during this time.

Terry Harrison was one of the students training at the Cheadle dojo, and what he lacked in physical ability he more than made up for in fighting spirit and determination. He also had the gift for fundraising, and this was to prove invaluable in securing regular visits from Tomiyama sensei. For an initial outlay of just thirty pounds, the dojo was able to run a small lottery. We had to have the local council's approval first in order to do this, but that proved simple enough to obtain. The extra monthly income the dojo gained by selling just one box of scratch cards came in at seventy pounds, and this was enough to ensure a visit from Tomiyama sensei each month. As well, there was enough money left over to create resources, like a library for the dojo. Kick pads and full contact sparring gear, including helmets, were also acquired, although the gloves, pads, and helmets received little use once the novelty wore off. The restrictions to breathing, movement, and vision began to outweigh the benefits of being able to hit your training partner with full force, and so within a few months of the 'armor' arriving, it took up permanent residence in a box under the stairs in my home.

When Tomiyama sensei came to visit the dojo, which was every six weeks, the training was thrown open to all non-dojo members who wanted to attend and, who, for a small fee, could learn about karate from one of the best karate teachers in the country. My students and I practiced free of charge, as Tomiyama sensei's fee came from the dojo funds. By now, the night school class I was running in a local high school gym had come to an end, and as far as instruction was concerned, I was focused solely on teaching at the Cheadle dojo. The dojo was proving popular, so much so that I moved the training to a slightly larger and more modern public hall about a quarter of a mile away. The dojo at the old Scout Hall had character and a wooden floor, but it also had loose floorboards that lifted nails, many of which lay in ambush to tear at the feet, ripping the flesh and causing the blood to flow. The new location had a concrete floor covered in tiles that offered no 'spring' when moving and no soft landing when thrown to the ground, but it was a trade-off between getting your break falls right or the very real possibility of going home from training with one toe less than you arrived with.

It was my custom to visit Europe every Easter to take part in the annual week-long European gasshuku organized by the Shukokai European branch. Although the yearly gatherings began in Belgium, they had shifted to France in recent years. Back then, I was for the most part blissfully unaware of the politics that seem to be ever-present the moment karate moves from being a dojo-based activity to that of an organized gang. The short-sighted pyramid structure adopted by many in all spheres of life is, ironically, the very formation that guarantees ongoing discord and the eventual failure to achieve the goals for which the structure was formed in the first place. I was to learn years later that the relocation had come about because of a disagreement between the local Belgian organization that arranged the gasshuku and the Japanese instructors stationed in France and England. The Japanese instructors solved the matter by simply moving the venue to France. When I heard the story for the first time, I was reminded of my childhood, and how kids would take their ball home if they couldn't win. The Easter of 1980 saw me, as usual, headed for Europe.

This time I was traveling in the company of Tomiyama sensei. Our destination was the small French town of Charlesville-Mezerie in the northeast of the country not far from the border with Belgium: but far enough. As usual, Suzuki sensei was in control of the whole event, and as usual, he was assisted by sensei Omi, Tomiyama, Okubo, and Kamohara, all of whom were ranked 5th dan. This year the gasshuku was going to be a particularly interesting and nerve-wracking time for me. I had been invited to test for the rank of nidan (2nd dan), and knowing the method Suzuki sensei employed when testing candidates, it was difficult to see how I was going to pass. Having said that, I was more than prepared to give the test my best shot and in the end that was all I could do. Suzuki sensei was a quiet man, not prone to overawing those he was trying to teach. He would provide a short demonstration of what it was he wanted you to learn and then let you get on with trying to learn it. As the number two ranked executive with the Toyota Corporation in Europe, Suzuki sensei did not make his living from karate and was therefore free of any concern he might have regarding the happiness of his students. He just taught the things he felt we needed to know and that was that.

I believe he had a subtle sense of humor though, which he clearly demonstrated at an earlier gasshuku, when the training took place in the village of Pepinster, Belgium. On the evening before training began, Suzuki sensei arranged for everyone to attend a village dance hosted by the mayor. This we did and enjoyed the company of the locals and their famous Belgian beer, which is among the most potent of beers on sale anywhere in the world. Belgians love their brew and are not shy about sharing it with visitors. The following morning, having drunk and sung our way into near oblivion, it was a very sorry-looking gathering standing in the dojo, feeling the worse for wear and fragile beyond belief. Suzuki sensei was as sharp as ever and, with a great smile on his face, began a training session that still ranks among the most difficult I have ever done. The next two hours were all about survival, with the only consolation coming from the knowledge that almost everyone around me was feeling just as bad as I was. By the end of training, no one was suffering from a hangover, although everyone was clearly suffering. Since that gathering in Belgium, I have taken great care not to over-indulge again. Socializing outside the dojo is fine, but in all things there should be balance and the village dance in Pepinster taught me a very clear lesson in its importance.

As the days passed and the gasshuku in France progressed, I grew increasingly nervous at the thought of testing in front of Suzuki sensei. His way of testing students was to ask for a kata, and if he detected a lack of spirit or more than the smallest of mistakes, he would call a halt to the proceedings and send the candidate on his way. I watched him do this once to a well-known Scottish karateka who was testing for *sandan* (3rd dan), the dismissal coming after just three moves into his first kata. Testing for promotion under Suzuki sensei was often a short, sharp shock for those not able to meet his exacting standards. And so it was, during an afternoon kata class with Kamohara sensei that the call went out for everyone taking a dan test to come forward. As well as myself, four other students left the class and presented themselves to Tomiyama sensei; he checked our names and the ranks we were attempting to gain, and he assigned each of us a number: mine was number five.

Of the five karateka hoping to be promoted that afternoon, three were attempting to gain shodan (1st dan) while I and one other student were testing for nidan (2nd dan). The shodan candidates stepped up one by one, bowed to Suzuki sensei, and did one kata each from the Higaonna and the Itosu traditions (Naha-te and Shuri-te respectively). A short conversation ensued between Suzuki sensei and Tomiyama sensei, and then, Tomiyama sensei addressed all three candidates. With great tact, he explained Suzuki sensei's opinion of their kata, apologized for not being able to promote them on this occasion, invited them to please try again, and then asked them to return to the class. Although this outcome was not entirely unexpected, I recall looking across at the young man about to take his nidan test with me. I think he shared my thoughts. If this was the way the afternoon was going, we too would soon be back practicing our kata with Kamohara sensei.

After another short conversation and a little shuffling of papers, number four was called forward to perform his first kata. My fellow candidate got only halfway through it before being stopped. The look of anguish on his face was doing my confidence no good at all, and in disbelief and an ever-growing sense of numbness in all four of my limbs, I watched him walk back across the gym to the group he had left only a short time earlier. In a daze brought on by an avalanche of nerves, I stood before Suzuki sensei. I was fighting hard to maintain my composure, breathing deeply, and telling myself to just do my kata and not to worry about the outcome. Tomiyama sensei asked me what my favorite kata was and I said, "*shokosokun*,"[33] which he then asked me to do. With one final deep breath, I assumed the yoi (preparation) position and then launched into the kata. Although I was aware of what I was doing, I felt like I was watching myself from outside my body. The kata came to an end and I drew one last deep breath. At the table in front of me, a discussion got underway; as the two sensei talked, I composed myself and got ready to make the long walk back to class.

But the walk never came; instead, I was asked to pick a kata from the Higaonna tradition: I chose *seiyunchin*.[34] Again, the kata seemed to perform itself, with me watching on from a distance; it felt like I was dreaming but conscious at the same time . . . very strange! Following the second kata, Tomiyama sensei asked me to stand sideways to Suzuki sensei and perform various kihon techniques. Punching, blocking, and kicking combinations followed for the next twenty minutes or so before, finally, I was asked to move to the side and sit down. While I worked on recovering my composure, Tomiyama sensei walked over to the senior class and from the line, chose Andre Boutleroff, a French karateka of 3rd dan rank who had an international reputation within the European Shukokai community. Andre was one of Omi sensei's senior students from his Paris dojo. I had seen him fight in tournaments, although, until now, never had to face him. As there were no other candidates left but me, Andre and I were going to engage each other. He was a much better karateka than I was, and I knew as soon as I saw the look he was giving me that I was in big trouble. But what could I do? Where could I go? I had no place to hide . . . even if I wanted to. My only option was to stand and fight, and so I took my position opposite my opponent and made ready to engage him.

Within seconds of Tomiyama sensei shouting "Hajime!" ("Begin!"), a kick from Andre landed heavily in my stomach, sending me reeling backward across the floor. This was exactly what I expected. Panic began to join forces with my deepening sense of uncertainty to consume me. Standing up, I walked back, gingerly, to the starting line. Tomiyama sensei looked each of us in the eye in turn, and then gave the command to start. Off we went again. Andre let fly with another lightning fast front kick, and even though it found its target, it did not land well. I was able to respond to his attack with a flurry of punches and kicks of my own that pushed my antagonist backward. Tomiyama sensei called us back to the start point, and it was then that I began to understand that I was the only one being tested. Suzuki sensei was scrutinizing only me: my technique, and my fighting spirit. From that point on, I brought the fight to my opponent with as much spirit as I could gather. When the combat was brought to a halt, I stood there exhausted, but happy. I had given a good account of myself, and if that wasn't enough to gain promotion then I could do no more. Andre and I bowed to Suzuki sensei and then to each other. We shook hands, and as I watched Andre walk back to his training, I stood and awaited my fate.

The longer the conversation between the two sensei continued, the more convinced I became of my failure. Finally, after what seemed like an hour, but was probably closer to five minutes, Tomiyama sensei turned his attention to me and began to speak, "Mr. Clarke, Suzuki sensei says you are now nidan." No fuss was made as Suzuki sensei handed back my membership license, now signed and endorsed with his *hanko*,[35] a small red stamp placed next to the little box that said nidan. We shook hands and I bowed deeply to Suzuki sensei. Tomiyama sensei also shook my hand and offered his congratulations, and then asked me to return to training in the kata class. The postscript to my promotion saw a little more celebration, but I was never allowed to feel like I had achieved something of great importance. Instead, the obligation of my new rank was explained to me in no uncertain terms: there was no place for pride in my achievement. Rank was only a very small part of the ongoing conversation conducted between teacher and student, and to confuse progression through the ranks in the same light as making progress in karate would be a big mistake. Inside, I was feeling elated by my achievement, but thanks to Tomiyama sensei, I was also aware of the inconsequence of my new status. In Japan, they have a saying: "Deru kugi wa utareru," which means, "The nail that stands up, will be knocked down." Although I came to dislike the accepted wisdom behind this proverb, I did come to appreciate more and more the value in another: "Keizoku wa chikara nar," meaning, "There is strength in perseverance."

Returning home from France gave even less cause for celebration. For some time now, my involvement with karate as both a student and a teacher was growing. At one point, I was running two dojo, a night school class, and a special Saturday morning class for the Boy Scouts Association. On three Sundays each month I made the one hundred and sixty mile round trip to Nottingham for senior or squad training and, on top of that, I was in negotiation with a private school to provide karate lessons for its pupils. In all this time, I had been neglectful of my marriage and let the balance slide heavily in favor of karate. With hindsight, the stupidity of the situation is all too clearly seen, achieved by a lack of understanding and maturity on my behalf. If only I could have foreseen what was over the horizon, I might have had the sense to back off a little from my commitment to karate, and instead, focus more of my efforts on my life outside of training. I didn't, and like many other people involved with the martial arts, I was blindly rushing headlong into an emotional brick wall, the impact of which was going to leave me deeply bruised and in pain for many months to come. Stephanie had always supported me in my karate, but had a difficult time dealing with what she saw as my addiction to it. She had become the quintessential 'karate widow', but like many a good woman, it was a role she was not willing to play forever. The writing was on the wall, although for a long time I was too busy looking elsewhere to see it.

That same year, 1980, Chojiro Tani sensei, the founder of Shukokai karate, arrived in England with a group of instructors and students from Japan. To meet the founder of the karate style I was training in was a very special moment for me. Tani sensei's karate was smooth and very fast, and belied his age: he was fifty-nine years old. This was Tani-ha Shito-ryu in its purest form on display by the very person who developed it, and I was honored to be on the receiving end of his instruction. I even managed to have a private conversation with Tani sensei for a while, although little was transmitted to me about karate due to his limited English and my complete lack of Japanese at that time. He did, however, sign a number of his books for me, and kindly gave me an example of his skilled penmanship (*shodo*).[36] Having the opportunity to watch Japanese karateka training, many with a senior dan rank, gave my karate a boost. We British were, on the whole, very good at what we did, but the Japanese were so much better: I wanted to be more like them. It was easy to see why so many karateka in England switched to the Shukokai style back in the late 1960s. In Japan also, the Shukokai way swept through the karate world like an autumn wind sweeping away fallen leaves, sending other methods of training tumbling before it, or so I thought. The forty-eight kata taught by Tani sensei originate from the three main streams of karate in Okinawa, namely, Shuri-te, Naha-te, and Tomari-te. As with other Japanese schools of karate, kata preserved by the Shukokai had been infused with concepts that were not present in the original. This was nothing new, of course; the Okinawans did exactly the same with the kata they imported from China. The kata found within the Shukokai have been imbued with Tani sensei's revolutionary concepts of double hip twist, kick shot, zero, snap, shoulder shock, and more.

At this point, it is perhaps appropriate to explain the difference between Tani-ha Shito-ryu and the Shukokai. Many people outside of Japan confuse the two, as if the two are in fact the same, but they are not; the former is a weaponless fighting art, the latter, simply the name of Tani sensei's organization. When Tani sensei began training, karate in Japan was in its infancy. At Doshisha University in Kyoto, the style of karate being taught was Goju-ryu, and the head of instruction was the Okinawan, Chojun Miyagi, the founder of that style. As Miyagi sensei did not like being away from his native Okinawa for very long, he asked his friend and fellow Okinawan, Kenwa Mabuni, to take over teaching duties at Doshisha. Out of respect for his friend, Mabuni sensei continued to teach only Naha-te karate at the university. Mabuni sensei already had a dojo in nearby Osaka where he taught his own brand of karate: Shito-ryu. A few of the students from Doshisha, including Tani sensei, also went to the Mabuni dojo for extra training, and slowly, they changed their karate from Goju-ryu to the Shito-ryu style of Mabuni sensei. Chojiro Tani eventually became one of Mabuni sensei's leading students and in 1948, while working as a schoolteacher in the city of Kobe, Tani sensei founded his own dojo and karate organization, naming the latter, Shu-ko-kai[37] (which means the association for people who train the same way).

This translation should not be taken literally, as Japanese cannot be translated verbatim into English, but I feel it gets closer to the thinking behind the name chosen by Tani sensei and is preferable, in my view, to the rather lazy translation so often used: "The way for all." The type of karate Tani sensei taught, however, was Tani-ha Shito-ryu, Mr. Tani's version of Shito-ryu. The 'ha' in Japanese is the important bit here, as its use indicates that the karate in question is a distinct version of something bigger: in this case Shito-ryu. Many people today, who believe they train in and teach Shukokai karate, misunderstand the meaning of the word; and if this is the case, I cannot help but wonder what else they have misunderstood about the martial art they are passing on to others. If you are not affiliated with the Shukokai in Japan, either directly or indirectly, then you should not use its name. Likewise, if you do not practice your karate using the same principles and ideas developed by Tani sensei, then you should not use his name either. Cultivating ignorance has no place in karate and is, in my opinion, only one short step away from dishonesty. It is my belief that if you cannot trace your personal lineage back more than one or two generations to the founder of the karate you are teaching, then you should refrain from calling your karate anything other than 'new'.

The visit to England by Tani sensei and his entourage flew by, and soon all I had was a set of wonderful memories plus the commemorative medallion he gave to each of the senior members of the English association. It is interesting to note that today, nidan would not be considered a senior grade in many organizations; however, like monetary inflation, the value of rank in karate has changed over time, and these days what you see in many karate organizations at 5th dan is similar to the average 2nd dan of old: inflation! I returned to my normal training invigorated from meeting and training with Tani sensei, and now, more than ever, I was determined to go deeper into the traditional philosophy of karate. I rejected the sporting aspect of karate and the preoccupation with competitions that I now began to see in evidence all around me. I didn't make the shift in thinking very well, I'm afraid, as is so often the way when youth and inexperience combine. I let my emotions run away with me at times, and this opened a rift between Tomiyama sensei and me. It was a small one at the moment, but it would get worse. As the months passed, I grew to dislike karate tournaments more and more. All the shouting and clapping as spectators supported their champions only caused me to recoil from an activity I once thought to be an integral part of making progress in karate.

I also came to believe there was a level of dishonesty prevalent throughout the entire sport karate world, from top to bottom; and this led me to turn my back on it completely. Things came to a head between Tomiyama sensei and me at the SWKUE's annual general meeting later in 1980. My feeling was that too much time and effort was being spent on competition-related activities, but my argument did not win the day, and my proposal to use association funds to sponsor worthy students on training trips to

Japan, instead of the expenses incurred organizing tournaments, was passed over in favor of the status quo. A week after the meeting I wrote a letter of resignation to Tomiyama sensei. In it, I thanked him for his instruction and friendship over the years but told him I would have to look elsewhere for the karate I wanted to devote my future to. He was very understanding, though somewhat disappointed by my action, and in his reply, gave me the benefit of his opinion regarding my views and my behavior. It was a difficult letter to read (I still have it, and occasionally read it even now), full as it was with many home truths that needed to be placed before me. I must have read it a hundred times over the following weeks; it brought me to tears on occasion and other times made my blood boil. Eventually, I stopped beating myself over the head with its contents, put it away, and began focusing my attention on what to do next.

I decided to travel to Liverpool about thirty-five miles away, once a week, with my Shotokan friends, Tommy and Steve, to train at the dojo of Terry O'Neill sensei. From the first time I saw him, he impressed me a great deal. Not only because he was a giant of a man who had built and shaped his body similar to that of his good friend, Arnold Schwarzenegger, but also because his physical skill with karate was simply breathtaking. Terry's way of teaching was excellent and never failed to bring out the best in me, so the long drive there and back seemed a reasonable price to pay for such a training experience. Wednesday nights became my 'Shotokan' night, not because I was trying to learn the style, but because of my weekly visits to Liverpool. One Wednesday I arrived home as usual at around eleven o'clock in the evening to find my house empty and in darkness. Where could my wife be? There was no note to explain and no sign of any disturbance, and for the life of me, I could not understand why she was not at home. In a supreme act of childish immaturity, I became angry.

I was tired from the long day at work and the drive to and from Liverpool, bruised from the kumite training, and hungry, as I hadn't eaten since lunchtime. So when the telephone rang I snatched the receiver, heard a familiar voice on the other end, and began yelling down the phone like an idiot. The caller was my wife, Stephanie, and she was upset, but not at my tirade of abuse. In a gap between my screaming, she managed to tell me her mother had been found dead that night: her voice broke and she began to cry. Jacquie was only forty-eight years old and had suffered a massive heart attack that killed her almost instantly. Divorced and living on her own, she lay dead and undiscovered in her home for three days during the height of summer. The alarm was raised only when neighbors began to notice a smell coming from the apartment and called the police. When they forced entry and found Jacquie, her body was already in a state of decay and almost beyond recognition. The circumstances of her mother's death only added to the sense of devastation Stephanie was feeling. And in her moment of need, where was I? Training!

I felt numb, as if my senses were turned off. The shock of the news I just heard, together with the overwhelming realization of what I had just done, hit me like a train. I put the phone down and drove to my father-in-law's house where the family were gathered together in grief. The short time it took to drive the few miles from my home brought into focus the depth of selfishness I had sunken to in my egotistical enthusiasm for karate. As a husband, I was an utter disgrace, a sorry excuse for a man too, and what did all this make me as a karateka . . . well, not much! Regardless of how good things were going with my karate, I was in serious danger of losing who I was: the man I wanted to be. What use were strong techniques if my character was lacking to such a degree that I had little awareness of what was happening to the people I loved? I thought by training harder and more often I could place my demons in a box and lock it. I could stop the angry outbursts that led to conflict with the police and make myself a new life, free from the worry of being arrested and wasting more of my life being locked up. That Wednesday night I suddenly realized just how little progress I had made these past six years; my sense of disappointment and self-loathing was absolute. Just six years after beginning my climb from a very low place, I had fallen to rock bottom once again. Would I ever learn?

Over the following year, I made a concerted effort to be more mindful of how I was living, and with frightening regularity, the mistakes I had been making up to that point began to reveal themselves. I had been making major errors without even noticing, believing that my transition from thug to good citizen could be accomplished simply by training harder in karate. It was a mistake of monumental proportions, born from egocentric thinking that allowed me to see only how good life was going for me. At home, I was now making every effort to be a better husband and friend to my wife, and hoped beyond hope that I was making progress. My karate training, now somewhat curtailed from my previous schedule, was going nowhere. Training with Terry O'Neill was wonderful, but after the death of my mother-in-law I traveled less and less to Liverpool. My other commitments to karate also took a backseat as I invested more and more time and effort into my marriage. There were now many days each month when I didn't train or teach karate. Instead, I tried to turn that energy into becoming a better husband, a better friend, and a better person altogether.

Time passed, and though I thought myself content with the role karate now played in my life, I was in reality making little or no progress. This only consolidated my appreciation for the mistakes I had made in the past and the impact those errors were having on my life now. I came to understand that there is no decision made without consequence, no choice made without responsibility, no privilege without obligation, and no change for the better without torment. I was going to have to do something to change my situation as far as karate was concerned, or throw it all away and find some other path through life. Perhaps for the first time, I began to appreciate that when things became difficult in life, I had to look for ways through and not for ways out. Problems had to be solved, not put off for another day: I had to put the problems behind me for good so that my way ahead was clear. After long hours of conversation with friends and lengthy contemplation on my own, I knew what I had to do: I had to ask Tomiyama sensei if he would accept me back as his student. I could think of no one else in karate with whom I wanted a student–teacher relationship. All I had to do was figure out a way of making it happen. I deliberately chose not to phone him, or write a letter. Both methods felt like I was looking for an easy way back. No, I would go and meet my former teacher face to face and receive his answer to my request like a man.

The Shukokai European championships of 1981 were held in Edinburgh, Scotland. I knew Tomiyama sensei would be there, and so I was determined to be there too. The difficulty of meeting him face to face again did not feel like the 'easy' option to me, but what choice did I have? If I were ever going to change my way of dealing with life, to grow up, then what else could I do but meet awkward and unpleasant situations head on? I had been imprudent enough to make a mistake. Now I had to be a big enough man to rectify it. I told none of my former training partners I was going to be in Scotland and did not let Tomiyama sensei know either. I wanted the meeting to be spontaneous, uncluttered by previous thoughts and misconceptions that could have developed in the days leading up to it. Thus, the long drive north to Scotland was filled with trepidation and worry. In truth, I had no idea what Tomiyama sensei's reaction would be to my being there, let alone the question I was planning to ask him. My stomach was in knots as I walked into the Meadowbank Stadium, though the feelings of nausea were relieved a little by the friendly reception I received from old friends who were there to compete. The European championships that year were made special by the presence of Chojiro Tani sensei, the founder of the Shukokai, who was in Scotland as part of a tour of Europe and Scandinavia that he was making with a number of his students from Japan. For an hour or more, I sat high in the auditorium's seating, away from the activity going on at ground level. I told myself over and over that Tomiyama sensei was far too busy to have time to talk with me, but even as I was doing that I knew what the real reason was for avoiding him. The truth? I was scared of being rejected and scared of the feeling of humiliation that would follow.

I had talked myself into driving all this way to rectify an earlier mistake, and now, at the very moment of dealing with it, I was about to bolt and run away. The first real test of my resolve to be a better man and I was already faltering. Paradoxically, it was this very thought that turned things around in my head: I was sick of running, sick of giving myself permission to fail, and sick of the problems in life that such thinking had provided me to date. From my position, high in the stalls at the back of the stadium, I could see Tomiyama sensei in the center of the arena. Indeed, there were many things going on and he was very busy, but none of that was stopping me. My inertia was because of my own fear to act. But as overwhelming as that inertia was, I knew I could no longer live that way. I could no longer hope that change would happen of its own accord. I had to do the things necessary to accommodate change, to take responsibility, accept the obligation, suffer the torment, and in doing so, earn my freedom to live a better life. My legs were physically trembling, my mouth had lost all its moisture, and my heart was pounding so powerfully in my chest that I could feel it pushing against my ribs. In all the hundreds of fights I had engaged in on the street and in bars, I never felt such an overwhelming feeling of dread. But I feared my inability to act more than my possible humiliation, and so I stood up.

A short break in the proceedings provided me with a window of opportunity. I was not about to return home having failed to face either Tomiyama sensei or my fear of being rejected. Walking toward my former sensei seemed to happen in slow motion, and as I approached him he turned to face me. His expression was warm, almost smiling, but not quite. It was as if he knew what I was about to say, as if he himself had been waiting for this moment to arrive. He looked me directly in the eye and for a second I froze but then gathered myself enough to bow: deeply. He acknowledged the bow and I took a deep breath before blurting out the words I had planned to say: "Sensei, I have come to ask if you will allow me to become a student of yours again." His reply to my request was as brief as it was welcome, "Yes, everything is forgotten." And with that he asked me to contact Terry Murthwaite, the SWKUE secretary, and rejoin the association. Nothing more was ever said again about my departure or my return, but even as my karate began to improve due to the instruction of my teacher, a seed of uncertainty was already beginning to germinate. It would take a few years to grow, but grow it would; and when it did, I would once again part company with my Japanese sensei, and Japanese karate altogether.

My home life had settled into the fairly typical suburban existence experienced by many young couples making their way in life: work, mortgage, and an annual vacation to somewhere hot if you were fortunate to have a well-paying job. Stephanie and I had all of these things. We both worked hard, I in the tool store at the Ingersoll-Rand engineering plant in Wythenshawe, and Stephanie, as a legal secretary with a major London law firm that had offices in Manchester. Our combined income provided us with a modern home, a nice car, and plenty of opportunities to eat in nice restaurants; in general, we had a 'nice' life, comfortable and free from financial stress. But none of this proved to be enough to offer us contentment. With a single dojo and only a small number of students, karate no longer dominated my life to the same degree as before, and because of that I spent more time at home than ever. Perhaps, in a funny kind of way, it was the increased time spent together that exposed the cracks in our marriage. Whatever the reasons for the unhappiness were, it would be safe to say that the early years of the 1980s were not exactly my happiest, but they would prove to be the starting point of something better. I read an article around that time that said, "We cannot go back and start again, but we can start again and do things differently." Somehow, that thought stayed with me.

Easter, 1982, spring was in the air and once again, I was in France to participate in the annual SWKU European gasshuku. Sitting on a train with Tomiyama sensei as it thundered through the French countryside toward the town of Charlesville-Mezerie, I was looking forward to another four days of training with sensei Omi, Okubo, and of course, Tomiyama. Due to various delays during our journey Tomiyama sensei and I arrived late at the youth hostel that served as accommodations for the gasshuku participants. We had already missed the first training session as well as the evening meal provided by the hostel. We had also missed out on room allocation too, or should I say, I had. Tomiyama sensei's room had been reserved for him, so I was left to do the best I could to find a bed somewhere within the hostel to call my own for the next few nights. Normally, this would not have been a problem as the three-story building had large dormitories and many smaller bedrooms located across its three floors. This year, however, the hostel was in the midst of major renovation work, and a lot of the space usually taken up by visitors was out of use. After some searching, I eventually found a room on the third floor that I thought would do nicely. Most of the other rooms on that level were still being worked on, as was the corridor and the shower room. But my room was clean, and the showers delivered piping hot water by the gallon. So, pleased with my situation as the only resident on the top floor, I moved in and looked forward to the training to come.

Without a promotion test to distract me, I could relax and enjoy all the gasshuku had to offer, only a part of which was the actual training. Because of my frequent visits to Europe over a number of years, I knew many of the regular participants well and they knew me. We had collective memories of training together and socializing afterward, of sitting down to eat and engaging in conversation, often with unintentional hilarity, as we grew ever more imaginative in our attempts to hold a dialogue. We played practical jokes on each other, and engaged in friendly patriotic banter, with my recalling the English triumphs over the French at Crecy in 1346, and Agincourt in 1415, in the voice of the late Peter Sellers imitating Sir Laurence Olivier. In return, I was hit with more contemporary reminders of just how shockingly bad English cuisine was compared to that of France and the suggestion that this was no doubt the root cause of the English propensity for grumpiness! Of course, our exchanges were conducted in fun; back then, there was a very real sense that we were involved in something special.

Training hard together and relaxing afterward fostered a marvelous sense of achievement and camaraderie. I don't recall anyone crossing the line into impropriety as so often happens these days. I'm not suggesting it never happened. I'm sure with individuals in some groups it did, but today, the personal discipline and humility required to prevent such things happening are seen as rare commodities in a world where karate instructors compete for the dollar and the largest number of followers. Concepts such as *shingitai*, for example, have long since slipped from the lexicon of martial virtues, replaced by best business practice and a plethora of market strategies borrowed from the 'Fitness Industry'. It must seem to karateka with only a few years training, say less than twenty, that it was ever thus; but even as recently as forty years ago, karate made available a very different education to the one for sale these days. Shoshin Nagamine sensei, the founder of Matsubayashi Shorin-ryu karatedo[38] had this to say about shingitai when I interviewed him in his dojo in Okinawa in 1992:

> "In karate we have a principle called Shingitai. Shin means your spirit, Gi means your technique, and Tai means your body. To do karate well and to understand it properly you have to harmonize these three things within you. Today in karate training there is an overemphasis on Gi and Tai, the techniques and the body. The Shin, spirit, of a person is often left behind while the other two aspects are worked on. Technique and power seem to be the reason why some people are doing karate these days; this is now a much bigger problem than it was some sixty years ago. We should not forget the building of a student's spirit and character. This point is very important and I want to emphasize it. The decline in karate has come about because people want to do karate just for sport or business. To adopt the principle of Shin throughout your karate training is very hard and to be successful takes a long time. It is much easier to train your body without the discipline of Shin. Your ability to do karate techniques comes from your body and your knowledge and practice of them, but wisdom comes from your mind and your heart. Your ability to make the techniques work comes from your feeling for karate, not only your knowledge of it. I would like to see more attention put on education; we must educate students on the importance of achieving a good feeling for karate through the development of Shin."

Although no longer alive, Nagamine sensei's words continue to offer sound advice to karateka searching for more from karate than physical skills or fighting techniques.

After a wonderful week of karate, I returned home to England full of new ideas and began to plan the innovations I was going to introduce to my students. As always, however, the best laid plans of mice and men have a way of being usurped by nature, and just when I thought I had my world back in balance and under some control, life stepped in and hit me, brutally: right between the eyes. Two weeks after my trip to France, I was at my parents' house enjoying my usual Saturday morning visit. They were getting on in years, and I was now old enough to appreciate the hardships my siblings and I, especially me, had brought to their door. My daily phone calls and weekly visits came from a deepening sense of respect and love for them as I grew older, that, and a deep feeling of remorse for the particular hurt I had caused them during the years when I was often out of control. I could at least be a good son, now, today!

This is what I was doing when the virus hit. I was, in fact, sharing a joke with my mother at the time, and we were doing our best to confuse my father, which wasn't that challenging a task if you picked your moment correctly. Suddenly, amidst the laughter, I began to feel unwell. I became extremely hot and a little breathless, and every joint in my body began to hurt. In spite of my mother's pleas to stay and to go upstairs and lay down, I decided to return home and so left my parents' house before the symptoms grew any worse. As the afternoon passed, my condition deteriorated seriously, with the onset of diarrhoea and a steadily rising temperature. Remembering my previous experience with internal bleeding, this time a doctor was called sooner rather than later; he took one look at me and called an ambulance. In the hospital, I was isolated while the medical staff worked feverishly to stabilize me and address the battle I was losing to breathe and stay conscious. The speed with which the symptoms had come on was cause for great concern among the doctors and nursing staff. A cannula (a small plastic valve attached to a needle) was inserted into the skin on the back of my hand, through which medication was administered regularly.

Still, I was growing weaker by the hour and concern for my welfare was turning into anxiety over the chances of my surviving. I first became aware that things were looking grim when the doctor suggested my family come to the hospital to be with me. In one of my less lucid moments, a priest issued the last rites of the Catholic Church, an act that was done without my permission and something I later complained about, but received no apology for. I had no need for their rites or superstitious beliefs. Stephanie had filled out the admission forms declaring my religious status, but it was done in error, in the stress of the moment, when all she wanted to do was expedite the care I needed. The priest chose to work his magic in the time it took Stephanie to go home to get some personal items and return with them. But my soul, if indeed I ever had one, did not need saving by an institution that is so rightly described in my opinion as 'the whore of Babylon'. It was only days later, when the fever broke, and I began making the slow climb back to good health that my doctor explained the condition I had been struggling to overcome was Legionnaire's disease.

Apparently, it was introduced to my body via the contaminated water from the shower I was using during the gasshuku in France. It was explained to me just how close my death had been, and how I wasn't to worry about that now because I was well on my way to recovery. Odd, but I have no recollection of ever being worried or fearful about dying. Death will come one day. I have always understood that, and although I have no desire to go early, when the grim reaper does come to call, he won't find me cowering under the covers—or asking for a priest! According to the doctor, my survival was due, not to divine intervention, but to my high level of fitness; this, he told me, proved the deciding factor in my recovery. Had I been old, a smoker, overweight, or just plain unfit, my chances of survival would have been cut to almost nil. If anything can take credit for my triumph over this particular challenge, then it must surely be karate.

A great deal more is known these days about Legionnaire's disease, its cause, and how the bacterium runs its course once it has entered your body. It is now known to be a type of hard-hitting pneumonia, caused by a bacterium named in 1976 as "legionella," following an outbreak of the disease at a conference of the American Legion in Philadelphia. To people unlucky enough to contract the disease it makes it no less dangerous or unpleasant to deal with, but at least the medical professionals know what they are up against, and hospitals are far better equipped to handle it. The only treatment available to me was to be pumped to the gills with antibiotics for days, and that, together with the natural resilience of my body, proved to be enough to see me through. Even so, once out of the hospital my convalescence took many weeks, and to this day, my lung capacity has never returned to its pre-illness level. In later years, I came to develop a chronic lung condition known as bronchiectasis, a widening of the airways within the lungs that prevents the naturally occurring mucus to rise from the bottom of the lungs and clear them of miniscule dust particles and bacteria.

Because of this, high levels of bacteria are constantly present at the base of my lungs, leading to frequent infection and a decrease in function. As I write this, I am fast approaching my sixtieth year, and the condition is beginning to make its presence felt more and more; for example, I am often left breathless after a spirited performance of kata. Legionnaire's disease also brought to an end my long-standing commitment to the British Red Cross and my role as a blood donor. Until my trip to France, I made eighteen regular donations of blood a year, as well as extra donations on special occasions to aid the sufferers of leukaemia. Apparently, the white cells in my blood contain something fairly rare, making my blood of value in combating this particular form of cancer.

Found in only a small percentage of donors within Great Britain, I was always very happy to help when asked. I felt really sad and disappointed about no longer being able to provide blood to those who needed it. Perhaps somewhere in the back of my head I was trying to give something back for all the blood I had spilt and wasted over the years. Who knows?

I had plenty of time to think about my involvement with karate as I recovered, and from that reflection, I knew that I wanted to move deeper into karate and not just climb further up the ladder of promotion. To do that, I was going to have to cultivate my character far more than I had been willing to do previously. It would take time, balance, integrity, and no small amount of courage, and in truth, I was not sure I had enough of these things within me. Time would tell, I guess. All I could really do was make a start. As well as my physical training, I became an avid reader of books on many different schools of karate and other martial arts, as well as—but to a lesser extent—various world religions and Eastern philosophies. Although I looked at many, none came close to capturing my imagination like the concept of Zen. I realize how cliché it sounds for a karateka to be drawn to the teachings of Zen, but I was not drawn to it. As I began to read and think . . . I simply recognized it. No, I am not a Buddhist, nor a Zen master, but then, show me an individual who truly believes he has mastered Zen, and I'll show you a narcissistic personality giving free reign to his own delusions. Simply put, the more one tries to contain Zen in ritual practice, or words, the further from its essence one becomes. Zen is not a religion, nor is it a sect of Buddhism. It simply "is" and you either accept the clarity of that thought or you don't.

Tomiyama sensei was a great help to me during this time, not only in the way he helped me fill in the gaps regarding my knowledge of karate's history, but also as a source of information on many of the underlying concepts found in budo, many of which often fail to come to the surface during a student's education in the dojo. We often talked late into the early hours of the morning during his monthly visits to my dojo. Staying overnight at my home was meant to give him a chance to rest before making the long drive home to Leicester. Instead, due to my thirst for information, he often drove home tired anyway. My curiosity back then was simplistic and childlike, closer to that of a six-year-old than an adult, and to his eternal credit, Tomiyama sensei somehow managed to put up with my questions to his explanations with remarkable patience: "How come?" "Who said?" "So what?" Tomiyama sensei was also helpful in teaching me how to become introspective, an attribute I found almost impossible to adopt at first due to the ugliness I saw when I began to take a close look at exactly who I was. I often thought my teacher unfair and brutal in his criticism of me, and at times, I am ashamed to say, I even hated him. But such feelings lasted for only an hour or two before the truth of his comments began to land in my consciousness like snowflakes landing on a rock. Slowly, and one by one, the ideas he put to me and the truths he exposed began to cover my thinking in a new layer of understanding. It was a process that took time, years in fact, and though I was destined to walk away from him a second time, this time for good, Tomiyama sensei's teaching has remained with me to this day. We remain friends, and although I am no longer connected to him through the physical practice of karate, I continue to respect, with a deep sense of gratitude, the efforts he made to teach a very poor student.

In August 1982, Tomiyama sensei returned to Japan due to the sudden illness of his father. Always a good son to his parents, as well as a good sensei to me, he was destined to be away for quite some time, running his father's business. Over the three years that he was in Japan, I felt alone in England. My connection to the SWKUE was not a strong one; I was in it because I felt I had to be for my sensei's sake. With him gone and his return uncertain,

I felt adrift with no particular direction. Had I thought about my connection with karate differently I would have, no doubt, helped keep the organization going, and like everyone else, dreamed of his return. My education in karate and my faith in myself were still quite fragile during this time, slight, and easily lost. I was still some years away from fully grasping the concept of *kai un,*[39] developing my own fate.

At home, my wife Stephanie and I decided to divorce just a few weeks after Tomiyama sensei's departure, and so it seemed to me that the collapse of my life was once again complete. Emotionally, I was at the bottom of a very deep hole, and from where I was standing, there seemed no chance at all of ever getting out. It was apparent that no matter how often I managed to get my life on track, I still managed to find myself in a bad place. Clearly, I was doing something wrong. This was not the fault of anyone else, and there was no grand design to keep me from a life of contentment. I was just not good at discovering the means to live well. Somewhere, but I don't remember where, I read that a seeker will find a teacher when he is ready for the lesson. I was in desperate need of a teacher back then and as if by the law of some greater truth, I found one. Walking into my friend's dojo one evening, I met John Boyle, a karateka I would come to respect and admire, and feel privileged to call a friend. He trained in Okinawan Goju-ryu and told me of the coming visit to Liverpool of Morio Higaonna sensei, a 7th dan instructor from Okinawa. I decided to attend the weekend of training, little knowing the life-changing effect that decision would have.

The break-up with my wife, when it came, was as amicable as possible given the gravity of the event. It was nevertheless a tearful episode for us both. So what went wrong? Maybe we had married too young, or maybe we had failed to struggle sufficiently to move us beyond the early years and into middle age. Unlike many newlyweds, we had not jumped into parenthood or incurred debts we could not afford to pay. We had been, in many ways, a model young couple who had saved diligently for years before we married, taken on a mortgage, and settled into domestic life with a burden of debt that was easily managed. I recognize now that it is never enough to simply work hard to achieve the things we want in life. If we want to hang on to our achievements, we have to be prepared to work even harder. People often want a big wedding, but give little thought to achieving a successful marriage; they want babies, but then treat parenthood as an inconvenience; and they want celebrity, without the skill or talent to deserve it. It took me many years to learn this particular life lesson: 'Shallow desires bring shallow rewards', and although I accept it now, I understand how unconvincing it must sound to people still trying to achieve the things they want. When our home was sold and the mortgage paid off, Stephanie and I divided our belongings equitably, and split the remaining money into equal amounts.

We hadn't actually divorced at this point, as that would take some additional time in order to comply with the law in England back in the early 1980s. However, between us we made the decision our marriage was over. I helped her move back into her father's house, and then two days later I flew out of Manchester bound for New York. Was I running away? Of course I was, although it did not seem that way until after some time had passed; still, it did not take me long to realize nothing could be achieved by avoiding the truth of my situation. I spent several weeks with my cousin in Connecticut, and it was the friendship and love I received from Frank and his wife, Pam, that helped me recover, at least enough to begin planning for the future. We hiked in the hills around Torrington and further afield, walked the streets of Lower Manhattan, and ate pizza in Little Italy. We visited great libraries, museums, and universities, and stood atop the World Trade Center, looking down upon the Statue of Liberty and watching the sunlight dance on the surface of the water where the East and Hudson

Rivers meet in the upper bay of New York Harbor. I was having a great time, but it wasn't real: this wasn't my life. My life was waiting for me back across the Atlantic Ocean, and the longer I put off returning the longer I was keeping alive the sadness I felt. I had to go home and I had to rebuild a life worth living.

Four days after arriving back in Manchester I took off again; this time I headed for the island of Jersey in the English Channel, just a few miles from the French coast. Jersey was home to Dave Moss, 4th dan and chief instructor of the Shukokai in the Channel Islands. We first met and became friends during my frequent visits to the continent. Originally from England, Dave had lived in Jersey for almost twenty years and was married to a local woman, Vanessa. Together they had a young son and lived in a small apartment in Millbrook just a short drive from the island's capital, St. Helier. Dave was kind enough to invite me to stay with him for a while until I got back on my feet, found a job and a place to live, and could begin to put the mistakes of the past behind me. I was very pleased to accept his offer, as I was still making the adjustment from 'married man with own home' to 'single guy of uncertain means'.

The generosity of Dave and Vanessa to invite me, practically a stranger, into their home was a wonderful gift, a gift I was keen not to take for granted. Their apartment was small, and I was acutely aware of not outstaying my welcome, so I began looking for accommodation in the classifieds of the local newspaper on the very day of my arrival on Jersey. Finding somewhere to live was a task that proved a little more difficult than I had imagined, due entirely to the island being a tax haven. Only people born on Jersey had the right to buy or rent property, and all others were subject to the laws governing 'housing qualifications'. Essential workers from outside Jersey could rent homes and apartments, but only for as long as they were working; if they lost their job or resigned, they lost their home too! People like me who wanted to live on the island but whose occupation was not considered essential, had no alternative but to rely on friends or rent a single room in a house owned by a local. Having a lodger or two was a thriving industry and a major source of income for many who were Jersey born and bred.

With an income tax rate of only one percent, the island has always been a magnet for the British, and without such draconian housing laws, Jersey would be swamped by people looking to keep more of what they earned. I believe the laws have changed somewhat since my time there when I would have to live on the island permanently, working and paying tax for at least twenty years, in order to qualify for the right to rent an apartment. Renting a house would have remained impossible unless I had a family with two or more children. Nonlocals, like me, had no access to unemployment benefits, so without a job, remaining on the island would quickly become a problem. If, as indeed Dave has subsequently done, I would have remained on Jersey for thirty years, I would have gained 'full qualifications', the term used to describe the rights and privileges bestowed upon the locals on the day they are born. I had no actual idea of how long my stay on the island would be, but my instinct told me it wouldn't be much longer than the time it took to get a good suntan and a healthy bank balance, and to have a little fun along the way.

I moved into my own accommodations after just two days. Vanessa had a friend whose family owned a small hotel that was closed due to impending renovations, so I was allowed the use of one of the rooms. It suited them to have someone living on the premises until the work began, and for my part, it was 'interesting' to have an entire hotel to myself. My stay didn't last long, only a few weeks, but the solitude I experienced there allowed me the time I needed to take stock of my new situation. The hotel stood on its own grounds in a heavily wooded valley and, in many ways, provided the perfect location for me to come to terms with my changed circumstances. It was a peaceful place, the silence only broken by the chatter of birds and the occasional dog barking somewhere off in the distance along the valley. At night, the blackness and silence was complete!

Springtime, March 1983, and within days of my arrival on Jersey I began training on a regular basis again at the St. Helier dojo, combining the dojo training with runs along the many beaches and country lanes around my new lodgings at the hotel, and for a while the sadness, which had enveloped my life, began to weaken. The sky was blue again, literally, and my surrounds were tranquil, fresh, and new. It would take some time for me to fully move on from my former life to my new one, but as the days and weeks passed by, I found my heart was less heavy and each new day brought with it the promise of something better. I entered the dojo one evening and was surprised to see Andre Boutleroff, my sparring partner from my nidan test, warming up in a corner of the dojo in his own typically robust way. Our meeting this time was less of a confrontation, and after training was over we shared a few beers and a few memories of our first meeting and the many subsequent times we had trained together since. He was on holiday in Jersey and stayed for only a short time; still, it was good to see him again, although I cannot say I gained the same level of enjoyment from being reacquainted with his kicks. Andre was always a hard hitter, and I was never able to defend myself fully from his attacks. The strikes that got through my blocks always left their mark, some for more than a week!

Yet it was refreshing to be a student again, free from the concerns and obligations that accompany students and their problems. I had no trouble at all letting the title 'sensei' slip, and on the odd occasion when I was asked to teach for the evening, I always felt slightly disappointed at having to step back into the role of instructor. Still, helping out was the least I could do in return for the kindnesses coming my way. Spring gave way to summer and the temperature, just like the number of tourists to the small island, rose steadily week after week. I had a brief respite from both when, along with Dave, I flew to Paris on route to Charlesville-Mezerie for yet another gasshuku. We had arranged to meet up with Andre in Paris but instead found another old friend waiting for us. This time it was Kenny Johnson from England. Andre would be along to pick us all up later, so for a while we had a chance to take a quick look around our immediate surroundings.

From what I saw, I liked Paris; it reminded me a little of Copenhagen and was in complete contrast to New York where I had been only a few months earlier. Andre eventually arrived, and with all four of us safely tucked up in his car and with typical French '*joie de vivre*', we drove out of the city at speeds the cobbled streets were never designed to handle. Over the length of the gasshuku, Omi sensei led the training with the help of Okubo sensei. We ran and trained, ate and drank, and slept and renewed old friendships for the next four days until the gasshuku was over. I was a little wary of taking a shower at first, given the outcome of my previous visit, but the hostel was no longer in a state of work-in-progress, so I crossed my fingers and hoped that lightning would not strike twice. Besides, the doctors who treated me said I was probably immune to Legionnaire's disease now, due to my body having fought it off and built up antibodies in my blood. At least that was good to know.

Back in Jersey, the summer rolled by. Days, weeks, and months of sunshine had a rejuvenating effect on me and I began to adjust to my new reality. But it wasn't all fun. Proving more difficult than I imagined was dealing with the lingering feeling of emptiness I carried around with me, invisible and undetectable by others. I had no difficulty looking after myself in a practical way, cooking, cleaning, or living within my income; I had no problems finding girlfriends either, but I missed the sense of companionship I had with my wife. Ironic, then, that I had been so careless with the emotional security I had when married; now I no longer had it, and emotional security seemed like the most valuable commodity in the world. The people I worked for owned and operated a string of jewelry shops across the island's capital. Business was good and a new shop had just been refitted and stood ready for its grand opening the following week. To celebrate the end of the fitting-out process, I joined several of my work colleagues at a seventeenth-century pub, the Smugglers, next to the beach at Ouaisne Bay. Good food and several jugs of beer between us ensured the celebration flowed smoothly on from afternoon to early evening.

That's when I met Kathy, a young woman visiting Jersey to spend time with an old girlfriend of hers from college who was now working at the pharmacy in Jersey Hospital. After a somewhat shaky start, a combination of tiredness, alcohol, and, at least in my case, an overwhelming of my senses, I left early. That night I lay in bed, unable to sleep, wondering what was happening to me. For reasons beyond my control, I could not get it out of my head that I already 'knew' the young woman I supposedly met for the first time earlier that evening, and yet I seemed to recognize her. The following day I returned to the pub to meet a friend and have lunch. I had no idea where Kathy was staying, how long she would be on the island, or if I would ever see her again. If indeed there are miracles to be found, I found one while sitting at a small table next to the sea wall with my friend, discussing what to eat for lunch. At the precise moment I looked up from the menu, who should walk past but Kathy and her girlfriend. They had also returned to the bay to walk along the beach and dip their feet in the warm waters of the gulf steam. My heart was pounding so hard I could hardly breathe. I wanted to call out to her, shout her name, but nothing would come. Finally, my friend did what I could not, and invited them over to join us.

That evening Kathy and I met again and had a chance to talk at length, and from that moment on we dropped the posturing, acknowledged our mutual attraction, and began to get to know each other. By the time she was due to fly home, two weeks later, we already knew we would spend the rest of our lives together, and with that in mind, we took the necessary steps to make it happen. Before arriving in Jersey, Kathy had already gained a placement at teacher-training college, as well as a position as a trainee-midwife. On her return to England, she withdrew from both courses and returned to Jersey. Although her choice was a cause of concern within her family, we were in no doubt of our commitment to each other. As I write these words, more than thirty years have passed since that day on the beach. Kathy and I have been through much together; we both knew then what we both know now—our life was never going to be 'normal', at least as the world would have it. But it would be true and genuine, and full of love for one another.

When I was young, I truly believed anger and aggression were the most powerful of emotions; possessed of either it was possible to achieve anything, to get my way in almost any situation. But I have come to learn how small a view of power that is, and over the years since meeting Kathy, I am reminded constantly of an emotion powerful enough to calm my anger and subdue my aggression: love. I'm not talking about romantic love or the infatuation that draws two people together and then fades like the darkness of night before a rising sun. The love I speak of empowers you to endure the unendurable and to face insurmountable odds and hardships. The extremes of life are often met in unequal measure: adversity and disappointment can outweigh the good; but met together, extremes can be navigated and life returned to better times. It was the Russian writer and dramatist, Maxim Gorky (1868–1936), who, back in 1914, wrote, "When one loves somebody, everything is clear—where to go, what to do—it all takes care of itself and one doesn't have to ask anybody about anything." Even in those very early days, when our love was indeed still young and full of excitement, we both understood that regardless of what lay ahead we would face it together. Today, our eyes still light up when the other walks into the room.

On our first 'real' evening together, I planned to take Kathy to watch the sunset in its usual spectacular way at the lighthouse on Corbiére Point, and then on to a romantic candlelight dinner at one of the island's many beachside restaurants. However, earlier in the day I was asked to teach the evening class at the dojo; although I could hardly say no, I immediately realized this would make reaching Corbiére before sunset a little tricky. Still, if all went well and the class finished exactly on time, I knew we would just about make it. Kathy, who had never seen karate before, came with me and was happy to watch the training. She already knew how much karate meant to me and was eager to get a proper look at it. Everything was going well and about an hour into the class, I asked the students to gather around me while I demonstrated an important detail from their kata.

Without warning, one of the students threw himself violently to the floor and began convulsing. Right away, I recognized his epilepsy for what it was and knew there was nothing to worry about. In such cases, it is advisable to allow the seizure to play out, making sure the airways remain open and there are no hard objects around to be impacted if there is excessive thrashing of the limbs. Most epileptic seizures last for only a few moments, after which the sufferer recovers and slowly returns to normal. Yet as I began to assist him, I noticed blood flowing across the floor and knew immediately something was wrong. His face had taken the full force of the dive to the ground and the impact had split his nose and upper lip wide open. I became concerned he might have difficulty breathing if he swallowed his blood, so I dashed into the changing room to grab some coins from my wallet and sent two students out to the nearest public phone to call for an ambulance, as there were no cell (mobile) phones back then. I returned to the dojo and was taken aback by what I found.

In quiet approbation, I stood and watched as Kathy, a registered nurse, comforted the student while making sure his airways remained clear until help arrived. When the paramedics got there, around fifteen minutes later, the student had all but recovered from his seizure, and Kathy had done all she could to halt the flow of blood from his mouth and nose. By the time I closed the dojo for the night and checked at the hospital that the student was okay, the sun had well and truly set. Kathy's skirt had been soaked in blood and even though she did her best to clean up, she was no longer in the mood for a romantic candlelight dinner. Instead, we stopped by a hamburger stall on the promenade and then drove up the hill to the children's playground within the walls of Fort Regent; there we sat on the swings until late, talking, eating our burgers, and laughing at the moon about our 'unforgettable first date'.

As the first half of 1983 unfolded, my techniques improved due in no small part to the balance between teaching and training, now tilting more toward training. That and the opportunities I had to mix with some very strong karateka were making a difference. But there was a sense of dissolution creeping into my thoughts each time I went to the dojo. More and more I found myself thinking, "Is this it? Is this all there is?" If all karate consisted of was learning more and more kata, did I want to spend any more time doing that? There had to be more to karate than just kicking and punching! I wanted more than just a good sweat session, more than just a good knock-about with friends; there had to be something else, something that would add value to my life in ways that I could not get from other sources. All of my karate and philosophy books were packed in boxes and held in storage at my parent's house in Manchester. Jersey's library was devoid of books on karate, although there were a few on judo and jujitsu, but there was little on the shelf that captured my interest.

I knew there must be more to karate; I had read that there was. Connections between the physical training and the moral education provided by authentic karate training were out there, somewhere: what I needed to do was seek them out. As the weeks and months passed by Kathy and I settled into life in Jersey; Kathy took a nursing job at a nursing home that catered to the rich, or famous, or both; and I continued to work in the jewelry business. I was never suited to my employment, but it paid well, and it was secure, so I was happy to stay. In November that year, I flew to Nottingham to train with Tomiyama sensei. He was making a rare visit to England from Japan and together with Omi sensei and Okubo sensei who had flown in from Paris, a weekend of instruction lay ahead. On the first day, the training was spread over three sessions, each of two hours duration. With only short breaks in between, I climbed into bed on Saturday night, totally exhausted. The second day proved a little less demanding, with only two training sessions scheduled.

Over the weekend, an invitation had been issued to those who were eligible to take part in a promotion test, and at the suggestion of Dave Moss, I put my name forward to take the examination for sandan (3rd dan). When the weekend's training was finally over, the applicants were divided into small groups, each relating to the grade its members were attempting. Besides me, there were two others taking the test for sandan; for all three of us, our ordeal would be over very quickly: one way or the other. Each of us had one chance, and one chance only, to display the depth of our understanding and the scope of our abilities. We knew that one slipup would be one too many and result in our dismissal from the proceedings. When my turn came, I was asked to choose a kata from the Shuri-te tradition; I chose the kata *dai kosokun.*[40] Ever since I was introduced to kata, my preference had always been kata from the Naha-te tradition, but I wanted to display a Shuri-te style kata first. All schools of Shito-ryu use kata from both traditions, and in this respect the Shukokai was no different from any other school of Shito-ryu.

My theory was this: if I were still in the test after a display of Shuri-te kata, I had a good chance of success. I performed the kata and much to my surprise was not asked to retire. For my next kata, I chose seiyunchin, a longtime favorite of mine from Naha-te, and a kata I believed I had a good feeling for; on completion, I bowed and waited. I was devastated when told I had done the kata incorrectly: I simply couldn't believe it! I had done the kata exactly the way it was practiced in Jersey; Dave Moss was *yondan* (4th dan), so how could he teach the kata incorrectly? Standing there ready to be dismissed, a brief discussion ensued among the sensei; then, completely unexpectedly, I was asked to choose a different Naha-te kata. The situation took me by surprise and in my confusion, I chose to demonstrate the kata *tensho*, although to this day I am not sure why I did that. It was a kata I had little feeling for and as a consequence, my performance was a poor one; the criticism that followed was entirely justified. Like that of the other candidates, my fate was sealed, and together, the three of us left the room shortly afterward: a trio of disappointed souls.

Tomiyama sensei returned to Japan shortly afterward, and I returned to Jersey; but before we parted, he told me of his plans to return permanently to England the following year. I was pleased to hear the news, but a small part of me was not at all sure I would be involved in Shito-ryu by the time he got back. My growing dissatisfaction with Shito-ryu had nothing to do with a failed promotion test. I had failed a promotion test before; the dilemma I faced had less to do with what was happening in my karate training and more to do with what wasn't. On Jersey, I was training less at the dojo and more on my own. My thoughts continually returned to the weekend I had spent training with Higaonna sensei almost a year earlier. Kathy and I had decided to return to England to live, but before we did that, I wanted to go to Japan. The dream to make the trip had been with me for years, but until now I had neither the time nor the funds to make the dream a reality.

Rather than the Japanese mainland, I decided, after much thought, to travel to the island of Okinawa instead. Why? Well, as the saying goes, "When the student is ready, the teacher will appear" and it was right about then that a series of landmark TV documentaries concerning the martial arts of Asia began to air on the BBC. Called *The Way of the Warrior*, each episode took an in-depth look at a different martial art, and for people like me it was manna from heaven. The episode on karate featured Morio Higaonna, the sensei I trained with in Liverpool only a year earlier. It began with a close-up shot of Higaonna sensei training his hands by slapping a heavy stone and later, showed him descending the stairs on the outside of his mother's home and entering his dojo that was in the converted garage under the house. I took the documentary to be a sign and instinctively knew that Okinawa, and not Japan, was the place to go to discover the essence of karate.

Without delay, our plans were made and tickets booked, but the journey would not be easy. Unlike today when airplanes can fly long distances in one go, back in 1984 flights were shorter and took longer. Once in Okinawa, my plan was to find Higaonna sensei's dojo and seek permission to train with him. I just wanted to go deeper into karate, to discover the undiscovered that I knew existed. Kathy and I left London for Okinawa on February 2, 1984.

CHAPTER FOUR

"What we hope ever to do with ease we must
first learn to do with diligence."
–Samuel Johnson

THE NAME, Naha-field, as the international airport in Okinawa was known in the early eighties, did little for my confidence that we would have a safe landing. Arriving tired, hungry, and in desperate need of a shower, thankfully, Naha-field, was a bit more of an airport than I had feared, not by much though. The arrival hall was a single-story building that looked as if it had been constructed in a hurry after the end of WW II; apart from the rest-rooms and one tiny food outlet, the airport offered no facilities at all. Still, Kathy and I were happy to be back on terra firma.

Planning for the journey was, well, 'basic'; but I thought only of the good that might come from following my dream: Kathy was less enthusiastic. Apart from her trip to Jersey, where as fate would have it, she met me on her first day on the island, Kathy had never left England, so to travel to the other side of the planet was a little more daunting for her. Still, she felt good that at least we had a contact in Okinawa, so no matter how strange a place it was, we wouldn't be on our own. I revealed the truth of our situation thirty-five thousand feet above the subcontinent of India. Kathy wasn't happy, but she was too tired to complain, so I got off lightly. Higaonna sensei had no idea we were coming, nor did anyone else for that matter; my 'grand plan' to locate Higaonna sensei's dojo rested solely on the clarity of my memory. I was certain if I could get to Naha, I could find his dojo. How difficult could it be to find a dojo with two huge karate signs hanging outside the door? Innocence can be a beautiful thing sometimes. The scale and layout of Naha never figured highly in my plan, nor did the prospect that Higaonna sensei might well be overseas; and I never even imagined that I could be refused entry to his dojo. Stupidity on my part perhaps, but I believe an honest heart often appears simple, and my motives for journeying to Okinawa were as simple as they were honest.

The trip had been a long and tiring one, thirty-two hours in all, and had taken us from London to Amsterdam, then on to Bangkok via Dubai. From the Thai capital, we flew to Taiwan and finally, to Okinawa. Today the same journey from England and Europe is more direct with fewer stopovers; Okinawa is no longer an awkward place to reach, and for most travelers, the cost involved falls well within their means. As a result, the island now has several thousand visitors each year, arriving from all over the world to train in karate and kobudo. Recently, an entire "Package Holiday" industry has sprung up to cater to a new breed of karateka: the karate tourists. They travel to the island in large groups organized by a third party, and they sample karate and kobudo before returning to the comfort of their Western-style hotel rooms. To complete their visit, they are bused to various "karate sites of interest," and later, presented with a certificate of completion at the end of their stay. Thus, they perpetuate the myth that they have trained in karate in Okinawa.

Clearly, the people who take part in these tours fail to gain an authentic experience of being in Okinawa, let alone engage with karate or kobudo in a meaningful way; and the training they do is too short, too orchestrated, and too general for anything worthwhile to emerge from the time they spend in the company of their instructors. Perhaps if the participants were new to karate it would be a different story, but they are not. The majority already wear a black belt and so clearly believe they are already well skilled in the art. Back in the opening weeks of 1984, Okinawa was still isolated from the rest of the international karate community by cost as well as distance, and for the most part, the only foreign karateka were American service personnel stationed on the island. Less than a handful of karateka from England had made it to Okinawa before I arrived, and of those who had, most went there to train at the Uechi-ryu dojo of Kanei Uechi sensei. With the notable exception of Mark Bishop,[41] hardly anyone else had traveled to Okinawa to train in Goju-ryu.

The heat of the day had subsided a little by the time we landed at around seven-thirty in the evening, but the air still felt warm to us. With no clear idea of what to expect, the tropical nature of Okinawa only added to its mystique and to a growing sense of being a long way from home. The eight-hour time difference between England and Okinawa did little to ease the yoke of exhaustion Kathy and I carried. Oppressively tired, all we wanted to do was take a shower and sleep for as long as possible, but before we could do that we first had to negotiate the formalities of entry into Japan. I had hoped for a speedy passage through quarantine, passport control, and finally customs, but had not taken into account just how fastidious the officials could be. Our progress was delayed a little as Kathy and I had to fill out a number of cards declaring that, among other things, we had no explosives or dangerous animals in our luggage. The quarantine officer didn't just look at the cards we handed him, he studied them; as a result we were the last to go through passport control and therefore the last to pass through customs too.

All had gone smoothly, if a little slowly, and thoughts of a warm shower and a comfortable bed grew stronger. The passport check was concluded without incident, and we had cleared the second hurdle standing between us and a good night's sleep, but every silver lining has a black cloud attached to it, and ours appeared in the form of the customs officer we found ourselves standing in front of. He was scrupulous in his approach and watching him from the end of the line, he seemed to be checking everyone's luggage right down to the lipsticks in women's purses. In horror, we both groaned quietly as our line shuffled its painfully slow way forward and brought us closer to our meeting with him. We had thought of jumping to the end of another line, but as soon as the last passenger had gone through, each line was closed down, and the officer simply disappeared.

In an effort to expedite our passage through the final checkpoint, I undid the locks and straps securing our luggage and, confident the officer wouldn't find anything to concern him, tried hard to remain awake. Finally, it was our turn. Placing our bags on the low bench in front of the officer, we handed him our passports and waited for our final ordeal to begin. He spoke to me in broken English.

"Where you come from?"

"England."

"How long you stay Okinawa?"

"I'm not sure . . . at least a month."

"A month . . . this long time vacation?"

"I've come to train in karate with Higaonna sensei of Goju-ryu."

"Ah so, karate! Higaonna sensei very strong."

The customs officer continued on to tell me that he had trained in karate when he was younger. His body language changed. He was less stern now, more animated and friendly. When he asked to see my hands, he was clearly disappointed; they did not bear the two large knuckles associated with training on the *makiwara*,[42] a staple for karate men on Okinawa.

"How long you train karate?"

"Ten years, Shito-ryu."

"Ah, Shito-ryu, no Goju-ryu."

For some reason this made all the difference in his mind and stepping back a little, he bowed and sent us on our way with his warmest wishes for a pleasant stay. So taken aback by what had just happened, it wasn't until we were outside the terminal building that we realized he had not even looked in our luggage!

This was not the only example of how my involvement with karate altered the way we were treated during our stay in Okinawa. It was as if my ten years of training in karate was a statement about my character. In Okinawa, karate was taken seriously, and to the local people it was as much a part of their cultural heritage as their traditional dance, music, or architecture. I found that once people knew me, I could walk into the little convenience store opposite the Higaonna dojo, pick up the things I needed, and be trusted to leave the correct amount of money on the counter. Often, the only sign of life came from the greetings returned to me through a curtained doorway that separated the shop from the living quarters at the back of the building. Karate, in the land of its birth, held a special place in the hearts and minds of the general public, more so than it did back home.

Leaving the airport and falling into the first available cab gave us little relief. I asked the driver to take us to a Western-style hotel, nothing too expensive but one with "proper beds." For the first night, at least, we wanted to forgo the pleasure of sleeping on the floor in the traditional manner. It was dark now, and the city streets were alive with traffic and people, all rushing about at a frantic pace. Arriving at the Hotel Ekka around 9:30 p.m., we checked in and retired to our room to clean up and get the sleep we were so desperate for. Not being met at the airport was bad enough as far as Kathy was concerned, but not to have so much as a phone number, an address, or any other way of contacting Higaonna sensei, well, she thought that was just plain stupid! Thankfully, she was too tired to scold me too much, and we both drifted off to sleep. When the morning came, I awoke, still a little groggy.

Finding Higaonna sensei that day was essential because I knew our funds would not last forever, and the cost of staying in the Hotel Ekka would deplete them within a week. Although I was making things up as I went along, behind the apparent disorder I always knew things would work out. My first step was to obtain a tourist map of the city from the front desk. Then, I asked the duty clerk to look up 'M. Higaonna' in the phone book. It never dawned on me that half the population of Okinawa would have the same surname; well, maybe not half, but there were a lot of people called Higaonna in Naha. Surely, they couldn't all teach karate though, so I asked the clerk to see if any of the listings gave a number for a karate dojo. Eureka! Of all the people called Higaonna in the phone book only one mentioned Goju-ryu: that had to be him. My next task was to identify where in Naha the dojo was, and for this I asked the desk clerk to point to the street on my tourist map. Here I hit my first hurdle; Okinawan phone books only gave the district, not the street, of the number listed. Undaunted, I asked the clerk to mark out the district. It was called Makishi and as luck would have it, it was not that far away. Things were looking promising again.

I just needed to find Higaonna sensei's dojo and ask for instruction and with that done, someone was bound to know of a less expensive place to stay. I was optimistic everything was going to work out fine, and feeling more relaxed, I decided to leave Kathy sleeping and to take a short walk to get my first proper look at Okinawa. The Hotel Ekka stood on top of a rise in the land on the main north-south highway that is known to all as Route 58, or sometimes just "58." Not far from the port of Tomari, the morning traffic was heavy, as was the pollution coming from it that hung in the air in a pale blue mist. The pavements were full of people walking quickly to work and schoolchildren, in their sailor suit uniforms, making their way with less enthusiasm through the bustle going on all around them. Every now and then one of them, confusing me for an American, would wave the victory sign and shout, "Hey, Joe" or "Peace, Man." So uncommon were foreigners back then that during our stay people always assumed Kathy and I were Americans. A look of surprise would wash over their faces when they discovered we had traveled all the way from England.

My walk took me south, in the direction the taxi came from the previous evening; it was downhill and brought me to the Tomari port complex. Turning right, away from the main highway and the heavy traffic, I found a small European style graveyard and ambled in to satisfy my curiosity. I knew Christianity had been introduced to this part of the world four hundred years earlier so expected to see headstones with Japanese and Okinawan names, but instead I found the names of English, American, and even people from the Philippines. Many had been laid to rest long before the decisive battle that took place here in 1945; the cemetery was the final resting place for men who lived in a different time and a different world. My mind wandered to times long ago, when Queen Victoria was on the throne of England and the American naval commodore, Matthew C. Perry, appeared without warning one morning in the bay not far from where I was standing.

I spent a fascinating half hour reading the headstones and trying to imagine how Okinawa must have looked to those early visitors. But the graves were not all ancient. Quite a number of servicemen had been interred here too. I could only imagine the love they must have had for the island, so much so that they would want their earthly remains to be buried in Okinawa forever. But I could not stop and dream for long. I had an important task to complete that day, if I could, and with this in mind left the solitude of the little cemetery and made my way back to the hotel. On the way, I witnessed a uniquely Japanese pastime that was a common sight back then—the company morning exercise program. Workers from a large car dealership on the opposite side of "58" were on the lot, being led through their paces by the management team. A common company bonding exercise as much as anything else, it is something I saw less and less of during subsequent visits to the island; these days I'm not sure any companies still do things like this.

Armed with my new plan, which bore a remarkable resemblance to my only plan actually, I returned to our room to wake Kathy. She was still sleeping soundly, but we had to move quickly. We had a lot to achieve today. First, I wanted to find Higaonna sensei and gain entry to his dojo, and then I needed to find somewhere to sleep that night and hopefully every other night for the length of our stay. Kathy dressed quickly; we gathered our belongings and vacated the room. In typical Okinawan fashion, the hotel staff had taken an interest in our adventure and insisted we leave our luggage at the hotel until we found somewhere to live. Usually, there would have been a charge for this after 10:00 a.m., but that was waived. Many small acts of kindness like this were extended to Kathy and me throughout our stay; their frequency often left us both momentarily speechless, and feeling very grateful. The duty manager escorted us outside and waved for a cab to come forward from the small number waiting outside. He told the taxi driver where to go, Makishi, and told us how much the fare should be. This was a deliberate move on the part of the manager because some Okinawan cab drivers took advantage of unwary Westerners, in a belief they are all Americans and all wealthy. A cab could often travel a few more miles than it had to, to reach its destination. Of course, Kathy and I were neither rich nor American, but the taxi driver wasn't to know that.

A few miles from the hotel the cab pulled to the side of the road, and the back door, which in Japanese taxis opens at the flick of a switch from the driver, swung open. "Makishi, Makishi," he said, pointing to the houses on the opposite side of the street. Perhaps irritated at being unable to work his scam on us, we paid him the amount the manager advised us to: he wasn't happy! No sooner had our feet hit the pavement than the cab door closed and the taxi launched itself back into the busy traffic. Kathy and I stood silent for a while, trying to take in our new surroundings. Alone, and with no idea where to start, we crossed the busy four-lane road to reach the other side. Narrow streets ran into a labyrinth of wooden houses all topped with heavy clay-tiled roofs. If there were street names, we could not see them, but even if we could, neither of us could read Japanese anyway so they would have been of little use. In my head, I had a picture of Higaonna sensei walking down a flight of external concrete stairs before entering his dojo. I would know that doorway if I saw it again. I was sure I would. All I had to do was walk down the right street. It was hot and humid, and with nothing looking remotely like the picture I had in my mind, we decided to stop for a while and rest in the shade. On the other side of the street, opposite us, an old man sat on a *tatami*[43] floor mat and watched us from the front of his bicycle shop.

The front of the shop was made of large wooden slats that had been opened up to the elements so that the bicycles on sale were on display to the public. The old man looked busy fixing a puncture in a small inner tube, but I could see he was also casting a curious eye over the two foreigners standing across from him. After a while, we left our shelter from the heat and I decided I would try my very limited skills with the Japanese language to ask for help. With a smile on my face, I took a deep breath and approached.

"Ohiyo gozaimasu." "Good morning."

"Eigo o hanashimasu ka?" "Do you speak English?"

No? Okay, then, this was going to be fun.

"Higaonna no karate dojo wa, doko desu ka?' "Do you know where the Higaonna karate dojo is?"

A huge smile spread across the old man's face, and I could tell he was having as much fun listening to my attempt at Japanese as I was squirming at how bad it was. His answer was quick and animated and far too detailed for me to grasp much information from. I did, however, manage to gather that he was telling me it was not far away and also got the general direction he was suggesting we take. He then confirmed it was the correct dojo by pointing to his thumb and then to his little finger before asking if the dojo I was looking for had a teacher with a foreign wife. In former times on Okinawa, the thumb and the little finger were often used to indicate a man and woman; back then, older people were still doing this.

"Gaijin desu ka?"

"Hai, gaijin desu." "Yes, a foreigner."

Close now, our sprits rose with the prospect of finding Higaonna sensei's dojo so early in the day. I thanked the shopkeeper for his help, and Kathy and I continued in the direction he had pointed to. It took no longer than two or three minutes to cross the little intersection at the top of a small rise and drop down into the street housing the Higaonna dojo. Though not immediately visible from the direction we came upon it, due to the surrounding houses having high walls, I recognized the external stairs that led to the dojo entrance as soon as I saw them. This was it, the place we had come halfway around the world to reach . . . . We found it!

Some years later, in an interview Morio Higaonna sensei gave to the owner of an American martial arts magazine, the story of how I found his dojo was put to Higaonna sensei as an example of how famous his dojo was in Okinawa. With typical humility, Higaonna sensei sidestepped the notion of fame that the interviewer, for his own purposes I suspect, was trying to cloak him in, and put the story down to "youthful enthusiasm" on my part. The magazine did not transcribe Higaonna sensei's words verbatim in the interview; rather, I believe the owner allowed his own motives to put words into Higaonna sensei's mouth, so in the magazine this is how Kathy and I supposedly found the Higaonna dojo. It reads like this:

Interviewer: In fact, your dojo is so well-known in Okinawa that a British karateka who went to train there wrote about it in *Fighting Arts International Magazine*. He said that after clearing immigration, when he asked how he could get to the Higaonna dojo he was actually put in a taxi by the officials who had processed his visa, and the driver given instructions to go to the Higaonna dojo.

Higaonna: I saw that article as well, and I think he exaggerated a little, a case of youthful enthusiasm perhaps . . .

Having now read my account of what actually happened, I'll leave it up to you to decide who was exaggerating, and whose "enthusiasm" was most on display in the magazine.

For an instant, standing outside the dojo, I didn't know what to do next. Time slowed down and the world became quiet, and in that moment or two of silence as I stood looking into Kathy's eyes for a sign that I had done the right thing, I tried hard to gather my composure as the enormity of what I had done washed over me. Taking a deep breath, I stepped up to the dojo door and knocked. Someone was in there. I knew that from the sound of training going on inside, and now that I had knocked I began to wish I hadn't. What if Higaonna sensei was in the middle of the best kata he had ever done, or was just about to block a powerful punch to his face? My knock might have distracted him at a crucial moment and he may have lost his concentration or worse, a tooth! Through the frosted glass doors, I could make out the shape of someone coming closer. Taking half a step backward, my nervousness grew and I swallowed hard to clear my ears. The door slid open from left to right revealing the familiar interior I had last seen on television; the face greeting me, however, was unknown and did not belong to Higaonna sensei. The man who answered my knock was Kazuo Terauchi, a 5th dan student who was visiting from Tokyo. I bowed and asked to speak to Higaonna sensei. Unimpressed, Terauchi did not bow back, but instead grunted something in Japanese and then in broken English told me that Higaonna sensei was not in the dojo and I should return at four o'clock if I wanted to see him. With that, he simply slid the door closed again, and from the sound of things continued with his training.

This was not exactly the kind of reception I was hoping for after traveling from the other side of the planet, although in truth I was never sure what kind of welcome, if any, I would get. My appearance, after all, was unannounced, and I was not a member of Higaonna sensei's organization. Now what? We could not afford to hang around all day until four o' clock; there was a need to get things sorted out sooner rather than later, before my lack of planning threatened to bring the entire trip to an abrupt end. Terauchi had not been particularly welcoming, and it was dawning on me that this whole business might in fact turn out to be a huge mistake. If Higaonna sensei was not in the dojo, perhaps he was at home. Knowing he lived above the dojo I decided to call at his home on the first floor, and climbed the two short sets of stairs that led to his front door. After our reception at the dojo, I felt very unsure that I was doing the right thing by calling at Higaonna sensei's home, and having knocked gently, we stood waiting in total silence. The door opened, and a very spritely old lady wearing a huge smile was clearly surprised to see a couple of foreigners standing before her. I bowed deeply and in my very limited Japanese, asked if her son, Higaonna Morio, was at home. My inquiry produced a reply that was too difficult for me to grasp, and noticing the blank look I was now wearing, Kathy and I were ushered inside.

Stepping through the front door, we removed our shoes in the *genkan*,[44] before entering the house proper; wearing the house slippers provided by our host, we followed her directions into the living room, and sat. Within minutes, tea and biscuits were placed on a small table in front of us by Mrs. Higaonna, who was anxious we take some refreshment. I tried to explain we had come from England and that I wanted to train in karate with her son, but I'm not sure she understood my dreadful attempt to make conversation. She did grasp some of what I was saying, I think, and was delighted that we had traveled so far. Mrs. Higaonna then excused herself and made a phone call. A short conversation ensued before she beckoned me to the phone. My heart began to race. What if it was Higaonna sensei asking me what the hell I was doing in his home disrupting his mother's peace and quiet?

I took the receiver and held it to my ear, "Hello." The voice on the other end of the line was that of Higaonna sensei's wife, Alanna. Because she is American, I could explain exactly who we were and what we were doing in her mother-in-law's house; I was also able to explain why we had come to Okinawa and asked if she thought it would be possible for me to train with Higaonna sensei. Alanna was "amazed" by what I had to say, and even more so that we had managed to find the dojo. She shared her thoughts that we were "Nuts" to do what we had done, but also expressed how pleased she was. She went on to say that Higaonna sensei was with her and that she would explain everything to him; he would be making his way home soon so Alanna suggested we wait for him in the dojo. We talked a little more before I handed the phone back to Mrs. Higaonna. It might have been my imagination, but her tone seemed to be different when talking to her daughter-in-law: less friendly.

When the call was over, the three of us finished our tea and biscuits, and before leaving, Mrs. Higaonna pressed a small bundle of traditional Okinawan sweets into our hands. Her beaming smile was infectious, and it was easy to see from where her son had inherited his trademark smile. We thanked our hostess, bowed deeply, and descended the stairs we had so hesitantly climbed just an hour earlier. Sliding the dojo door open, we were relieved to find Terauchi had finished his training and had gone, leaving the dojo empty. It was a strange feeling to be standing in a space I had visited so many times while watching and re-watching *The Way of the Warrior* video. The dojo looked bigger on TV, but now that I was actually standing in the place, the size hardly mattered. The dojo had everything needed for training in karate: a smooth wooden floor, mirrors to check your form, a couple of makiwara in the back corner, a heavy kick bag for developing impact, and a whole host of different weights to build up strength.

Kathy and I sat on two chairs at the back of the dojo next to a small office. Instinctively, we spoke in whispers, although at the time I was not sure why. Later, as I thought about our reaction, it seemed quite natural. For me, dojo hold the energy that is generated within them during practice, at least for a while; on reflection, whispering felt appropriate in order to keep the peace and serenity of the empty dojo intact. Suddenly, the door slid open and without warning, in stepped Higaonna sensei, wearing that trademark smile of his. We stood quickly and bowed. He bowed in return, and then offered his hand. I shook it using both hands, as a sign of respect.[45] I introduced Kathy and myself, and began explaining what we were doing there and what I hoped to achieve as far as training was concerned. Higaonna sensei was very happy to have me train at his dojo.

According to some, 'ignorance is bliss', and certainly, had I known of the accepted protocols and etiquette expected of visitors to a dojo in Okinawa back then, I would have walked a different path to the place I now found myself. Looking back, I can see that my ignorance was, in fact, wrapped in a wide-eyed blanket of innocence and a belief that all it took for great things to happen in karate was a good heart and a willingness to act. I still believe in the fundamental truth of that today, although I'm no longer so confident about the amount of 'great things' there are out there for young karateka to experience. The essence of karate is approached through quiet achievement, with reflective thought backed by action, and adopting a calm resolve to face whatever comes your way—and deal with it! I had no idea what was waiting for me in Okinawa when I boarded my flight in London, but I went there anyway.

If you think about the 'headline' events promoted by the media in 1984, history will tell you that Ronald Reagan announced his intention to run for a second term as the President of the United States, Torvil and Dean captured the world's imagination ice dancing their way to gold via the *Bolero* at the 14th Winter Olympics in Sarajevo. Oscar winners Robert Duval and Shirley MacLaine celebrated their roles in *Terms of Endearment*, and Michael Jackson was badly burnt while filming an ad for Pepsi. But as far as I was concerned at the time, the most impressive achievement of mankind in 1984 was the first untethered space walk by the American astronaut, Bruce McCandless. I expect there are few reading this who remember him or his unbelievably courageous achievement, but have little problem calling to mind one or more of the other events from that time. Confirmation, I believe, that history continuously fails to credit the achievements of individuals who did great things, and instead, merely records the exploits of people who made the most noise.

With the question of training now settled, the conversation shifted to how we had come upon the dojo, as apparently even visiting Japanese karateka found it almost impossible to locate. He asked where we were staying, and once I explained everything, he told me of a place we might like to stay. It was inexpensive and not too far from the dojo, a local *minshuku*[46] close by the city's main fish, fruit, and vegetable markets. Higaonna sensei was a little concerned it would not meet our requirements, but I did my best to convince him it would. Leaving the dojo, Higaonna sensei, Kathy, and I walked through the narrow backstreets of Makishi, past the tiny bicycle shop where we had earlier sought directions, and a number of seedy bars and brothels of Tsuji, Naha's red-light district. Our walk took us along the boundary between Tsuboya, an area of the city famous for manufacturing Ryukyuan pottery on the left, and on the right, the Heiwa dori market, originally the heart of the local black-market economy that grew up after WWII. And even now, the market is still the place to go, to find everything you might need—at a good price.

As we walked, Higaonna sensei asked questions about England and about my history in karate. Taking a small detour, we called in on Alanna. She was the owner and operator of a large new aerobics studio close to the market, and she was very welcoming; she, conversing freely in English, made Kathy and me feel less isolated by language, a feeling we had missed over the past twenty-four hours. Sagi, their son was also there, putting on a display of high-octane, boundless energy that only young children are capable of. I wondered, as I watched him race around the large open space of the empty studio, would he follow his father into a life of karate someday. Since that first meeting, Sagi, or Eric, as he prefers to be known these days, has indeed grown up to become a karateka, and although we have never met as adults, we did meet again a few years later when in 1989 I traveled to San Diego, California, to take part in a three-day seminar hosted by Higaonna sensei.

Leaving the aerobic studio, we continued our walk to the minshuku, and a short time later crossed a busy intersection that brought us into the city's wholesale fish, fruit, and vegetable market. This was not the kind of place you would find on a tourist map; it was a rough and gritty place full of ruddy-faced characters scurrying to and fro, with gravelly voices and bodies that bore witness to a lifetime of hard work. Water washed along the gutters in front of the fish stalls, carrying with it pieces of matter I didn't easily recognize, nor stare at long enough to satisfy my curiosity. But for all that, it wasn't a threatening place, far from it. For among the hive of activity going on all around and the cacophony of noise coming from the sellers as they did their best to attract the attention of buyers, I was, over the coming weeks, greeted often by warm smiles and the nod of a head from perfect strangers as I walked through the market each morning on my way to the dojo. One street farther on from the market, the minshuku nestled tightly in between a mixture of low wooden houses and the various level concrete buildings that made up the untidy streetscape so typical of this area of Naha.

The entire neighborhood had seen better days. As if cobbled together quickly in the rush to rebuild after the devastation of WWII close to forty years earlier, there was now a recognizable sense of decay that comes over a place when its time has passed and demolition is its only salvation. I had grown up in a similar decaying, inner-city environment, so in many ways this part of the city was familiar to me, but not to Kathy; her childhood had been spent in much less confrontational surroundings. The sewer system that ran along one side of each street was covered over by a series of flat concrete blocks that rattled when you walked on them. Depending on what side they walked, it was possible to lie in bed and hear people stroll the entire length of the street, the Doppler Effect allowing you to work out not only how quickly they were moving, but also in which direction they were heading. Every now and then, the concrete slabs were replaced by an open metal grill, allowing for pedestrians to experience the full aroma drifting up from the contents swirling along just below their feet. A casual observer was also likely—as we did countless times—to witness the large rats that inhabited the sewers, scurrying along, oblivious to the world going on above and around them. It took Kathy and me a few days to figure out that it was always better, where possible, to walk on the opposite side of the street.

The minshuku itself was a favorite stopover (as we were to discover during our stay) with Japanese tourists making a circumnavigation of Okinawa by bicycle. It was owned and operated by Mr. and Mrs. Kinjo, a Christian couple, who for many years after our visit, sent Kathy and me Christmas cards decorated with a curious mix of Okinawan art and the Christian Christmas message.

Higaonna sensei seemed a little worried our room might prove to be too basic, and once again asked if we were okay about staying there. My thinking was the less money that had to be spent on things like accommodations, the longer we could stay in Okinawa. If Kathy had any reservations, she was keeping them to herself. As a nurse, there wasn't much she had not already seen and dealt with as far as discomfort or the human condition goes, and so the absence of all the creature comforts expected in a good hotel was, if not entirely desirable, then at least, bearable.

Our six-mat room[47] was on the second floor, and it was spartan, containing nothing but a small table and a cupboard that housed our bedding during the day. But it was clean and dry, and safe; and as a place to retreat from the hectic pace of life outside and rest my body in between the demands of training, it would do just fine. On a corner of the building, the room had two sliding windows, one opening onto the street and the other onto the building next door. So tightly were the dwellings pushed together it was possible to reach out and touch the side of the building next door. Thankfully, within a week of our taking up residence, the neighboring building was demolished. It happened almost overnight and with such speed and practiced execution that I was left amazed. The effect of the open space outside each window meant we could now open both and allow what breeze there was to flow through our room and bring with it a little respite from the humidity and heat that neither Kathy nor I was used to.

Each of the two floors in the minshuku that contained the guest rooms had two communal bathrooms, one for men and another for women. Each consisted of a small number of showers and toilet cubicles, only the first of which was familiar. The prospect of a daily shower was a welcome one, but if I wanted a hot shower, then I had to give Kinjo-san at least half an hour's notice, so the water heater could be turned on. As it was rarely practical to do that, I got used to cold showers. The actual toilet, still used across

Asia today, was a 'squat', and consisted of a ceramic trench set in the ground that was something under a meter long. At the front end, a sturdy chrome-plated pole was set in the ground, attached to which was a lever that provided a means to flush the trench when you were finished with it. The method of use was quite straightforward; you straddled the trench, squatted on your haunches, and held on to the pole for balance. At the end of the working day, you pulled the lever and washed everything away, down the opening at the front of the trench.

I have to say that initially I found the experience to be a little more intimate than I was used to. Growing up in the Victorian slums of Manchester, in England's industrial heartland, I was no stranger to living with only the basic needs being met, in conditions where visiting the outside lavatory at night meant bringing with you three things: a flashlight or candle so you could see where you were going, some old newspaper so you could clean up after yourself, and a stick so you could fend off the rats that often lingered about the place. But even in such appalling conditions, I always had something to sit on! Higaonna sensei negotiated a good price for the room, an act that was to prove typical of the way he looked out for us and tried to make our life as problem-free as possible. After explaining how much we needed to pay each week he left us, telling me before he left that training started at seven-thirty the following morning.

I returned to our room and as we sat there working out what to do next, I began to wonder . . . was I ready? In truth, I wasn't sure if I would be able to take the level of training the Okinawans did. And what if the locals took a dislike to me and I found myself walking into a lion's den? The momentary doubts passed; besides, it was too late now. We were in Okinawa and I had no choice but to go to the dojo and take whatever came my way. Kathy and I made our way back to the Hotel Ekka and collected our bags. The day had worked out perfectly for us and though the butterflies in my stomach were already beginning to flutter at the thought of what was ahead, I knew there was no turning back. I had made it to Okinawa and found the dojo and the man I was looking for. All I had to do now was face the doubts and fears that my uncertain but immediate future was holding. I knew others had been in this situation and I drew strength from that fact. If it were possible to step into the dojo and come out in one piece, I would give it my best shot. By ten o'clock that evening, I had already showered and had my dogi packed ready for the morning; I rolled out the futon[48] and settled down for a good night's sleep, but it never came, of course.

Our second full day in Okinawa dawned slightly overcast and with a level of heat and humidity bordering on uncomfortable. Looking out across the surrounding rooftops from the communal bathroom window, I began to wonder whether training would be a problem if these conditions continued. With my dogi rolled up and placed in the leather carry bag I had bartered for a few years earlier with an Arab trader in the Canary Islands, I left Kathy sleeping and slipped quietly out of the minshuku. Sunday or not, the shops were open and people were already going about their business. Only the absence of schoolchildren on the streets marked the difference between today and any other day of the week. Walking through the busy market, trying to live in the moment, my senses took in what they could of the sights and sounds going on around me. As well as the unfamiliar visual and audible sensations, the smells too were strange and not always pleasant. But for the most part they enhanced the feeling of being in a foreign land far from home.

Having the only non-Okinawan face in the crowd attracted some attention as I passed through. Once their surprise at seeing a foreigner in this part of the city faded, my presence usually brought a smile or a giggle, while others just looked on in bemusement. I become aware of portly old ladies in overalls scraping the scales from that morning's delivery of fish, cackling with laughter at some unspoken joke only they were aware of. A porter cursed a box of fruit for falling from his cart as one wheel managed to navigate the curbside and the other didn't. And in the background, a collection of voices were holding their own sale and speaking in that phonetic Esperanto[49] spoken by auctioneers the world over. If I could have stayed longer and soaked up more of the atmosphere I would have, but I had somewhere I needed to be and I was not about to arrive late. So leaving the market behind, I made my way along the streets Higaonna sensei had walked Kathy and me down the day before. The landmarks I picked out then looked different now as I approached them from the opposite direction, but I managed to keep to the correct route and arrived at the dojo with plenty of time to spare.

My walk had brought home the gravity of my situation; here I was in Okinawa, the birthplace of karate, and thoughts of being rejected by members of the dojo returned to fill my head. What if the students in the dojo took a dislike to me? What if I could not cope with the Goju-ryu way of training? And what if the black belt I wore counted for nothing? Stories of foreigners arriving in Japan and being beaten close to death were part of the folklore of European karateka. Only the best of the visitors had survived, and I considered myself a long way from being good, let alone one of the best. To counter the negative thoughts trying to overwhelm me, I held on to the thought that the choice to be where I was standing now was made weeks ago. By putting myself in Okinawa, the time for doubt had already passed; regardless of what was to come, my focus now had to be on doing what needed to be done—and that's all. I had made a commitment to myself and now had no choice but to see it through.

Entering the dojo, I paused and bowed toward the main wall, the *shomen*, before slipping behind the curtain at the side to change into my dogi. Only two other students were present, Kazuo

Terauchi, the person whose training I had interrupted the previous morning, and a young man from the island of Penang in Malaysia, whom everyone called Virra. Virra, short for Vildrasidarem, was training at the Higaonna dojo prior to the arrival of his sensei from Malaysia. Virra was due to test for shodan before returning home. He was a tall, athletic young man, extremely fit, with a friendly disposition. Virra's only problem, as far as I could tell, was his tendency to suffer quite badly from homesickness. Not surprising really, for he was no more than nineteen or twenty years old and had been in Okinawa for two months by the time I arrived at the dojo. Being a stranger in a strange land brings with it only so much excitement, and for many who travel alone, a point is reached where the familiar holds a stronger place in the psyche than the urge to experience the new and exotic. I believe the way we deal with situations similar to this makes us stronger, and I pity those without the courage to leave their comfort zone and test themselves in ways that hold a mirror to their character. Their inability to observe what is reflected means they miss out on so much about karate that cannot be explained to individuals who have not endured such things.

Higaonna sensei entered the dojo shortly after I had changed into my dogi, and my time for worrying came to an abrupt end. Whether or not I could produce the level of karate my grade promised was about to be revealed. The previous day, as we walked to the minshuku with Higaonna sensei, he asked me what grade I held. My answer, rather childishly, contained a hint of pride to it: "Nidan!" As usual, however, overt pride was setting me up for a fall, for it led me to believe that Higaonna sensei was suitably impressed, and that belief was confirmed when my offer to wear a white belt when I came to the dojo was refused. Instead, I was told to wear the belt I normally wore, and I took that to mean his acceptance of my rank—but it was hardly that. In Higaonna sensei's mind, I had made a statement and he expected me to back it up with ability and action. Though I didn't know it at the time, he was already looking to my education, and what better way to do that than engage with my ego from day one. So armed with a false sense of security planted firmly in my head, sitting silently in mokuso, I prepared for my first karate lesson in Okinawa.

The *junbi-undo* (preparatory exercises) consisted of postures and movements designed to foster both strength and flexibility and preceded every lesson. I was familiar with many of them, but not all; still, I was able to maintain the pace set with little trouble, and easily followed Higaonna sensei's lead. Twenty minutes later, we paused and a brief discussion followed between Higaonna sensei and Terauchi. We were then directed to swap our gi jacket for a T-shirt, and amidst some confusion on my part, left the dojo and set off for a run. Turning left out of the dojo, we headed down the narrow street and then an even narrower alleyway, before emerging onto Himeyuri dori, a busy road that ran south from Azato toward the river and industrial port of Naha. As we ran through the morning crowd, I recognized the spot where the taxi had dropped Kathy and me rather unceremoniously the day before. Little could I have imagined then that the next time I would pass this way I would be jogging behind the man I had flown halfway around the world to see. A clear and almost overwhelming sense of being in the moment washed over me. I was here, training; I had achieved what I set out to achieve. Could life get any better than this? We continued at a fairly easy pace until arriving at Yogi Park on the opposite side of the busy four-lane road that was now bumper to bumper with morning traffic.

Once inside the park, we turned right and began to run its perimeter. I lost count of how many times we passed the entrance where we came in, but certainly enough to find myself hoping that the next time we reached it we would make the turn and head for home. By now, the strain of keeping up with Higaonna sensei and the other students was beginning to tell. The heat, coupled with high humidity, was sapping my stamina, and as we continued running, my mind began to engage in that conversation familiar to all who find themselves approaching their physical limits. I was very happy when, finally, we followed Higaonna sensei back through the gates and turned toward the dojo. Crossing the busy road for the second time, we stopped running when we reached the other side, and instead began walking on tiptoes all the way back to a spot about a hundred yards from the dojo. From there, the street ran uphill, and though the slope was not very steep, it was enough of an incline to register on a pair of already tired legs. Higaonna sensei lined us up as we prepared to sprint to the dojo door. In my mind, I had delivered a lackluster performance so far, and so I was determined to get to the dojo first. As soon as Higaonna sensei indicated the race was on, I launched myself forward. Maybe Virra knew better or maybe he was just tired, but the race to the dojo door was only ever between Terauchi and me, and I won. He was not pleased at all. In fact, the look he gave me would have soured fresh milk; and it was then that a little voice in my head whispered, "You haven't heard the last of this."

At that point, I was still naïve to the man's ego, but I was in Okinawa to learn. And even though I had no idea of just how steep the learning curve was about to become, I knew there was no going back. Back in the dojo, we had a drink of water and swapped our sweat soaked T-shirts for our gi jackets. The rest break didn't last long, however, and within minutes of our return to the dojo we began a second round of exercises, this time even more strenuous than the first. Beginning with the *chiishi,*[50] we manipulated the tool through a series of exercises that left me struggling to keep up. Nothing in my previous ten years of training in karate had prepared me for using tools like the chiishi. It wasn't so much the weight of the tool that was causing me problems, it was the lack of harmony of body, breath, and intention that was required to control the tool and make its use relevant to the basic principles of karate that Higaonna sensei taught. Twenty minutes later, the chiishi were put to one side, and we began a sequence of push-ups, squats, and sit-ups, in that order; each exercise was done in repetitions of one hundred, but seventy-five sit-ups into it, my stomach began to cramp, and an overwhelming sense of nausea began to envelop me. I had to get to the toilet, and quickly! Indicating my situation to Higaonna sensei, I jumped up and dashed for the small toilet, *benjo*, at the back of the dojo, reaching it with no time to spare.

The heaving emptied the contents of my stomach, but produced nothing except digestive juices, the acid in them burning the back of my throat. Still, my body continued to contract violently, long after the spasms had evicted what little content was there to begin with. Finally, the heaving stopped and I was able to swill my mouth with water; even so, it took a few moments for me to regain my composure before returning to the dojo. When I opened the door, Higaonna sensei was waiting for me with a glass of warm water in his hand. He directed me to the open door of the dojo and had me sit, in seiza. From there I watched the other students complete their training while I did as I was told and sipped the warm water: slowly. Looking on as Terauchi and Virra worked their way through various kata, I sat, furious with myself at my inability to take the kind of training being asked of me. There I was, declaring myself a serious student of karate, nidan no less, and yet I could not get through a morning's training!

Embarrassment turned into anger and then shame. When the training finally ended, I approached Higaonna sensei, bowed deeply, and apologized for my lack of stamina. He told me not to feel bad, saying there was no disgrace in pushing myself to my limits. It was people who hold back from pushing so intensely, he told me, who should feel ashamed of themselves. I saw the sense in his words, but that did little to relieve my ego of the battering it was experiencing. I knew I had given everything I had, tried my best; even so, I couldn't help feeling I had let myself down. Looking back on that morning from the vantage point of time, I see clearly why my strength and fitness deserted me. Quite apart from the eight-hour time difference my body had yet to adjust to and the heat and humidity the likes of which I had never experienced before, I realized, as I made my the way back to the minshuku, that with the exception of the tea and biscuits Higaonna sensei's mother had served us the day before, neither Kathy nor I had eaten in two days.

It was not only the climate I was going to become accustomed to, I also needed to find a source of nourishing food, high enough in calories to give me the energy to train as often as I had planned to and cheap enough not to deplete our funds too quickly. For now though, any kind of food would do to take away the stomach cramps. Deep in thought about my training and where I was going to get some food, I passed by the bicycle shop Kathy and I had called into the day before to seek directions. The owner smiled and then bowed before calling out his greeting of good morning. I returned all three before continuing on my way, buoyed by the realization that, finally, I was living the dream I had dreamt for so long. Quickening my pace, my thoughts turned to where Kathy and I were going to find breakfast.

A cold shower back at the minshuku rid me of any sleepiness I might have felt from the afterglow of tough training. Within an hour of my returning to the minshuku, Kathy and I set out to explore our surrounds in more detail and to find a place to eat. We soon discovered that Naha, like all other cities in Japan, was not built like cities in England. Roads and streets were not laid out in a grid system; instead, they seemed to run off in all directions. Roads meandered to their destination in anything but a straight line, and streets were often so narrow we wondered how anybody would have a clue finding an address in an unfamiliar neighborhood. All the wider roads carried heavy traffic, and even some of the smaller side streets suffered from the Okinawan equivalent of gridlock. The pace of life was frantic and took a little getting used to, but neither of us felt uneasy, as the Okinawan people themselves were friendly to a fault. To illustrate what I mean, let me relate a story that typifies the way Okinawa is the 'Land of Propriety'. On that first day, exploring our new surroundings, I stopped to ask an elderly doorman, standing outside a bank, if he could direct us to where we might find something to eat: "Chotto matte kudasai." "Please wait a moment," he said, before dashing inside the bank only to return a few seconds later. Then, with the biggest smile you have ever seen spread wide across his face, he escorted Kathy and me through the Heiwa dori market and onto Kokusai dori, Naha's main retail area. Its name, Kokusai, means 'International', a place where all manner of goods and food from around the world can be found.

Merely saying "Thank you!" to our guide felt totally insufficient given the trouble he had gone through to assist us, but over the coming weeks we came to learn that his keenness to help was not unique. Many Okinawans went out of their way to help us during the course of our stay, and Kathy and I often wondered how the average Okinawan would fare on the streets of London or Manchester. Would the average English person go out of his way to help a stranger who was lost and couldn't speak the language? While I had no doubt there would be a few individuals who would help, I was certain the majority would leave a visitor stranded. Outside Shuri-jo, the former royal palace of the kings of Ryukyu, stands a replica of the world-famous Shurei-mon, (Shurei gate); set in the center under the eaves of its heavy roof, a sign proclaims to all who enter the palace through the gate that this is the 'Land of Propriety'. Today, with their royal family long since passed into history and the modern world encroaching ever more deeply into the minds of the young, the Okinawan people remain living examples of a maxim by which their homeland has been known for centuries.

The first familiar name we saw connected to food, I'm sorry to say, was McDonald's. With neither of us particularly big fans of their menu, our hunger at the time was as big as the golden arches standing like sentinels above the door. Stepping inside, we were greeted by a sea of nodding heads followed by a well-rehearsed chorus bidding us welcome and directing us to place our order. A young man stepped forward and in a perfect American accent said, "Hi, can I help you sir?" He certainly could! An order was placed for four egg-and-bacon McMuffins, six large portions of French fries, a large tub of coke, no ice, and two cups of tea, all of which arrived only a few minutes later. Everything on the table was consumed with an indelicate enthusiasm that is no doubt typical when two hungry people sit down to eat their first meal in two days.

Monday morning found me once more on the way to the dojo for the seven-thirty training session. I walked to the dojo slowly. I had plenty of time and wanted to enjoy where I was, to live in each moment just a moment longer. Feeling much better after our feast of muffins and fries the day before and having found a grocery store where we bought bread, ham, tomatoes, and some cheese, I was now well fed and felt confident I would finish the training this time. Giving thought to my first training experience, I also decided to let Terauchi win whenever we lined up for a dash to the dojo. I had made my point by winning, but saw no advantage in alienating the toughest student in the dojo. Besides, this was going to be the first of two training sessions today, and I did not want to leave myself too exhausted for the evening training. The wind picked up and my hair, wet from my shower, was drying nicely as I ambled along the narrow back streets through the local red-light district and over the rise into Makishi.

Higaonna sensei introduced me to the kata, *gekisai dai ichi*,[51] explaining the timing and pace he wanted me to appreciate. My breathing too came in for scrutiny, and his explanation of how my mind, body, and technique needed to harmonize to produce maximum power was as simple to understand as it was difficult to implement. It was pointed out to me many times that the ongoing study of kata was the real challenge of karate, and to neglect the kata or settle for only a shallow understanding of them was a great mistake. Higaonna sensei initiated the idea in me of experimenting with the timing of a kata, encouraging me to be deliberately slow sometimes and use strong *kime*, that is, focus; the same kata was performed as fast as I could while keeping correct form and technique. Finding the point of balance that kept each element present and working in harmony during the performance of a kata, even a simple one like gekisai dai ichi, was difficult. Switching my concentration to different parts of my body—legs, arms, hips, shoulders—also gave me much to think about. The morning's training had been strenuous but very enjoyable, and a real eye-opener as far as how to study my kata was concerned. I left the dojo feeling excited and ready for more.

After breakfast, Kathy and I ventured forth once again onto the streets of Naha; this time we wanted to locate a number of buildings and businesses that were going to make our stay in Okinawa more convenient, places like the local post office, a bank, and if possible, a cafe where Kathy could indulge her passion for drinking tea. We managed to find examples of all three and over the coming weeks made frequent use of each of them. The Heiwa dori market was only a ten-minute walk away, its maze of narrow streets and alleyways housing hundreds of tiny shops and stalls, each selling a vast array of goods, from food to fine silk and everything in between. Stalls selling mundane items like pots and pans stood alongside family-run businesses, offering a more esoteric line in stock. Kathy loved the market and often spent hours wandering through it. I, too, found a few interesting items there, ranging from a replica samurai helmet to a beach towel depicting Kiyomasa Kato's part in the invasion of Korea in 1592.

The market sprang to life shortly after the end of World War II, as a place to buy goods that were in desperately short supply, or banned altogether. It was a cash-only location that facilitated the ebb and flow of a black-market economy; so while the commerce underway along Kokusai dori was sanctioned by the ruling American authorities, in Heiwa dori the shops and stalls found their support directly from the locals. The day was not completely our own, however, as I had more training to go to at seven-thirty that evening, so after a few hours of retail therapy for Kathy, we made our way back to the minshuku where I rested for a while in the late afternoon before returning to the dojo. I rolled out my futon and tried to relax, but with little success. Unlike my training earlier that day, tonight the dojo would be full of students, many of whom were long-time students of Higaonna sensei; I would have to find my place among them, and I wasn't sure I had it in me to do that.

Arriving at the dojo in plenty of time to change and loosen up before training, the number of karateka coming through the door began to worry me. The dojo was small with few windows and only one door, so when the training started it was going to get hot and I already knew I was going to suffer because of that. The one pleasant surprise was the arrival of Christina Larsen, a New Zealander, who came to Okinawa for a six-week stay a year earlier and had been unable to pull herself away from the life she was living here. Holding the rank of nidan in Goju-ryu, she was a great source of information for me and the two of us became good friends from our first meeting. Higaonna sensei arrived and the noise level in the dojo from people talking dropped to zero; he called us into line, but I was unsure of exactly where to stand. As Christina was nidan and she was in the second row, I figured I would stand behind her, in the third row, but in front of the kyu grade students on the two rows that lined up behind me.

Higaonna sensei soon put an end to my confusion by ushering me to the left-side end of the front row, a move I was to discover the true significance of at a later date, but right now, I had more pressing things to think about, like how I was going to survive the next two hours. The feeling of dread I experienced walking to the dojo the first time, which I thought had passed, returned with a vengeance. Beads of sweat brought on by the huge wave of doubt filling my mind began to trickle down my face. The names of everyone in the dojo would become easier to remember as the weeks passed by. A few names however, like Terauchi, Uehara, Yonezato, and Yamashiro, would be etched into my memory forever, some because of a kindness shown, others because of the training we did together, and one because he was a dangerous bully.

Beginning with a comprehensive series of preparation exercises that lasted around fifteen to twenty minutes, the training moved on to a huge number of repetitions of basic techniques. Punches, blocks, strikes, and kicks were performed in the hundreds; first, on the spot, and then again with movement from one stance to another and back again. The training was very demanding on a physical level as well as difficult on a psychological level. As the training continued, some began to weaken, but in a strange way, their struggle to continue gave me the impetus to continue. I wanted to prove to myself that my first experience in the dojo had been nothing more than an anomaly brought about by the alignment of tiredness, hunger, and a great deal of apprehension about what I had let myself in for. So I pushed on and drew strength from knowing that there were others in the dojo not coping as well as I was. The training was to prove a good example of the physical level I would be expected to work at, and over the course of that first week, I was pushed to my limits repeatedly by the other yudansha during training. After the formal training ended, senior students often stayed behind to work on their technique in a less formal way; and it was during such times that I was often asked by Higaonna sensei to face the half dozen or so senior kyu grade students in kumite. They clearly wanted to prove their mettle by taking down a foreigner wearing a black belt, so they fought with a spirit that sometimes outweighed their sense of control.

At times, I reverted to a few tried and tested methods from my days fighting on the streets of Manchester and found the judicious use of a head-butt here and there had a way of reigning in their fighting spirit to a level that worked more in my favor. The occasional thumb in the eye did the trick too, as did a knee between the legs. Although none of the tactics and techniques were looked upon as orthodox or proper during my Shito-ryu training with Tomiyama sensei, they found a home in Okinawan karate, and if Higaonna sensei was aware of my using such methods and disapproved, he said nothing about it. Knowing him as well as I eventually did, I can't imagine he missed very much at all, and looking back, I get the feeling he was probably enjoying the struggle he watched me going through each night after training. Apart from extreme fatigue and the masses of bruising over my whole body, little permanent damage was caused, and slowly, bit by bit, my attitude and understanding began to change. My tormentors too, learnt quickly that they could not take liberties without facing consequences. I was happy to spar with them, karate style; but if they wanted to fight, I was ready to do that too!

The conditions Kathy and I were living in were difficult, and the training I was experiencing was even more so; therefore, I had to adjust quickly to both or return home knowing I had been unable to cope. Walking back to the minshuku after my first night of training, not coping was far from my thoughts. It was late, and I was bathed in the warm afterglow of a long and demanding training session. The gentle rain falling from a pitch-black sky was keeping people inside, leaving the world a quiet place. Only the odd stray cat, often with a tail missing or an eye lost in a fight with a rival, shared the tiny backstreets with me as I made my way quietly along streets that were already becoming familiar. The illumination of the infrequent streetlights placed a shine on the wet walls and houses along my route home, giving them an attraction that was instantly lost in the dry, stark light of day. As my first week of training at the Higaonna dojo progressed, my resolve to face whatever came my way had faltered a number of times. I was already accustomed to hard physical workouts, but I was finding the Okinawan approach to training much less symbolic of fighting than the karate I had been practicing up to then. Sparring with members of the Shukokai had been fierce at times and as a result, injuries did occur. But the basic premise of sparring had simply been to continue an exchange of techniques for three minutes, and in that time, gather as many 'points' as possible. Mentally, it was an exchange that suited a sporting contest more than reality, for in a genuine altercation, three minutes is a lifetime. In my experience, a fight, once it turns physical, is decided in a matter of seconds and ends shortly thereafter.

At the Higaonna dojo, we trained in a manner he called *irikumi*,[52] a kind of all-in method of fighting that allowed for grabbing, pulling, and even groundwork just so long as it didn't degrade into a wrestling match. I felt irikumi brought karate closer to the actual dynamics of combat and required a different mentality to the one adopted during most other methods of sparring I was used to. Although I found irikumi a more realistic approach to practice fighting and much more to my liking than regular *jiyu kumite* [53] sparring, I always knew it was still a very long way from engaging in an actual fight. The way the kata was performed also had a feeling that was unfamiliar to me. Although the Shukokai used all of the kata found in Goju-ryu, the execution and technique—and therefore the information encoded within them—had gone through a number of changes at the hands of Kenwa Mabuni and later his student, Chojiro Tani. Thus, it bore only a passing resemblance to the original kata of the same name. My education, or should I say 're-education', in the kata of Naha-te was mostly carried out during my morning training with Higaonna sensei, which took place each Monday, Wednesday, Friday, and Sunday. As time passed, I also received encouragement from Terauchi and Yonezato who, each in his own way, kindly took the time to push and prod me into correct postures while all the while uttering disapproving grunts that had an unsettling effect on my concentration.

Friday night at the Higaonna dojo back then was given over exclusively to kumite and was not a place to be if you were in any way shy about hitting or being hit. My experience of the intensity of "Friday night fighting" began toward the end of my first week in the dojo. I remember vividly the feeling that something special was in the air when I noticed the many new faces coming through the door. I thought I had already met most of the students, but a good number of the karateka coming through the door were yudansha from other dojo. What I was about to take part in for the first time that night was a gathering that echoed Okinawan training from a long-gone age when karate teachers would send their students to learn specific aspects of karate from different teachers whom they either admired or felt had a better understanding than they. The reputation of Higaonna sensei was enough to attract many students from other dojo, and all who came knew what to expect. As the students were called into line, it seemed that I alone had no idea of the hurricane to come, and so, oblivious to events that were fast approaching, I lined up and bowed. Training began with a strong warm-up session led by Terauchi-san. Higaonna sensei prowled around the dojo, every now and then stopping to correct a student's posture or to encourage him to go a little deeper in a stretch.

As I worked my way through the exercises, I began to detect an atmosphere in the dojo that felt different from previous nights. After about half an hour, Higaonna sensei took over the instruction, and we launched into literally hundreds of repetitions of basic blocking, punching, striking, and kicking techniques. After an hour, the sweat was rolling off everyone and the dojo had taken on the atmosphere of a greenhouse, but it was a greenhouse where the windows were closed, for there was little oxygen to be had from the sweat-laden air. The heat and humidity was deliberate; it added to the stress of training and the worsening conditions we students had to deal with. Higaonna sensei was well known in Okinawa for his ferocious training sessions and the length of time they would sometimes run. A student fainting was not an uncommon sight in the dojo; the same was true of blood, and sometimes tears too. In time, I would learn to pace myself, but on that first Friday night I had little inkling of what lay ahead. Pairing off, each couple found what space they could and made ready to begin the gradual transition toward irikumi. Starting with *sanbon kumite* (three-step sparring), we advanced to ippon kumite (one-step sparring), and then on to *yakusoku kumite*[54] that allowed for numerous prearranged attacks to be delivered with speed and with some power. Finally, having changed partners many times up to this point, the training turned to *randori,*[55] a light, continual form of kumite conducted without a prearranged attacker and defender and without stopping until Higaonna sensei called "Yame!" ("Stop!").

With everybody now past their 'comfortable' best, the kyu grade students were allowed to finish for the evening, although they were free to stay and observe what came next. What followed was as much a test of mental endurance for me as it was my physical abilities, and I look back on those days now with a quiet satisfaction that my capacity to endure such training to the end did not desert me. Although conducted without malice or ill will, most of the time the fighting from that point on grew ever more intense in its application. And even though excessive force to the face and genital area was frowned upon—but not unheard of—heavy blows to the body from fist and foot were expected, with impact heavy enough to knock you off your feet. It was quite common to see people going to the ground in any number of different ways; in fact, I discovered a few interesting ways that I could hit the floor myself during that first Friday night of kumite at the Higaonna dojo.

In spite of the grueling pace and the accumulated punishment being taken and given, I was doing well until a call to change partners brought me in front of a young man, Yamashiro, from the dojo of Ko Uehara sensei. Yamashiro and I subsequently developed a mutual respect for each other, although on this, our first meeting, the potential for that was not immediately obvious. From the very start of our engagement, I knew he had something other than irikumi in mind. This guy was out to make a point at my expense, and if that meant my getting hurt, then as far as he was concerned, so be it. I, of course, took a different view and very quickly decided that I too was going to have to prove a point of my own. Things began civilized enough, but that changed very quickly, and Yamashiro began to fight as if I'd insulted his mother, and time and time again his attacking combinations pushed me backward along the length of the dojo. At first, I was puzzled by the intensity of his attacks, and for a moment had no choice but to suffer the onslaught of his kicks to my thighs. But without realizing it, I was slipping back into a mindset I had not held since my time fighting on the street. It was as if my brain divided itself in two, one-half good and one-half bad, one side sensible, the other side chaotic. While the sensible part of my brain tried to make sense of what was going on in front of me, the chaotic half fought for dominance, and once the tipping point was reached, all hell broke loose. I was sufficiently aware of my surroundings to try to keep a lid on my emotions, but I was slipping, and not at all sure I could contain the rage that was building inside.

Yamashiro was employing a strategy often seen in the modern Kyokushin knockdown tournaments, where fighters try to literally kick the legs out from under their opponent by landing heavy roundhouse kicks to the thighs and downward-driven punches that shook the body to the core. It was a method of sparring that required a great deal of tenacity to stand against and trade blows while taking the punishment. My mind was racing with the realization that I was once again in familiar territory. Mentally, I was under real pressure, and everything I had learnt about fighting from my days on the street was screaming at me to fight back. I had hoped not to experience such feelings again and never expected to experience them in the dojo. A voice emanating from the chaos inside me said Yamashiro was out to hurt me, and from that moment on, something in me changed. If someone was going to get hurt during this exchange, it wasn't going to be just me.

My opponent's confidence was on the rise as I crashed against the wall of the dojo for a second, third, and fourth time. But things were about to change. The momentary easing of hostilities that followed my smashing into the wall allowed me to shoot forward with a flurry of kicks of my own: hard, forceful, kicks that would hurt if they landed, and I was doing my best to see that they did. Pushing my antagonist backward along the length of the dojo, my last combination ended with a leg sweep that lifted him off his feet and sent him tumbling to the floor. Without missing a beat, Yamashiro bounced to his feet, and that's when I knew for sure that someone was going to get hurt: this guy wasn't going to stop. I knew then I would have to land a blow powerful enough to take the fight out of him. In the back of my head, I knew also that this was an important moment for me in the dojo. I didn't want future challengers to spot a weakness of spirit in me, for that could easily be interpreted as an invitation to 'try their luck', and the potential for such confrontations to spiral out of control was all too real.

The fighting continued, within me and around me, and as in former times, my world grew silent and slow. Scientists and doctors can no doubt explain the psychological shift that takes place in the brain during moments of high stress brought on by physical confrontation. Like one tectonic plate giving way to another, something snaps, and the resulting release of energy is enormous. With Yamashiro standing before me only slightly shaken from his visit to the ground, I drove my next attack home, I am ashamed to say, with little care for my sparring partner. A second leg sweep hit both his ankles with such force that his body lifted off the ground in a sideways twist that left his exploding punch falling well short of its intended target. The event was unfolding in front of me in slow motion, and I felt I had all the time in the world to slam my mawashi geri (roundhouse kick) deep into his stomach while he was floating, weightless, in the air. He hit the ground hard, landing with a dull thud that could be heard over the surrounding noise of others engaged in battle. This time Yamashiro did not bounce to his feet. Instead, he stayed there for a moment before trying to stand.

My final kick had found its mark and done its job well. My foe lay on the ground, arms wrapped around his stomach with his knees pulled up to his chest. I stood back, waiting for him to come again, but from his fetal position, he could only lift himself onto one knee while continuing to keep both arms around his body. His face told me everything I needed to know. I had hurt him; and I knew that if he stood up and continued to fight the way he had, I would do my best to hurt him again. It had been a long time since I had felt a desire to hurt someone. Like an unwanted guest who shows up years later, I thought my temper was a relic of the past, a symptom of a way of life I no longer lived nor wished to return to, so the feelings that resurfaced that night were totally unwelcome. I had worked diligently to bury my temper and change my character, but that first "Friday fight night" illustrated just how shallow a grave I had dug in my efforts to lay my temper to rest. Clearly, more time was needed, but I was convinced I had the tools and the discipline to keep digging. What I really needed was guidance, and at that time, I believed Higaonna sensei was the right person to provide it.

Yamashiro did eventually get to his feet, his character more subdued now than before. Over the coming weeks, we faced each other again many times in the dojo, trading blows that were at times difficult to deal with, but never again did he try to hurt me, or I him. As I had suspected at the time, others in the dojo had been paying attention to the outcome of my first meeting with Yamashiro. The following day, Yonezato told me how pleased the dojo seniors were that I had not let them (or the dojo's reputation) down by yielding to Yamashiro's attacks. He told me that each Friday night visitors to the dojo tried to dominate Higaonna sensei's students during kumite; as I was new and also a foreigner, it appeared that I was considered an 'opportunity' to take things a little further than usual. By stopping Yamashiro's onslaught so decisively, I had demonstrated that even a guest at the Higaonna dojo could not be taken lightly. It was reassuring to hear Yonezato say such things, for I was beginning to think that my presence in the dojo was not exactly to everybody's liking. While most of Higaonna sensei's students were welcoming, a small number deliberately kept their distance. They were never antagonistic, but they were never openly friendly either. From what Yonezato had said, at least the seniors were warming to me, and I was glad of it.

The soreness in my legs from Yamashiro's kicks hung on for days and the bruising that followed looked horrendous, but in truth, it looked worse than it was, and apart from a little stiffness and soreness to the touch, I was happy to deal with it. I had read somewhere that pain was only fear leaving the body; but it always sounded like the kind of self-promoting nonsense used by the military to groom new recruits. Even so, in a peculiar way I came to think that my first week at the Higaonna dojo, with all the physical and mental stress that was brought to bear, could be summed up in that slogan. The feelings of doubt that had threatened to consume me were well and truly banished, replaced by a bruised and battered body that, in spite of all the punishment, housed a mind that was looking forward to more training. Nothing could dampen the sense of confidence that was now growing inside me.

I had just experienced the toughest week of karate training I had ever lived through, and though I did not know it at the time, I also passed the test put in place at the beginning of the week by Higaonna sensei when he motioned for me to stand on the front row with the dojo's senior students.

Sunday morning training gave way to a pure exchange of information that would, if I worked diligently enough, transform my physical efforts into knowledge and perhaps in years to come, even wisdom; and as the morning progressed, *hojo-undo* training—working with the traditional tools that promote health and strength—led to kata practice. Higaonna sensei always took pains to make sure I understood the kata and the basic bunkai that provided a more complete picture of why particular techniques were being used, and why timing, angles, and the adoption of a correct distance from an opponent were crucially important. My education into the depth of kata and its true role in the learning of karate began to open before me. I discovered for the first time that karate was more than a list of techniques to be memorized and hopefully mastered. Rather, it was a set of principles to be grasped, internalized, and put into play whenever the need arose. I came to understand that the bunkai of any kata depends entirely on the depth to which a kata has been studied and understood. It began to dawn on me that there was, in fact, no such thing as an 'advanced' kata in karate, and that the concept of advanced and beginner kata entered the karate dictionary only after the art moved away from teacher and students training privately together in seclusion to the open system of teaching karate in a diluted form to schoolchildren. As karate was exported around the world largely by organizations that were created in mainland Japan shortly after World War II, the notion of basic and advanced kata also became a valuable marketing ploy.

If proof was ever needed of the physical decay of karate and in particular kata, since the art left Okinawa in the early years of the twentieth century, you need only consult the Internet. As YouTube will testify, kata is all too often a display of pretend fighting, far removed from the principles of combat the kata are there to teach. It is not the karate, but you, the karateka, who determines its usefulness, its role in society, and its place in your life. At the end of the day, karate condenses to little more than feelings, but for me back in the early weeks of 1984, my feelings for the karate I was now immersed in hardly existed. It was all I could do to remember the sequences Higaonna sensei was so patiently teaching me.

The Monday morning gathering in the dojo began not only my second week of training, but with Higaonna sensei announcing his plan to take us sightseeing: wonderful! Looking around the dojo I could see the other students did not exactly share my enthusiasm, and had I known what was in store I would have kept my big, 'gormless'[56] smile to myself and spent more time stretching and warming up my legs better than I did. This morning, Christina and Yonezato were also training, and together, our small group of eight or so, led by Higaonna sensei, left the dojo and began to jog at a steady pace. As we jogged along, I honestly began to wonder what all the fuss had been about. The pace was relatively easy and I was feeling so much more relaxed now than on my first run a week earlier. I was feeling supremely capable of continuing the steady pace. The thing I didn't realize about Higaonna sensei at that time was that although he never ran very quickly, he never slowed down much either. So whether the route took us up and over the huge pedestrian walkways that were a major feature in the urban landscape back then or along meandering backstreet passageways that followed the line of open sewers, in true 'Forrest Gump' fashion, we just kept running at the same steady pace, mile after mile.

The only time the group stopped to gain a collective breath was at the foot of the Ishi-Tatami—stone tatami—road in Kinjo-cho,

Shuri. This was once the tradesmen's route up to the original palace, the Shuri-jo, which was the main residence of the king of Ryukyu. The road forms the partial remains of a highway system that was laid with efficiency in mind rather than comfort, and as such, its direct course to the top of the escarpment from the valley below gave little consideration to the massive toll taken by the legs and lungs when ascending its torturous trail. The stones are roughly cut and only partially level, but this amounts to nothing when compared to the gradient of the road in places where the incline is so steep that steps replace the rising slope. The steps, made from large stone blocks only add to the punishing toll already taken by the legs just to reach them.

Higaonna sensei halted us all at the bottom of the stone road and allowed us to catch our breath in preparation for the lung-bursting struggle to the palace grounds at the summit. Once he felt enough time had passed for us to collect ourselves, typically around two minutes, he led the way. As before, the pace was easy enough, but now the gradient was such that it felt like running in water that was waist deep. For a while, Christina and I kept pace with each other. She had done this before, although I suspect she was finding this occasion no easier because of that. Looking at me, she said, "Never mind, it's good for your soul!" That was all well and good, I remember thinking, but right then I would have given anything to remain a sinner. This was my first climb to Shuri-jo by way of the Ishi-Tatami, and even though in the years to follow I would scale its rugged surface many times, on that particular occasion I was finding it difficult to believe the mental torment and physical suffering I was experiencing would ever end. As always, when we approach our physical limits, we arrive at the true battlefield upon which we must fight, and once there, begin to do battle with our ego. Budo is found in adversity, in the discomfort of the unfamiliar, and is absorbed into your character by the choices you make when all around you is not as you would like it to be. Your mind is where progress is made or lost, where character is developed or allowed to shrink in the face of hardship. In the end, the thought that pushed me to the top was the realization that there were others around me engaged in the same struggle. They were doing this too, facing the same difficulties as I was, and so how could I not struggle to find in me what they had found in them.

About three quarters of the way to the top, the Ishi-Tatami crosses a modern street, and Higaonna sensei had warned us to be careful not to run out into it, but to stay alert and cross the road with care. As I recall, this is where Higaonna sensei stopped his own strenuous push up the hill and from there took a more sedate pace to the top. We students, on the other hand, were encouraged to dig deep one last time and push on to the very top. Although this final section is fairly short, it is still very steep in places, and as such it was by no means an easy thing to 'dig deep'. But dig we all did, and with a collective effort, we grunted and groaned our way to the entrance of a small Buddhist temple at the top of the hill. The *roshi*[57] there, Sogen Sakiyama, was once a student of Chojun Miyagi, the founder of Goju-ryu.

On this, and subsequent visits to Shuri-jo, Higaonna sensei never took long to catch us up, scarcely enough time for us to catch our breath again. And once he did, the training continued. Reaching the palace grounds, we dropped to walking pace and continued to follow Higaonna sensei as he led us over bridges, through gateways, and along paths that skirted the large ornamental ponds within the palace grounds. The original Shuri-jo had long since disappeared, leveled by a bombardment from air and sea that lasted close to three months and was finished off completely during the battle for Okinawa that began, on the ground, on the morning of April 1, 1945. In 1984, a few small parts of the palace had been restored, like the Shurei-mon gate and the Enkakuji bridge, but the main buildings were still in the early stages of being returned to their former glory. I didn't know it at the time, but years later, in November 1992, I would stand within the walls of the newly rebuilt palace and witness Okinawa's most senior karateka demonstrate their karate as part of the palace reopening ceremony. Due to its prowess as a trading nation, the kingdom of Ryukyu was once known as the Venice of the East; and in an era when China was the only superpower in Asia, almost every neighboring country or kingdom paid homage, either directly or indirectly, to the Middle Kingdom.[58] In the years following the unification of Okinawa in 1429, Ryukyu stood out as a place of peace, art, and culture.

The walk around Shuri-jo came as a great relief from the hard slog up from the dojo in Makishi; the return, thankfully all downhill, proved only marginally less strenuous than the uphill climb. This was due in no small part to the congested traffic on the roads and the amount of smog and pollution we were forced to breathe. In places the air was, literally, blue from the exhaust of what seemed like a million internal combustion engines. Even before we reached the dojo, my eyes were red and stinging and I developed a sore throat; but as there was nothing I could do about it, I kept running and kept breathing and tried to focus on the kata I knew I would be practicing back in the dojo. The feeling of relief from drinking fresh water once we arrived at the dojo was overwhelming. Running in traffic was nothing new, but the level of pollution was, and I began to understand why no one else but me had expressed any excitement about going sightseeing. Changing into our keiko-gi, the following hour of kata practice passed quickly. On my walk back to the minshuku, I bought a liter bottle of cold lemonade from one of the tiny convenience stores I passed each day on my way to and from the dojo. The bottle passed from the cooler to my mouth in seconds and its contents gulped down with a relish seen only in the very thirsty. The liquid seemed to ease my throat, but later, gave me a truly awful stomach cramp. All that cold, carbonated water hit my hot and empty stomach and the resulting shock took a while to adjust to. After that, I never drank quickly again, no matter how thirsty I was.

When I returned to the dojo on Wednesday evening, I learnt that Higaonna sensei had gone to the airport to meet Virra's instructor, Michael Ch'ing, who was flying in from Malaysia. Terauchi led the training that night and at first, I felt a little uncomfortable about him being left in charge. Terauchi had an unpredictable nature; I had witnessed it and had been on the receiving end of his barbed comments and sarcasm. Ironically, as the weeks passed by, he also made it known that he liked me, but I was never one hundred percent sure he meant that. During training, he often stalked his training partners like a wolf circling a deer just prior to moving in for the kill. Back then, Terauchi was the Tokyo all-styles kumite champion and had a physique similar to an American pit bull. He seemed impervious to the powerful blows I witnessed him take from Higaonna sensei during *shimi*[59] and never once took a backward step that had not been calculated to draw his partner into a punch or kick that was delivered with frightening speed, power, and to be fair, control. I have no doubt at all that had he wanted to land his techniques fully, he could have done so unimpeded.

I took my place in the lineup and the training began. It was a difficult night's training and the pace began in fifth gear and stayed there for the next few hours. Terauchi led from the front, doing everything we were being asked to do. His strength and fitness proved too much for some, and when this happened, the student was directed to sit at the back of the dojo. Several times, I found myself experiencing internal conflict about whether or not to stop. Others had, and they were allowed to sit and rest at the back of the dojo. Granted, most of them were kyu-graded students, but a couple of the younger shodan were also sitting at the back . . . so I wouldn't be the first yudansha to quit. I now understand that moments like this are the most important part of training, for this is where the very essence of budo resides—not in the problem you face, but in the decision you make when facing it. Why is it that the path to further progress is trod by making difficult choices? Why is it that the easy option is most often the poorer choice? Is there some cosmic law that states progress can be made only through struggle? I didn't have the answer to any of these things back in 1984. All I knew then was that I could either stop or keep going, and for some reason, the thought of stopping always irritated me more than the thought of continuing.

Perhaps it was nothing more than sheer pig-headedness mixed with stupidity that kept me struggling that night. Instinctively, I understood that if I sat down I would soon become overwhelmed by feelings of regret and even shame; perhaps then, it was only egotistical arrogance and pride keeping me on my feet. I have thought about that night, and others like it that I have experienced over the years and concluded that it was more than a fear of failure, more than shame or ego that stopped me from sitting down at the back of the dojo. When moments like this unfold, they transcend conscious thought. Like a surfer riding a wave, you learn to blend with the power that is alive in the moment you are living, and by doing so you achieve the ride of your life. There is nothing vulgar about the strength found in budo. Rather, there is an elegance and beauty to how a kata is performed. Balance and a feeling of oneness produce simplicity of movement, which in turn reveals elegance and a level of sophistication denied to individuals who insist on the conscious possession of all they do. Smoothness comes from the steady pounding of the roughness collected at puberty, when the simplicity of childhood gives way to the unchecked exuberance of approaching adulthood. Authentic karate training provides a means by which the simplicity of living can be reclaimed, but only if you can develop the courage to remain in the fray and not look to rest at the back of the dojo.

The following morning I met Michael for the first time. He was a confident young man, older than me by only a couple of years, and had spent over a decade training in the Japanese style of Kyokushin karate. As a regular visitor to the Kyokushin Hombu[60] dojo in Tokyo, Michael was no stranger to tough training. Renowned for its no-nonsense approach to kumite, my original thought was that an experienced Kyokushin fighter was all I needed in the dojo on Friday night. Michael was scheduled to be training with us for the next two weeks, at the end of which he would take the examination for yondan, 4th dan. He was in Okinawa accompanied by his wife, TinNee, and they had moved into the same minshuku where Kathy and I were living. So we got to know each other quite well over the length of their stay. Kathy had someone to explore the sites and markets with, stop for tea with, and converse with, in ways that remain a mystery to most men.

When Friday night came around again, I wondered what lay in store for me. Would Yamashiro be there again, and if so would he try to pick a fight with me? Given the outcome of our first meeting, I didn't think he would; but I confess, I was no less worried that he might or that he had a few bigger and tougher friends at the Uehara dojo who he might bring along. Walking to the dojo with Michael, I dismissed all such thoughts as silly and self-defeating. I told myself I could handle—at least to some degree—anything that came my way, and this proved to be the case as the training that night got underway. There were individuals in the dojo that night, besides Terauchi, who gave me a controlled beating and returned at various times over the following weeks to repeat the favor. In retrospect, I learnt much about my physical skills and mental abilities from the encounters where I was not able to dominate my training partner. It is one thing to hit hard and fast, and grow in confidence when things are going well, but quite another matter to deal with the heavy impact of your partner's technique and to continue regardless. The first takes timing and coordination, accuracy, and even audacity; but the second takes all those things: plus courage.

Absorbing the shock and rushing back into the skirmish, displaying not an ounce of discomfort, is a characteristic of combat not trained for nearly enough. Although I believe boxers work on such ideas, karateka seldom do. As a tactic it works well, unnerving an opponent who has just landed his best shot and now finds you coming back, as if nothing had happened! When Yamashiro jumped to his feet the first time my kick dropped him to the floor, I felt my confidence faltering; had he recovered as well from his second visit to the ground, I am not sure what the outcome of that engagement would have been. Whenever I was on the wrong end of a fight in the street, I tried to focus on concepts like this to get me through. I knew about them from my father, long before I ever walked into a dojo. And even though he never fought much in the street like his wayward son did, he fought in the amateur ring with some distinction, and as a result, knew a thing or two about ways to give and take a hit. My previous experience of fighting did not make the blows I received in the Higaonna dojo any less painful, but in my mind, it did serve to devalue the suffering.

For the first hour and a half of training, Yamashiro and I managed to avoid each other, but when Higaonna sensei paired up the yudansha for ippon kumite, he and I found ourselves standing opposite each other once more. As I had anticipated, his strong attacks began immediately, but I was able to defend myself against them, and surprisingly, with more ease than I thought I would be able to. On some level, I felt like I already had the upper hand; given the way our last encounter had ended and seeing Yamashiro now trying with great intensity to land his techniques only added to my confidence. As far as I was concerned, he would never get the better of me again, and as the training progressed so too did his frustration. When Higaonna sensei called for a change of partners fifteen minutes or so later, Yamashiro found a young shodan no older than eighteen or nineteen standing before him. Bowing to my new sparring partner, I was still looking at Yamashiro, recognizing a look on his face that I had seen many times before on the street. It was a look that appeared when confidence bristled into a feeling of superiority, and the thought ran through my mind that Yamashiro was about to take his frustration with me out on his young opponent. Once the sparring began again, it did not take long for my premonition to become reality, and I was appalled to see the way he treated his partner. Higaonna sensei had seen it too and, in typical fashion, said nothing. Instead, he would deal with this matter in a calm and decisive way. Yamashiro was going to have a lesson taught to him, and when it was, everyone in the dojo would be on hand to learn from it.

At some point during the evening, the training was halted, and those who wanted to take on water were allowed to do so. No one ever passed up a chance to rehydrate, as the temperature and humidity in the dojo on nights like this were always high and everybody sweated profusely: we all needed a drink.

Looking at the clock, I saw it was almost 9:30 p.m. and if this had been any other night but Friday, training would be drawing to a close. But it was Friday. So once again, we formed pairs and began to engage in *ude kite*—arm pounding exercises. Already tired and bruised from the previous training, we spent the next fifteen minutes impacting each other's arms and legs in a variety of ways, all of which hurt. I felt sure my arms and legs would soon fall from my body, either that or simply crumble to dust on the floor in front of me. Once again, I had to dig deep into my reserves of tenacity. Kathy would laugh when I used words like 'tenacity' to relate what I was experiencing; she said it was sheer bloody-mindedness on my part, mixed with stupidity and a good helping of stubbornness. Well, whatever it was that kept me standing there I was grateful for it. Tenacity or stubbornness, it did not matter to me which word was used to describe what was going on inside me, only that I was able to last longer than my fear told me I could. For providing such a valuable life lesson, I thank Higaonna sensei, for without his constant encouragement I doubt I would have ever appreciated how important it is to keep going when faced with life's seemingly impossible demands.

Higaonna sensei had everybody sit around the perimeter of the dojo while he slipped his arms into two thick pads that ran the length of each of his forearms; then he called the yudansha out, one by one, to attack him with full power and focus. He called for a technique, a particular kick or punch, and it had to be executed as quickly and as powerfully as possible into the pad that he placed into position to receive it. This continued until he said "Stop!" but he never said stop until the person attacking was exhausted to a point where he could hardly stand, much less continue throwing heavy and damaging techniques into the pads. I had the pleasure of being in that very situation myself shortly after he called my name and I stood to do battle with my teacher. If Higaonna sensei felt you were holding back he would just keep you there longer, so the best thing to do was give it your all, and when exhaustion came, to call on as much spirit as you could to continue for as long as possible. I suspect this was the reason the yudansha were put through such training in the first place. It was becoming more and more clear to me that karate without spirit was like a Ferrari without its engine, nice to look at but not much use if you want to do anything with it. I wanted my techniques to not only look right but have substantial power too.

The clock was showing 11:00 p.m. when we finally lined up to end the training that night. Wending my way back to the minshuku, and my bed, I was sore; as my body cooled, stiffness began to make its presence felt. The Higaonna dojo has no shower so a rub down with a towel is all that is possible once the training is over. As a result, I took a shower at the minshuku. But such were the hours I was keeping at the dojo, the minshuku was often closed by the time I returned home, and Mr. and Mrs. Kinjo long since retired to bed. I had a key for the back door that led from a tiny side alley directly into the kitchen, and I became quite adept at navigating my way in complete darkness, from the door to the stairs. With no hot water available until the morning, I also became acclimated to taking quick and almost silent cold showers late at night or in the early hours. Sliding into my futon on the unforgiving tatami floor of my room often felt like a feather bed. My unyielding pillow, filled with beans, was as soft and welcoming as any my head had ever laid on before. At such times, I would drift toward sleep through thoughts of how others I knew back in England would cope with the training I was experiencing here in Okinawa.

Since becoming popular in the West, karate has followed a well-worn path that has taken it from an activity worthy of study to little more than an entertainment for the masses. I believe the karate training I experienced in Okinawa back in 1984 is now a minority activity on the island. In recent years, many Okinawan sensei, including Higaonna, have opened their dojo to groups of casual visitors, karate tourists who want to play at training in Okinawa. Turning a dojo into a 'tourist destination' and making karate a mere holiday experience cheapens both immeasurably. Karate should never be practiced for the convenience or entertainment of others.

Karate was introduced to the Western world through the lens of Japanese society, and in that society, many cultural norms exist that, outside of Japan, appear at best contradictory and at worst downright repulsive. Take the concept of *honne* and *tatemae*, for example. In public, you behave with tatemae, expressing opinions that serve you well in your work, family, or neighborhood environment. However, in private, away from your normal surrounds, you reveal your true thoughts and act without inhibition; this is honne. This kind of conduct is not exclusive to Japanese society of course, but I find it fascinating that they have conceptualized the behavior and made it acceptable by giving it innocuous-sounding names. Let's not forget that budo reflects the society in which it is practiced, and you bring to the dojo all of the social mores, as well as the emotional and ethical baggage you have gathered before arriving; budo exists to help you discover ways of relieving you of that burden. Apathy emerges from your lack of character and, once established as a part of your nature, induces a kind of moral torpor that dulls the senses and allows others to manipulate your future.

Within Japanese society, even at the very highest levels of business and government, there exist shadowy figures known as 'Kuromaku', which literally means 'Black Curtain', and alludes to the veil of darkness that keeps them from view. These shadow-men may possess a public face, but you'll never see the true nature of the person you are looking at. This inclination to control from the shadows, although wrapped neatly in the Japanese word, Kuromaku, is by no means solely a Japanese phenomenon. The desire to control, and the corrupt behavior that goes hand in hand with that desire, is a cancer that weakens much of the good that men do, undermining the wholesome, the positive, and even the great. Duplicity is the currency by which Kuromaku acquire their status. The recent revelations surrounding the inner workings of football's world governing body FIFA (Federation of International Football Associations) are understood better, not as an uncharacteristic anomaly, but as yet another example of man's inability to follow a straight course.

In the karate world, perhaps the most influential Kuromaku was the late Ryoichi Sasakawa,[61] the inaugural president of the World Union of Karate Organizations, which now operates under a new name, the World Karate Federation, an institution that bears, at least from the outside, an uncanny resemblance to FIFA. You can never be sure who are Kuromaku and who are not because the more successful they are, the less likely it is you will ever notice their hidden activities. There are a number of low-level Kuromaku, shadow-men, in karate today, individuals who live on the periphery of great wealth and influence, but don't quite have the intelligence or determination to fulfill the job description with the same level of success as their political and business world contemporaries. Nevertheless, their influence in the world of karate, said to have a population in excess of 50 million, is telling. Significant among karate's Kuromaku today is one particular shadowy character who hides behind an additional 'black curtain' for he is neither Japanese nor Okinawan, or even a karateka for that matter; and yet he exerts significant influence in Okinawan karate circles. The only reason I don't name him is because Kuromaku are as ruthless as Lance Armstrong in defending their duplicity. As society's addiction to technology grows, karateka routinely spend more time on YouTube and Facebook than they do in the dojo, and all the while, as they slumber under their blanket of apathy, enterprising shadow-men are hard at work shaping karate's future to suit their own agenda.

In the years since returning from Okinawa, I have been asked many times if my nidan in Shito-ryu was recognized by Higaonna sensei. Those who have asked me this have been yudansha, that is to say, karateka who have passed the required test to wear a black belt in the group to which they were members. I began to wonder why I was being asked; could it be that they felt a little inadequate about wearing the belt they wore? Whatever the reason, I would answer the question in one of two ways: with a quick "Yes" or with a story illustrating the point that it really does not matter what color your belt is because it's your skill and understanding that counts. The story I would tell to illustrate my point is about a young man who turned up at the Higaonna dojo one Friday night, the night when everyone gathered to train in kumite.

The visitor, an Okinawan, arrived a little late, after we had already bowed and sat in mokuso for several moments. When we opened our eyes, he was instructed to get changed. He emerged from the changing area a short time later in a clean white keiko-gi, the jacket of which was held closed with a black belt. As the junbi-undo—preparation exercises—began, I recall murmurings going on around me that grew as the exercises we were doing became more difficult. Although aware of something unusual going on about me, I had learnt to keep focused on just one thing each Friday, my own survival. A couple of rows behind me, the visitor was having a tough time keeping up the pace, and to those who could see him, something didn't seem right. His stamina too was lacking, and all this was causing a sense of agitation among those near him. With the junbi undo exercises over, the training moved on to *sandan-gi*,[62] an exercise where two people face each other. One attacks three times in a predetermined sequence, while the other blocks, also using predetermined techniques. Technically, it's a simple-enough training exercise, except it was often made less simple by a determined partner. After sandan-gi, the training switched to ippon and then to yakusoku kumite, one pre-arranged attack and counter to continual attacks and counters that were also pre-arranged.

All my efforts and focus were trained on the person in front of me. During such times as this it was dangerous to let your mind wander, and even though I was aware of something going on elsewhere in the dojo, I did not feel confident enough to turn my head and take a look. To do so may well have invited a powerful punch or kick, either one bringing with it a quick end for me to that particular kumite. The training finally stopped for a water break, and this was when I caught my first glimpse of the visitor who had arrived late. Already he was in a sorry state. The night was still young as far as the training was concerned; from here on it was only going to get tougher, and from the look of the visitor, I wasn't sure he was going to make it to the finish. Higaonna sensei called us back into line and the training switched to jiyu kumite—free sparring. A quick glance at the clock showed the time was approaching 10:00 p.m. We had been training for two and a half hours and finishing time was anybody's guess. It was not at all unusual for training, especially on Friday nights, to continue past midnight. Among the students, there was a joke going around about buying Higaonna sensei a watch for Christmas. It would do no good, as he obviously could not tell the time!

But Higaonna sensei had no problem telling the time, and even less of a problem pushing his students to ever-greater levels of difficulty; the visitor was now in a very dangerous position. None but the yudansha took part in the kind of training that was to follow. The fighting was fast and often rough, and not for individuals who could neither take nor give a little 'punishment'. Kyu level students, that is, everybody below shodan, spent this part of the evening as spectators. This was not an option for the visitor; he entered the dojo wearing a black belt. Given the reception he had received so far, I thought he was doing well to last this long, but the irikumi that was about to follow was going to be fierce in its intensity and brutal in its application. I had my doubts that he would cope with it. The senior students picked their partners and every seven or eight minutes, the fighting was paused, but only long enough to change partners and face somebody new. Eventually, I found myself standing opposite the visitor, and it was then that I managed to get a good look at him. When I did I was shocked; he had clearly taken several heavy blows to the face and body, and looked to me like he had been in a car crash. I felt sorry for the young man. It was obvious to me that he was out of his depth, and for reasons I was unaware of at the time appeared to be paying a very heavy price for an unknown misdemeanor. I did my best to handle the young man without inflicting any more pain or damage, although my clear impression was that I was expected to give him a very difficult time.

A few hours later, in a restaurant not far from the dojo, I complained to Terauchi and Yonezato about the treatment the visitor had received earlier that night. Over the course of our supper, they each explained the rationale behind the events of the evening, offering as justification the following explanation. As they saw it, they had to deal with the stranger harshly in order to preserve the standard of the dojo. They pointed out how new students start at the back of the dojo and spend many years of tough training slowly progressing their way to the front. Visitors who stand ahead of them have to match the standards set by the seniors in the dojo, and if they do, then everything is fine. But if they don't, then the seniors feel an example must be made of them . . . for the sake of the junior students. I was reminded, too, that the color of a belt does not bestow rank, it merely indicates it; and should the signal prove to be a false one, then the wearer has to be called to account. Yonezato reminded me of the treatment I had endured throughout my first week in the dojo, and how that treatment altered dramatically when I returned to the dojo on the second week. Because I told Higaonna sensei I had nidan in karate, he put me where one of his own nidan students might stand. If my karate matched the level indicated by the belt I was wearing there would be no problems. If not, the junior students would be provided with an example of pride coming before a fall, and I would be taught a very valuable lesson.

Yonezato's explanation suddenly made sense of the heated exchanges I had during jiyu kumite with the senior kyu-grade students after training, and the apparent indifference I was greeted with from many of the seniors when I asked questions. It was also the reason for the blank stares from my training partners and the absence of a smile or acknowledgment that we were all going through something difficult together. It made sense to me now. They were all aware of what it took to put on a black belt in that dojo; they just needed to be convinced by me that I did also.

The fact that I had done all that was asked of me and returned at the start of the second week for more of what I believed would be the same persuaded everyone that, as limited as it was, my karate was what I had said it was. Walking home in the early hours of the morning, past the revelry of drunken salary men[63] and tourists from the mainland, my mind drifted back to the visitor and the way he limped away from the dojo, silently and alone. I felt strange inside, realizing for the first time that I had passed an important test, not the kind that led to promotion and a new rank, but a test that marked a level of progress all the same.

The moral of the story is clear; if you wrap a black belt around your waist, then make sure it signals a depth of ability and understanding appropriate to that level. During our initial conversation, Higaonna sensei appeared to recognize my nidan in karate by allowing me to continue wearing my belt when I visited his dojo; but he also put me in a position where I had to demonstrate I could live up to it. I believe I passed his test because of the education in karate I received from Mr. Vickers, and later, Tomiyama sensei. Their schooling had encouraged me to continue during difficult times and to find ways to work through tough situations, instead of looking for ways to escape them.

Life on Okinawa was not all blood and bruises. I came to love my Sunday morning training, for example, as it was then that Higaonna sensei often spent time working with me on my kata. Sunday being the only day of rest for the Okinawan students, many chose to spend it with their families, and as a result the dojo was practically empty. Apart from foreign visitors like myself, and the occasional Okinawan youngster trying to make a little progress, Sunday mornings in the dojo were quiet and peaceful, an altogether different atmosphere from the rest of the week. From time to time, Higaonna sensei would announce special weekend training and the dojo then became less empty, but for the most part Sunday morning always brought with it a relaxed type of training. One time Kathy and I, and a few other students, were invited to Higaonna sensei's home for Sunday lunch. When Higaonna sensei retuned from Tokyo with his new American wife, Alanna, to live in Okinawa, they lived above the dojo with Higaonna sensei's mother. Alanna, however, was unable to settle into her role of 'daughter-in-law' in the way Okinawan culture expected her to, so they moved out and rented a small wooden house a short walk away from the dojo.

I was excited to be invited to Higaonna sensei's home, to sit at his table and eat with him. I believed I could see in him many of the character traits I wanted to adopt. I suppose my admiration for him stemmed from the way I believed he lived his life: his continual training, long after many his age had relegated their time in the dojo to nothing more than teaching. I was drawn to him, I think, because he was a great example to have in mind when my own life was proving difficult and the challenges ahead seemed impossible. I wanted to know if I could discover in me the character traits I was observing in him; and if I could, I would then consider a measure of success had been made in my efforts to grow as a person. Throughout that Sunday afternoon, as we sat together eating and talking about a wide variety of subjects, Higaonna sensei's warm and caring character came to the surface many times. It was difficult to reconcile his fierce nature in the dojo with the happy, laughing man sitting across the table from me, but I have come to learn that we are all multifaceted in nature, and that the true challenge of budo is to find a way to balance each aspect of our character in harmony with the rest.

I had the opportunity that day to observe my teacher, and then to look inside myself to determine if I was the kind of person to take advantage of the occasion or use the occasion to take advantage of my teacher. I was conscious of trying to see past the obvious lesson being taught by Higaonna sensei's hospitality and search for the deeper implication of what was going on around me. Over time, I have learnt a great deal about myself and others, as well as about karate, from appropriate socializing. The many physically tough sessions in the dojo provide a particular avenue for learning, but a more rounded education in karate is to be had from learning to navigate the time spent with your seniors and teachers outside the dojo. This existential element in the learning of karate is all but lost now; and the sensei–*deshi*[64] relationship that once oversaw the transmission of karate from one generation to the next has long since passed into history.

Appropriate socializing with your sensei and seniors has an important role to play as a counter to the tough training undertaken in the dojo. Doing nothing but harsh physical training can lead to an elitist view of karate and opinions that stem purely from high levels of physical prowess. Too much socializing with your teacher leads to a lowering of respect, and even contempt. Either way is unbalanced and both extremes must be avoided. Teaching, as opposed to instructing, is far less popular these days. The only attribute an average karate student needs today is enough money to pay his training fee, as the majority of karate instructors no longer look to form a relationship with the people they teach. To me this is a mistake and only serves to guarantee the continual decline of authentic karate. For it is my belief that all karateka have an obligation to strive for more than knowledge of karate's physical techniques, and, through hard work and personal sacrifice, to seek a profound understanding of themselves through the study of the art. Even as a younger man, when my ego often led me by the nose, allowing me to fall flat on my face as it did when I first tested for 3rd kyu, something inside was telling me that my feeling of defeat was of my own making. It took some time to understand that karate was not about winning—it was about not losing; but in 1976 such insights were mere whispers in my mind compared to my drill-sergeant ego. In many ways, the challenge faced in the learning of karate is to fade out the sound of your ego and learn to listen more closely to that soft whisper of truth you hear, but so often choose to ignore.

As Sunday drew to a close, Higaonna sensei presented Michael Ch'ing, Virra, and me with a signed copy of his latest book. Each copy had a personal message written in it, making the gift even more special to each of us. After washing the dishes and helping to clear up, Michael and TinNee, Virra, and Kathy and I thanked our host for a wonderful day and took a slow walk back to the minshuku via the dojo. Virra was living in the dojo, sharing his accommodation with Terauchi. It wasn't a situation I envied, as Terauchi often came home late and the worse for alcohol. A frequent visitor to the many establishments found in neighboring Tsuji, the dojo's senior student was no great example, not to me at least, of how to live. As ferocious as his karate may have been, in my mind, his importance as a karateka was never great. Feeling relaxed and happy as we arrived at the minshuku, I recall thinking how perfect a day it had been; training in the morning and then relaxing in the afternoon, good food and great company.

Although I had no way of knowing it at the time, that day became a template for my future personal training. At my dojo these days, students train mostly in the evenings, but I do my own training in the morning when the air is rich with oxygen and the sun is not yet in command of the sky. Because I am energized from my kata and strengthened from *kigu-undo*,[65] karate has established a place in my life that harmonizes perfectly with my other commitments. But all that was many years in the future. As my head hit the pillow on that Sunday night, my only concern was to get a good night's sleep and to ready myself for another week of training in the dojo. All the friendship Higaonna sensei had shown us as guests in his home would vanish when we met him again in the dojo.

The first training of the week began with another sightseeing tour of the city the Higaonna way: on foot. Higaonna sensei never ran very quickly, but he did run for a long time. The pace that morning was, as always, steady and continual whether we ran uphill or on flat ground. His apparent lack of exhaustion came, I learnt later, from the control he had of his breathing. An innate ability to harmonize his breath with the activity his body was doing was the key to Higaonna sensei's longevity as a runner. He never told me this. I stole it! What I mean by that is I watched him when we went running, and as much as I could, took note of exactly what he was doing. Higaonna sensei was forty-five years old when I was training with him in Okinawa. Physically he was in his prime and showed no signs of being middle-aged, whereas I was only twenty-eight years old and already felt that my youth was over!

Watching someone and actually seeing what they are doing are two very different things. For example, it is entirely possible to watch something being done right in front of you and not be able to describe what you just saw. A good magician or conjuror can perform many tricks that you cannot fathom, but I'm not talking here about card tricks or the art of misdirection. When you are trying to understand your teacher's karate you have to be careful not to watch him through the lens of your own preconceptions. Watching someone properly means that you take note of as much detail as possible, allowing your senses to absorb what is happening. In this way, you appropriate not only the obvious, but also the subtle aspects of what is going on in front of you. If you can learn to do this, then you have a chance to absorb what you 'see' into your own karate practice. In olden times, much of what passed between a sensei and student was transmitted in this fashion. The two-part process of transmission and receivership taught the student to come to grips with the concept of *ishin-denshin,* which roughly translated means something like 'vibrating at the same frequency as the teacher'. A failure to 'tune in' correctly to the lesson being transmitted will always leave a student vulnerable to failure, for without the ability to establish clear reception from his teacher, a student is left with no other alternative but to practice karate with the incorrect information he has at his disposal.

Our run that day ended as always with a dash up the hill to the dojo door, followed by a quick drink of water before training continued, this time with kata practice for another hour. Later that evening the regular training passed without incident, although as always, not without exhaustion. Even very fit students had to work diligently to get though a training session with Higaonna sensei, as he made sure we were working to our limits, regardless of what those limits were. Before leaving the dojo, Higaonna sensei invited a couple of us to join him in a visit to the local bathhouse[66] the following morning. This is not as strange an invitation as it might seem to readers unfamiliar with the ways of Japan or Okinawa. Bathing is more of a social activity than merely a means to keep clean. In fact, sliding into a Japanese bath while dirty is unthinkable. Washing and bathing may seem to be the same, but in Japan, this is definitely not the case.

Gathering at the dojo the next day, the small group lined up before Higaonna sensei and sat, Japanese style, in silence. Every day our teacher began with karate practice, and for the next hour he guided us through the finer points of hitting the makiwara. It may be thought by some that there is little to using this tool, other than hitting it as powerfully as possible, and in the process building up a set of heavily callused knuckles on each hand. Ultimately, nothing could be further from the truth, but as with everything in life, we began our approach to understanding through methods that may at first seem unrelated to the final objective. By the time we had finished working with the makiwara that morning, none of us had skin left on either of the first two knuckles of each hand. For me personally it was a difficult lesson, as until my arrival on Okinawa, the makiwara had played little or no part in my karate training. The everlasting impression I took away from my first serious engagement with the makiwara was just how formidable an opponent it was. Standing silently before the target, then repeatedly throwing my best punch into the small leather pad at the top of the post, it showed no reaction if I hit it well and as little as possible when I did not; it was a moment of singular clarity for me.

After an hour, we left the dojo and ate a light lunch together in a nearby *izakaya*[67] before heading off to the bathhouse about a mile away. Once inside, we undressed and washed ourselves using small buckets of warm water, which we refilled from a showerhead that stuck out from a tiled wall at hip height. Sitting on low stools and with a mixture of lathered face cloth and water from the bucket, we cleansed ourselves before entering one of the seven or so methods of bathing now available to us. I tried the hot tub, cold tub, Jacuzzi, whirlpool, waterfall, steam room, and sauna. I watched other bathers leave the sauna and immerse themselves completely in the cold tub. I decided to follow their example, and I almost had a heart attack! My personal favorite of all the baths was a warm pool; there I sat waist deep under a waterfall of equally warm water cascading down on my head and shoulders. When Higaonna sensei motioned to everyone that it was time to go, I had a hard time dragging myself away. My heavily tattooed[68] arms had caused quite a stir when we arrived, and even though it was explained to the management that this did not mean I was *yakuza* (a Japanese gangster) I suspect everyone was happy to see me leave all the same. My tattoos completely emptied the sauna when Higaonna sensei and I entered it and sat down. Not that I minded, as it gave Higaonna sensei and me a chance to swap stories about our various body scars, a moment of fun I will remember forever.

Although I was mildly aware that the Japanese and Okinawans looked down upon the idea of tattoos, at least in the way they were used by men to display an air of danger, the ink under my skin had been there for so long I hardly gave it a thought; and it wasn't until situations like my visit to the *sento* happened that I was reminded of its impact on others. I acquired my first tattoo while I was still under the legal age for such things in the UK and by the age of sixteen I had already begun to mark my body. The tattooist who worked on me in those early days often worked with a half empty bottle of Johnny Walker next to him. His 'studio' was situated in a small back street in Moss Side, a notorious district of Manchester, where crime was rampant and the police never patrolled alone. Between regular swigs from the bottle and the accompanying profanities that spilt from his lips, he introduced the ink under my skin, where it remains to this day. In time, the small designs he placed on my forearms would be joined by larger, more elaborate images on my upper arms and shoulders, put there by other tattoo artists who found they could work without reference to a bottle.

Why tattoos? It's a question I have been asked a number of times, and as yet I have been unable to provide a completely satisfactory answer to the people who ask. For me, the idea of tattoos is one I have always been attracted to. My first, on my left forearm was, looking back, an act of rebellion, although against what has long since faded from my memory. I do recall it brought a level of consternation to my parents that I found hard to understand at the time, but would relate to in a heartbeat today if I had a sixteen-year-old who came home having marked himself for the rest of his life. I have a vivid memory of the welcome I received from my mother when I returned home from my visit to Moss Side. "What's that on your arm?" "Nothing!" "Show me!" . . . . Whack! Her open hand made contact with the back of my head so hard it sent me sprawling. Visibly upset and no doubt utterly despairing of her youngest son, all she could do was cry and issue that classic line spoken throughout the ages by so many mothers to so many sons . . . . "Wait 'til your father gets home!"

The tattoos that cover my arms have no profound meaning for me. I just like them. Any imaginings I had that they would make me appear tough disappeared during my time as a guest of Her Majesty the Queen, when I witnessed several heavily tattooed inmates fail to live up to the reputation their multicolored bodies suggested. As I mentioned earlier, looking tough doesn't mean you are tough, and individuals who set out to appear that way by means of tattoos, shaved heads, and goatee beards often find their 'tough-guy' image shatters when faced with the quiet determination of the psychopath who just wants to hurt them.

My training settled into a familiar pattern of fatigue and excitement, each feeling alternating for supremacy and feeding off one another as the days merged into weeks in an endless round of training, sleeping, and finding enough time to eat. For Michael Ch'ing and his student, Virra, entering the dojo at the end of the week brought with it a further challenge. That Friday morning, the three of us practiced our kata together while Higaonna sensei checked and made corrections. Later, he took me to one side and taught me Shisochin kata for the first time. The kata appeared long and complicated at first, utilizing mostly open-handed techniques that I soon came to realize required a greater level of subtlety to execute properly than I had at my disposal. Following Higaonna sensei's lead, I tried my best to follow him and remember the pattern of movement he was walking me through. Eventually, the form was committed to memory, but it was going to be some time yet before I could draw anything useful from this kata. Remembering the postures and techniques in a kata is one thing, but understanding the principles at play is something else entirely.

The morning training passed quickly, and before I knew it, Higaonna sensei called the proceedings to a close. In a strange way, I felt like I was having a day off from the hard, physical grind of training. Morning training had been conducted in a very relaxed way. At times, even laughter broke out in the dojo as mistakes were made in the kata, usually by me. Because I was enjoying myself so much, I completely forgot about the tests Michael and

Virra were about to face in a few short hours. My inability to recall that neither of them appeared as happy about the day's events as I was meant that I was not aware of the different experiences we were having that morning. At the time, I was so wrapped up in my own thoughts that I failed to offer my dojo friends any emotional support for the tests to come. It may seem like a small thing, to be unaware of others in the dojo, but I now understand that without such awareness karate training becomes a selfish activity instead of a nurturing one. Being in the dojo is not just a matter of location; it depends entirely on your frame of mind. Being physically present is not the same thing at all as being in the 'right' place. But I had no sensitivity toward ideas like this back in 1984, and so I remained focused solely on my own experience.

In the early evening, students gathered in the dojo as usual, the training began as it always did, and for the first hour the now familiar pattern I had come to expect on a Friday night unfolded with predictable intensity. Higaonna sensei eventually called a halt to the training, and everyone took the opportunity to drink some water. Shortly afterward, the students sat cross-legged in a circle around the perimeter of the dojo while Michael and Virra took turns to stand in the center of the dojo and displayed their kata, one after the other. Virra was then asked to engage in ippon kumite with almost every brown belt student who was present. As well, he was asked to perform randori with two of the shodan students. His final challenge was to face the makiwara. Michael, having delivered a fairly nervous display of kata, fought all the yudansha present there that night. It was a difficult task set by Higaonna sensei, as there were perhaps fifteen or more yudansha in the dojo and all, including me, knew that nothing but a spirited challenge would be appropriate. During one particular exchange, Michael was hit with a powerful kick that swung in low and impacted him on the side of his left knee. It was a technique I had seen used a number of times to destabilize opponents before moving in with a flurry of punches to finish them off. Michael's reaction to the kick indicated that it had done its job perhaps a little better than expected, and Higaonna sensei was forced to stop the sparring and inspected Michael's leg. The initial examination failed to reveal any serious damage, no dislocation, and no blood. Nevertheless, there was obvious pain on display, and so Higaonna sensei sat Michael down to one side to allow him to recover.

You may recall the account I gave earlier of my first meeting with Yamashiro, the regular Friday night visitor from the Uehara dojo, and how, after a maddening exchange with me he decided to vent his frustration on a less experienced sparring partner. I was sure that Higaonna sensei was aware of what transpired that night, but I was less sure why nothing seemed to have been done about it; tonight I was about to get the answer. Calling Yamashiro to the center of the dojo, Higaonna sensei matched him up with Yonezato. The two men were of a similar age and both had nidan, so they were well matched. There was also a noticeable personal rivalry existing between the two of them that was often intense. When the command to begin was given, they set about each other like two pit bull terriers, and it was not long before Yamashiro had blood running down his face from a cut below his eye. Over and over, he was knocked to the ground only to spring back up as he had when I faced him. Yonezato hovered over his opponent, menacing Yamashiro with a clear message that if he stood up, he would be knocked back down.

Yamashiro did indeed jump to his feet, several times, but each time he was returned to the ground with a little more force. As the combat continued, I thought I recognized a moment when Yamashiro finally realized what was going on. It was as if a light had switched on among the many lights that were increasingly being turned off. When that happened, Higaonna sensei's lesson to Yamashiro, about controlling your emotions during kumite, had been understood and the kumite was brought to an end. I had always found Yonezato a difficult training partner to deal with, but only because his abilities were so much better than mine; away from the dojo he was a very easy-going character and great fun to be with. Watching the battle of wills unfolding in front of me that night, I was overwhelmed by the way Higaonna sensei had chosen to communicate that particular lesson to Yamashiro, as well as the serious nature of the role karate training has in the cultivation of the individual.

The injury to Michael's knee was such that he could no longer face an opponent; so instead, Higaonna sensei had him face the makiwara. Michael delivered punch after punch into the pad, each one as potent as the one before. It was evident that he knew how to generate great power, and as I sat there watching him and listening to the loud "thwack!" that echoed around the dojo each time his fist met the leather target, I envied him a little for being able to make the makiwara dance as it did. Michael's test came to an end with his final punch. Then we lined up in the same order we began the training three hours earlier; mokuso provided a moment of silence for everyone, and for some in the dojo that night, a time for somber reflection. Before the students left the dojo, dispersing in all directions, Higaonna sensei announced the results of the test. Virra had been successful and was delighted to accept his promotion to shodan. His teacher, Michael, did not do so well, and failed to gain promotion to yondan, 4th dan. He took the news as I would have expected, showing no emotion, instead a sense of determination to return the following year and try again. I knew, as I witnessed and experienced the events of that evening, they were providing me with an education. I was trying my best to live in the moment, knowing all too well that my time in Okinawa was finite. Soon I would leave behind me the island and nights like this, possibly forever.

A number of students later joined Higaonna sensei at a small restaurant nearby, and over some typical izakaya food and a number of cold beers, relived the events of the evening. Many happy memories were created that night, and I was thrilled to be there. The following weekend was Michael's last in Okinawa, so Higaonna sensei invited a small group of us to the Motobu peninsula for two days of training and sightseeing. Leaving early on Saturday morning, Kathy and I joined Michael and his wife, Tin Nee, Virra, Christina, and Yonezato-san; and together with Higaonna sensei and Alanna, we packed our bags, and ourselves, into two cars and made our way out of Naha traveling north along Route 58. We passed through Urasoe, going past the many American military bases that dominate the center of Okinawa. The heavily developed sprawl of southern and central Okinawa eventually gave way to a gentler, relaxed, and far greener landscape; here I caught glimpses of the natural rain forest and the wonderful beaches and coves that, all together, make Okinawa a true island paradise. The contrast between Naha and the scenery I was passing through came as a huge shock to me, and I found myself daydreaming about what my time on Okinawa would have been like had Higaonna sensei settled, not in Makishi, but in one of the small rural villages that were dotted across the this part of the island.

Eventually, our little convoy pulled into the car park of the hotel Miyashiro. Situated just a few miles north of the Motobu peninsula on Okinawa's West Coast and a mere stone's throw from a long stretch of sandy beach, it was a perfect location. We arrived later than expected, due to the insanely heavy traffic we encountered along almost the entire length of Route 58. Everyone was tired, so after checking-in we dispersed to our rooms to freshen up, with arrangements having been made to meet again in a couple of hours to have dinner together. Any thoughts I might have been entertaining of a relaxing shower and a quick nap were soon dispelled by Higaonna sensei 'suggesting' we students should join him in the hotel's empty dining room for some light stretching before dinner. So while Kathy was relaxing in our room, I was with my dojo buddies, contorting my body into various positions while wondering if our stretching session was going to evolve into something else. It was not unheard of for Higaonna sensei to become so engrossed in training that all else simply faded from his mind. I was hoping this wouldn't be one of those occasions . . . . I was hungry!

With our hour of stretching over, we returned to our rooms and cleaned up before dinner. The exercise had only served to hone my appetite and I was more than ready to devour the food that would soon be placed in front of me. But I was to be disappointed, when I discovered none of the restaurants in the village were open, and the hotel, whose kitchen had already closed for the evening, only had soup left to offer us. Don't get me wrong, I like soup, but right then and there I could have eaten a horse, hoofs and all. Karate training teaches you to make the best of what you have, so reminding myself of how fortunate I was to be in the situation I was that night, I enjoyed my soup and crackers . . . all three bowls of it! Over dinner, we discussed how the rest of the weekend was going to go. The plan was to practice karate on the beach the following morning, and then, in the afternoon, explore the many tourist attractions in that part of the island.

I slept surprising well considering how hungry I was; but there would be no rushing down to breakfast for me or the other students. At 6:00 a.m., a gentle tapping on our door was the signal to get up, get my dogi bottoms on, and get downstairs, all of which were accomplished in just a few moments, and along with Yonezato-san, Michael, Christina, and Virra, I slipped on my running shoes and stepped outside, ready to go when Higaonna sensei appeared. He soon came through the hotel door wearing his trademark smile that quickly spread through the group; we were fresh from our sleep and raring to go. A short walk through the village to gently limber up our joints was the prelude to a torturous two kilometer run through the soft sand of the beach. Removing our shoes and tee shirts, apart from Christina, we ran bare-footed as well as bare-chested. The air seemed extra rich with oxygen, the wind washed over and around me, and the sound of the surf pounding so close by added to the invigorating situation I was in. Immersed in this heady blend of nature, my senses became heightened, and for moments at a time, the burning sensation in my legs vanished. Being truly 'present' in the moment produced a kind of 'out-of-body experience', allowing me to observe the beach as if watching from a distance.

As the run progressed the group fragmented, and each of us found the physical space and inner solitude to experience that part of the training as if we were the only ones hurrying through the sand. When the run was over, we recovered for only a short time before turning toward the breakers, and together, performed sanchin kata. With Higaonna sensei leading, we performed the kata many times, too many to keep count. The concentration necessary to practice each kata as if it were your first is not easy. Again, I discovered the location played a decisive role in my ability to continue, kata after kata; I became lost in the overwhelming presence of nature. My taste buds could sense the salt in the spray coming up off the surf, my ears could hear the rhythmical crashing of the waves upon the shoreline, and my eyes, although moist from the wind, were working overtime processing the imagery of what spread out before me. My skin, too, was assailed by the wind that in turn either caressed or slapped my body as its direction changed, finding me to be either a wing to flow over or an obstacle to batter.

When the final sanchin kata ended, we stood for a moment looking out across the choppy waters of the East China Sea. Higaonna sensei told us stories of how Chojun Miyagi sensei, the founder of Goju-ryu, would sometimes practice his karate in such a setting, on the beach. As well as the physical training, he would train his powers of concentration by turning to the horizon and setting his gaze as far to one side as he could without moving his head. Then he would slowly begin to track the horizon from one side to the other with his eyes, taking in every inch of the line that separates the sea from the sky. We tried it, it proved difficult, but we persisted. The morning's karate was concluded with ude kite training. Standing on a beach in Okinawa with the wind blowing through my hair, my body glowing from the physical exertion we had been undergoing for the past few hours, I could think of nowhere else I would rather be. Yonezato-san and I were smiling quietly to ourselves as our arms collided over and over again. Karate training like this was, physically and in all other ways too, a world away from the activity I had been involved with until then. Walking back from the beach, my body soaked in sweat and speckled with sand, I knew there would be no returning to Japanese karate for me, but in the back of my mind, I also knew the changes that lay ahead were not going to be easy.

The time I spent with Higaonna sensei, on this and other occasions, gave me a candid insight into his life and what he was like away from the dojo and his many thousands of followers around the world, the majority of whom would experience him only in the context of karate training. By observing how he behaved around his students outside the dojo, I learnt a lot about how to conduct myself in the company of my own students. His fearsome personality in the dojo was matched and balanced perfectly by his friendly and approachable character outside of it, and I came to appreciate the true value of the education he was providing me. The lessons I was learning would prove every bit as valuable to me in later life as any I received in the dojo during training.

Cleaned up, and on the right side of a hearty breakfast, it was time to relax. Our convoy of two pulled out of the hotel car park and headed south for a few miles before making a right turn onto the Motobu peninsula. The old coastal road came with views over the sea, and because we were now at a right angle to the rest of the island, Kathy and I caught our first glimpse of the rugged coastline. Although we had been on the island for some time, this was our first genuine sighting of Okinawa's natural beauty. We were on our way to visit the site of the 1975 World Expo. It was in a part of the peninsula that had been completely transformed a little over a decade earlier to make way for the International Fair designed to showcase the world's relationship with the ocean. With the motto, 'The sea you would like to see', the Expo was opened with great fanfare by the American author and Pulitzer Prize winner, James A. Michener, whose novel, *Tales of the South Pacific,* was later developed for the stage by Rogers and Hammerstein to become the musical *South Pacific.* When the Expo was opened, it ran for six months and attracted three and a half million visitors; the Japanese government even issued a special 100-yen coin depicting Shuri Mon to mark the occasion. Today, the site is home to the world famous Churaumi Aquarium, but back then the technology to build such a structure did not exist, so we walked around the many exhibition halls and took onboard the information on display.

The live seal and dolphin show was something of a highlight, but only insomuch as there was movement and a certain air of unpredictability; though to be honest, I thought the enclosures were rather small and I found little satisfaction at all in watching intelligent mammals being coerced to perform for the entertainment of an audience that consisted of excited children and adults who, due to the cool wind blowing in off the sea, appeared only mildly interested. I was glad when the show was over and we could return to entertaining ourselves, rather than have other sentient beings do it for us. We left the Expo site and drove back along the peninsula toward Route 58, our road back to Naha. It was early evening, and the heavy Sunday traffic bore witness to the number of people who had spent the weekend somewhere other than at home. As painfully slow as the trip north had been the previous day, our journey back was even slower. Between us and our destination were the towns of Chatan, Kin, and Koza, home to the majority of the 20,000-plus US military personnel and families based in Okinawa. Of that number, it appeared to us as if all of them were driving back to their base that evening.

As we finally drew close to Naha, we stopped to eat our last meal of the weekend together at an American-style restaurant called the Pizza House, a landmark building that stood at the northern entrance to Camp Foster on Route 58 in Urasoe. Although the building has since been demolished, back in 1984 it provided Kathy and me with our first taste of familiar food in weeks, and our excitement at the thought of tucking into a steak with all the trimmings caused a great deal of amusement around the table. Don't get me wrong. Kathy and I love rice, and we found a great deal in Okinawan traditional cuisine that we enjoyed eating. Even so, beef and vegetables served with lashings of gravy and a cob of crusty bread proved an irresistible draw. The next hour or so brought the weekend to a perfect end. The beach training had been tough on the legs, and the ocean breeze had proven to be a significant element in the performance of sanchin kata; the experience as a whole had been unlike any other in my karate training so far. I felt like I was quite literally living my dreams! As we walked back to the cars, Higaonna sensei said he knew how tired we all were and that it was okay with him if we did not go to the dojo the following morning, but instead, stayed in bed. He was right, of course. With all our sightseeing and training, it had indeed been a busy weekend, and even though he was planning to be in the dojo early the next morning, here he was relieving us of the same obligation. I was never sure if he meant it as a gesture of concern or if he were testing our resolve. Either way, we all turned up at the dojo the next morning anyway. Although he said nothing about it, I suspected at the time that he was pleased to see us, all the same.

Quite by surprise, the Monday evening training ended early, or should I say on time, at 9:00 p.m. Michael, Virra, and I were told to get changed quickly, and then we accompanied Terauchi to the Junkokan dojo of Seiko Kina sensei in nearby Tsuboya. A student of the founder of Goju-ryu karate, Chojun Miyagi, Kina sensei was an impressive man. His advanced years and recovery from a stroke had done little to curb his enthusiasm for karate. His dojo, the Junkokan, was very small and situated above a coffee shop at the rear of Heiwa dori market. The coffee shop was owned and operated by Kina sensei's son, who was also one of the yudansha at the dojo. I first saw Kina sensei on the BBC television documentary series, *The Way of the Warrior*. His enthusiasm for karate then was obvious, and in person, he seemed even more enthusiastic. During our visit, Kina sensei had his son demonstrate kata from both the Shorin-ryu and Shorei-ryu traditions, and afterward, he took me to one side to explain the subtle differences found in the fighting philosophy behind each system. Kina sensei told me he was very happy to have a karateka all the way from England standing in his dojo and expressed his delight that Okinawa's martial tradition had found its way around the world. He saw karate and kobudo as a way of uniting people in a common bond of physical training and character building. For my part, I was feeling incredibly fortunate, privileged even, to be where I was, listening to the man who was talking to me.

Kina sensei was the first person I ever met who actually knew and received instruction from the founder of Goju-ryu. In the years that followed, I would meet five other students of Chojun Miyagi, talking at length with each of them about their early experiences, as well as their current thoughts on karate. I would take instruction from four of them and receive a promotion from two: Eiichi Miyazato sensei and Koshin Iha sensei. But all that was ahead of me. At the end of my visit, as I shook hands with Kina sensei, the thought passed through my mind that I was holding a hand that Miyagi sensei himself almost certainly had held also. An insignificant coincidence, I know, but as a young man, heady with the richness of Okinawan karate culture, it was a significant moment for me nonetheless, and I continue to believe that seemingly inconsequential moments like touching a hand that once touched another's can provide the internal drive needed to maintain the difficult struggle to make progress in karate. My visit to the Junkokan dojo has remained in my memory ever since. Kina sensei passed away just a few years later, and shortly afterward, his tiny dojo closed.

There was an air of change that came over the dojo after our trip to Motobu, a kind of watershed of sorts. Michael Ch'ing returned home to the island of Penang in Malaysia. Over his two-week stay in Okinawa, we shared a lot of hard training and we enjoyed many of the more relaxed moments of his trip together. The tough nights in the dojo, when our sweat came as much from the high humidity in the air as the often brutally high repetitions of techniques we were asked to perform, cemented a friendship that, unfortunately, lasted for only a few years. I fully intended to take up Michael's offer to visit him in Penang and would have done so had not my life been interrupted so severely within days of my own departure from Okinawa. By the time I had my life back in balance, sadly, Michael had died from cancer. He was only a young man and left behind a wife and family, as well as countless friends who mourned his premature passing.

Higaonna sensei, too, was set to leave Okinawa, as part of his commitment to provide instruction to his ever-growing international following. He would, over the coming years, spend almost as much time away from his dojo as he did in it. His imminent trip to India also signaled the return home of Virra to Malaysia and Christina to New Zealand. Virra had been on the island for three months, Christina for closer to a year. Their leaving triggered feelings in me to return home too, but I wasn't quite ready to go. Kathy and I had been in Okinawa for a little over a month and had only just begun to settle down, but Higaonna sensei's looming departure to India and shortly after his return from there to Europe and America triggered in me a sense of being left behind. I was on the island for a specific reason: to train with Higaonna sensei. Now that he was about to enter a period of traveling that would see him absent from the dojo for many weeks at a time, my desire to stay began to wane, and as Higaonna sensei's departure date drew closer, I began to think more and more about returning to England.

Our original plan included finding work and staying for as long as we could, but finding a job that allowed me enough time to train proved impossible. Kathy, a registered nurse by profession, pursued several options, even waitressing, but nothing came of any of her forays into the job market. All the time we were in Okinawa we lived off our savings. Arriving on the island with enough money to last for around three weeks, or so we thought, would give us more than enough time to secure employment and allow us to stay on the island indefinitely. I had given no consideration at all to specific visa requirements and knew nothing of the need to obtain a sponsor if we expected to remain on the island for longer than our holiday visas allowed. My thinking had taken none of these practical necessities into account; I just wanted to practice karate. I expected we would be eating at least two good meals a day and have enough money to buy as much water, groceries, and other supplies as we needed. The reality of our situation started to become clear as early as the end of our second week, when I realized work was not going to come as easily, if at all.

Together, Kathy and I reassessed our budget and cut out all non-essential spending. No more morning tea and no more luxuries like fruit. The two good meals we had budgeted for each day became one small meal each afternoon; and the unlimited water dwindled to four small bottles a day for me, and two for Kathy. The amount of sweat I was losing during training was the reason for the extra water I was consuming. The tap water was not as it is now in Okinawa, and relying on it to quench a thirst was asking for trouble. Our meager diet was supplemented by taking advantage of any kind offer of a meal that might come our way, and even though it was not a wise thing to do, we drank tap water to swell the small portions of rice we ate to keep our stomachs from aching too much. For the last week and a half of our time in Okinawa, Kathy and I existed on 500 yen each, and on the day we left, Kathy had just 16 yen in her purse—enough to buy exactly nothing! Our rather rapid descent into semi-desperation began to impact on my stamina in the dojo.

The planning for our trip to Okinawa had been far from detailed; in reality, there had been no planning at all. I trusted in fate a lot when I was younger, of everything working out and putting myself in the way of good things that might happen. I had no idea of how expensive the cost of living would be in Okinawa and just assumed we would be able to eat properly and keep ourselves sufficiently hydrated in the heat and humidity of the Okinawan climate. You could say that Kathy and I were wonderful examples of innocents abroad, and you'd be right! There was a balancing act going on inside my head, as my desire to continue training tilted me one way, and the need to eat and pay our way threatened to topple me the other. Learning that Higaonna sensei would soon be leaving became a kind of circuit breaker to my predicament; with him about to be away for weeks on end, the grip Okinawa held me in was loosening.

My final training with Higaonna sensei in Okinawa, that is, my last day in the dojo, was meant to bring with it a morning and evening practice. But that didn't happen. The day began well enough, although I'd had a restless night due to hunger and hadn't slept very well. Nevertheless, I was in the dojo early. At that time, Higaonna sensei lived with his wife and baby son in a rented house close to the former home of Goju-ryu's founder, Chojun Miyagi, a short walk away from the dojo. I was joined by just one other student that morning, and together we focused on kigu-undo,

Higaonna sensei having us spend the entire morning working with many of the different tools used by Okinawan karateka. My deteriorating physical condition became evident when I maneuvered one of the heavy *ishi-sashi* (stone padlocks) Higaonna sensei had in his dojo; the swinging motions of the exercise aggravated an old injury and the pain that followed was immense, enough in fact to bring my training that morning to an end.

Throughout the afternoon, I did what I could to rest, but by early evening, when I was meant to be making my way to the dojo, it was clear that I was in no position to train. I did attend the evening training, but only as an observer. In a strange way, the injury served as yet one more lesson in the learning of karate. In England, karateka will often turn up for training with a list of things that, for one reason or another, they cannot do. Injuries are sometimes used as an excuse to avoid aspects of karate that individuals find more challenging than usual. But in Okinawa, I learnt that if you turn up at the dojo for training, then you will be expected to train and do everything! Injuries do occur, of course, and it's not at all uncommon to see bandaged toes or fingers in the dojo, but a karateka, who has an injury and has chosen to practice, also has an obligation to protect himself from further damage. You cannot learn how to do that by asking everyone else to take it easy on you. So if you feel unable to do what is about to be asked of you in the dojo, then it is better to sit out the training and learn what you can as an observer.

Kathy came to the dojo that night also. She wanted to say her goodbyes to the students she had come to know, and to Higaonna sensei too. When the training was over, Higaonna sensei made a short speech to the gathering of students. He apologized for doing so little for us while we were in Okinawa and expressed his regret at not being able to do more, a statement that left Kathy and me speechless. Higaonna sensei had, in fact, gone out of his way to make our time on the island an experience neither of us would ever forget. He then presented gifts to us both and said he hoped we would return to Okinawa soon, and with that, the evening came to an end. Higaonna sensei was leaving early the next morning for Japan and his connecting flight to India. Standing together outside the same dojo doors I first knocked on so hesitantly a little over a month earlier, I bowed deeply and wished him a safe journey. I declared my intention to visit him again and assured him that I would do my best to put into practice the things he had taught me. Kathy and I walked back to the minshuku through a gentle rain, and like snow, its falling had brought a hush to the world. I was feeling sad that my Okinawan karate adventure was drawing to a close, but given my lack of planning and my utter naïveté, I suppose I was fortunate to have had any kind of meaningful experience at all. Even so, I do not believe my experience in Okinawa during the early months of 1984 can be attributed entirely to good fortune; courage, too, had something to do with it. Having the courage to leave my comfort zone far behind and to step into the unknown is no longer as common as it once was in karate circles, the preference now being to have others do everything for you so that you remain free to relax and enjoy what you have paid for!

Okinawan karate teaches how to look inward at your true nature, and not outward to compare yourself with others. Through years of authentic training, karate cultivates the courage to have faith in yourself and illustrates the problems inherent in developing a dependency on others to provide for you. Karate, as a way of engaging life, is unsuited to individuals who invest in excuses because to study karate requires a particular level of maturity. The aim of karate is to improve yourself as a human being and, in doing so, improve your life and that of others with whom you come into contact. Nothing I have written in this book will make one jot of difference to you if you do not take what you have read and use the information to chart your own course. Action alone is the key to experience, and experience has always been the real teacher of life.

Our flight home to England was long and tiring, and unknown to us at the time, potentially life threatening to me. The events unfolding silently around Kathy and me as we made our way home would, in the weeks to follow, test our determination to solve the problems life unendingly places in the way. Without doubt, much of the sadness and suffering seen in the world is, I believe, the result of not accepting responsibility for your current situation, or your future life. Your lot in life can be enhanced if you discipline yourself to find a balance and then maintain it. My teenage years stand as a testimony to the way a life can be so easily wasted. A life where violence and aggression are considered the two best options for solving problems is a life that is at best only endured. In karate, the saying "Nana korobi ya oki"—"Seven times down, eight times up"—points to the essence of karate training, and life. It's not important when you take a fall; the important thing is to get back up.

Arriving back in London, Kathy and I moved within days to the sleepy little town of Ilfracombe, on the North Devon coast. After a bumpy start due to my being hospitalized for a number of weeks, we settled down to our new life together. We married, bought and sold a number of properties, and I established a small but well-respected dojo. There I continued to practice what I'd learnt in Okinawa, introduced others to the ways of budo, and began my career as a writer, all of which I would subsequently describe some years later in my book *Small Steps Forward.* But here is where I must take leave of my story for now.

The original narrative in this book came from a time when my outlook on life was severely misaligned due to an almost nonexistent sense of balance. This was a time when my life was being wasted because I believed I already knew everything about matters I clearly knew nothing about: like how to live well. I did many dreadful things in my youth, and paid the price for doing so. As an adult, I continue my resolute efforts to pass through life without causing distress in the lives of others. This has been no easy task, especially as my writing often confronts the established order of things, as well as the inertia and apathy that almost always accompanies it. As a result I have, I'm sad to say, made enemies. Nevertheless, I take solace from the words of Winston Churchill: "You have enemies? Good. That means you have stood up for something, sometime in your life."

Since these days were lived, my karate training has continued without pause. Now, well into my fifth decade of karate training, I practice each morning in my private dojo at home and have returned to Okinawa many times over the intervening thirty years since the end of this chapter in my story. The irascible and callus nature of my youth has been erased by decades of dedication to the budo art of Okinawan karate. Change is possible, but only if you really want it.

"The difference between a successful person and others
is not a lack of strength, not a lack of knowledge,
but rather a lack of will."
–Vince Lombardi (1913–1970)

ENDNOTES

Chapter One

1. Craic is witty conversation, joking around.
2. Shebeens were unlicensed drinking clubs, similar to the speakeasies of the 1920s.
3. Slopping-out was the emptying of chamberpots full of human waste when the cells were opened up each morning. The practice was supposedly banned in British prisons in 1996, but it still continues in certain jails.
4. To be placed 'on report' involved appearing before the prison governor and receiving his punishment.
5. 'Borstals' were named after the village of Borstal in Kent, England. In 1902, 'Borstals' were special prisons established to house delinquent boys (aged 15–21) with the aim of providing work, education, and discipline. Some Borstals were 'open' and operated as a cross between a farm and a boarding school, while others, like Hindley, were 'closed'; prisons in all but name, they housed many of Britain's worst young offenders. The Borstal system was officially abolished by amendments to the Criminal Justice Act of 1982.
6. A 'roll-up' was a handmade cigarette. In an effort to make a tobacco ration stretch as far as possible, inmates became adept at constructing cigarettes that were only slightly thicker than the match used to light them.
7. The dojo is a place where a particular subject is studied and experienced.

Chapter Two

8. Aikido is a modern Japanese martial art developed by Morihei Ueshiba in the first half of the twentieth century.

9. Dan (literally, step or position), used to designate progress through various advanced levels of skill.
10. Kyu is a ranking system for beginners. Those with kyu rank are 'mudansha' (without dan); when they earn a black belt, they become 'yudansha' (with dan).
11. Budo means the martial way, a term more widely used to describe authentic karate training.
12. Kata (literally, form) are solo training patterns that, if studied deeply, allow karateka to experience the essence of karate.
13. Kumite includes various forms of sparring.
14. Karateka refers to the practitioners of karate.
15. Dogi is the most common word used to describe the clothing worn during karate training.
16. Sanchin kata is the foundation-training pattern for practitioners of Goju-ryu.
17. Sifu is the Chinese equivalent of the Japanese word 'sensei' and is used in the same way.
18. Sempai is a title used in karate to signify seniority. Your sempai are your seniors.
19. Seiza is sitting/kneeling in the traditional Japanese fashion.
20. Mokuso is the term used for a moment of contemplation at the beginning and end of training. Usually this is done while sitting/kneeling in the traditional Japanese fashion, with your eyes closed and your hands either resting on the thighs or loosely clasped in front of the navel.
21. Kiai is the term used to describe the 'shout' issued at the exact moment a keenly focused technique strikes its target.
22. Keiko-gi is the more correct term used to describe the clothing worn during karate training.
23. CBD (Central Business District) is the downtown in any big city.
24. Bruce A. Haines, born in California, 1934, became interested in karate in 1954, as a student of the art in Hawaii. His book, *Karate's History and Tradition*, first published in 1968, was a seminal work, breaking new ground for Western students of karate and other Asian fighting arts.
25. Gasshuku is a Japanese term meaning to 'lodge together'. It is used more commonly in karate to describe a period of time set aside exclusively for karate training.
26. Kobudo is a Japanese term meaning 'old martial way', but now refers to

the practice of weapons used in Okinawa following the ban on carrying swords.

27. Yudansha is a term used to describe anyone who wears a black belt.
28. Shodan is the first dan level, which is far from indicating mastery. Instead, it describes a karateka who has reached the 'first position' and is now equipped to begin learning.

Chapter Three

29. Bunkai refers to the fighting principles hidden within a kata.
30. Although commonly referred to as rice flails, nunchaku is a weapon thought by historians to have originated in Okinawa from the use of horse bridles.
31. Semi-detached describes the home my first wife and I purchased: one of two separate dwelling spaces built together in a single building. Called a duplex in America.
32. Karatedo is the 'way' of karate.
33. Shokosokun is also known as Kosokunsho in some karate schools. It is a kata from the Shuri-te tradition of Okinawan karate.
34. Seiyunchin is a kata from the Naha-te school of karate.
35. Hanko (Japanese) is a signature seal, made from wood, ivory, horn, or stone. They were first used in Japan in AD 701 for official documents, but became more common in the mid-seventeenth century.
36. Shodo is the Japanese term for the art of calligraphy using brush and ink.
37. Shu-ko-kai (Shukokai) is a combination of Japanese words. 'Shu' means to conduct oneself well, to study, or display discipline. 'Ko' means to associate with like-minded people. 'Kai' is the Japanese word for an association.
38. Matsubayashi Shorin-ryu karatedo was founded by Shoshin Nagamine (1907–1997) in 1947 and is considered one of Okinawa's leading schools of karate. Following Nagamine sensei's death, many branches and sub-branches of Matsubayashi Shorin-ryu have been established around the world.
39. Kai un means to develop your own fate.
40. The designations of 'sho' and dai' are used to differentiate two related kata, and 'kosokun sho' and 'kosokun dai' are examples of this. Different schools of karate place the designation in different locations, either at the

beginning or the end of the kata name. 'Sho' means first, and 'dai' means great.

Chapter Four

41. Mark Bishop is a well-known English budoka and author who lived in Okinawa for fifteen years.
42. Makiwara, also known as 'machiwara' in the Okinawan dialect, is a wooden post standing chest height, four inches wide, and is used to develop powerful punches.
43. Tatami are traditional floor mats made from compressed wood chippings and covered with a woven layer of soft rushes. Measuring just under one meter wide by just under two meters long, the ratio of one to two is important; room sizes depend upon it. I once had a hotel room in Tokyo that was a 'four mat' room. It was inexpensive and very small.
44. The genkan is the area where shoes are removed when entering a Japanese home and other buildings, such as a dojo.
45. As a mark of respect, it is customary to use both hands when shaking hands with your seniors or anyone who is deserving of respect.
46. Minshuku are low-budget boarding houses that offer only basic accommodations.
47. The size of a Japanese room is often quoted in the number of tatami mats it takes to cover the floor. A standard tatami measures roughly one meter wide (three feet) by two meters long (six feet). However, different regions of Japan have adopted slightly different measurements as 'standard.'
48. Now popular in the West, a futon is a thick mattress that is rolled out on the floor each night. The bed is made complete by a one-piece quilt and a small, sturdy pillow stuffed with beans.
49. Esperanto was developed in 1887 by the Polish physician and linguist, L. L. Zamenhof, as an 'international auxiliary language'; by 1999 it was said to have as many as two million speakers worldwide.
50. The chiishi (strength stone) is a strong piece of wood inserted into a stone and is used in lifting exercises to strengthen the body.
51. Geki sai dai ichi is one of two kata devised at the request of the Okinawan government in 1932 by Shoshin Nagamine, in collaboration with Chojun Miyagi. Seen as a way to introduce school children to the fundamentals of karate, its companion kata, geki sai dai ni, was the brainchild of Chojun Miyagi.

52. Irikumi is a term used to describe a kind of nonstop sparring where limited grappling and throws are permitted along with the usual punches and kicks.
53. Jiyu kumite is continuous sparring where only kicking and punching are allowed.
54. Yakusoku kumite is literally, 'exchange of hands', the term used to describe various forms of sparring.
55. Randori is a type of free sparring, allowing all the traditional techniques to be used during the exchange.
56. Gormless is a word from the Gaelic tradition, used to describe someone with a blank look, being clueless, or acting stupidly.
57. A roshi is a title of honor given to a venerated teacher in the Zen Buddhism tradition. Each Zen temple is headed by a roshi.
58. China, when referring to times past, is sometimes called the"Middle Kingdom."
59. Shimi is the term used for testing a karateka's level of concentration during the practice of sanchin kata. It involves karateka receiving strong slaps and heavy blows to various parts of their body while performing the kata.
60. Hombu, sometimes spelled 'Honbu', means headquarters in English.
61. Sasakawa was a class 'A' war criminal responsible for atrocities against the Chinese during the Japanese occupation in Manchuria, and he was the leader of the Japanese Fascist Party. Sasakawa was arrested after World War II, but later was released from prison and retained by America to help fight their 'War on Communism'. Allegedly, he was a Yakusa crime family boss and a friend to the rich and famous in his later years; in spite of intense lobbying, he failed in his attempt to be awarded a Nobel Prize.
62. Sandan-gi are a set of predetermined attack and defense drills used in the learning of karate.
63. 'Salary men' in Japan are usually office workers who labor unreasonably long hours, and who can be found drinking with colleagues into the early hours or sleeping on trains as they make their way home.
64. Deshi is commonly translated as student or pupil, but deshi implies more than merely learning from somebody and is closer in meaning to the English idea of being an 'apprentice'. However, even this word falls short of what it means to be a deshi.
65. Kigu translates as tool or apparatus. Kigu-undo is the act of training with them.

66. A neighborhood bathhouse in Japan is known as *sento*, not to be confused with *onsen*, which is a natural hot spring.
67. Izakaya are local, often family-run restaurants, offering home-style food, beer, and good company. They are extremely popular in Okinawa.
68. In Japanese society, with the exception of the aboriginal Ainu people of Hokkaido, and some firemen, only criminals had their bodies tattooed. In Okinawa, however, such adornment was reserved for the female village or spiritual leaders, who tattooed her hands and arms in designs that were passed on from generation to generation. The more ink under the skin, the higher a woman's status within her community.

About the Author

Michael Clarke was born in Dublin, Ireland, in May 1955, and moved to England with his family at the age of three. He grew up in one of Manchester's crumbling slums, and left school as soon as legally possible, at the age of fifteen. His later teenage years were fraught with violence: on the streets, at football games, in pubs and bars—in fact, anywhere a crowd gathered and an opportunity to brawl presented itself. It was a lifestyle that led to many arrests for violent and destructive behavior and saw him facing a court of law on more occasions than any young man should. His final conviction, following a revenge attack on three gang members, resulting in all three being hospitalized, led to his being incarcerated in Strangeways, one of Britain's most notorious prisons. There, he spent his eighteenth birthday. It was his first, and last, birthday spent behind bars.

Walking into a karate dojo for the first time in the winter of 1974 began a transition that would take years to unfold. It was a step in evolution for the author that often hung in the balance, as street fighting became a hard habit to break, and a return to prison often loomed large on the horizon. With the support of his parents, friends, and sensei and a desire to change, the author gradually left his violent world behind and moved toward a life worth living. He never stopped fighting; instead, he turned his aggression inward to face the belligerence that smoldered within. Turning his focus away from conflict with others and aiming his anger squarely at his own character, the transition was many years in the making. The author has been practicing karate for over forty years, traveling the world to do so, and in all that time, learning from karate's best teacher: experience!

Over his forty-plus years of physical training and research into the art of karate, the author's magazine articles and interviews have been published around the world without a break since 1985: an unprecedented literary contribution. As well, he has had five books published, including the multi-award winning books, *The Art of Hojo Undo: Power Training for Traditional Karate*, which has been translated into Italian, and *Shin Gi Tai: Karate Training for Body, Mind, and Spirit*. Often confrontational, the author's writing attracts both support and disapproval in large measure. Today, he remains one of the few internationally recognized karateka of his generation who continues to devote more of his time to practicing karate than teaching it. His relationship with karate points the way to a more meaningful future by observing closely the lessons of the past.

Since reaching the age of sixty in May 2015, the author continues to practice his karate and kobudo privately each day, and to act as sensei to a small number of enthusiastic and sincere karateka. With a number of new writing projects in the pipeline, his work remains in demand by magazine editors, and his blog, also translated into Spanish, is read by over 14,000 readers worldwide each month.

VIDEOS FROM YMAA

ANALYSIS OF SHAOLIN CHIN NA
BAGUA FOR BEGINNERS 1 & 2
BAGUAZHANG: EMEI BAGUAZHANG
BEGINNER QIGONG FOR WOMEN 1 & 2
BEGINNER TAI CHI FOR HEALTH
CHEN TAI CHI CANNON FIST
CHEN TAI CHI FIRST FORM
CHEN TAI CHI FOR BEGINNERS
CHIN NA IN-DEPTH SERIES
FACING VIOLENCE: 7 THINGS A MARTIAL ARTIST MUST KNOW
FIVE ANIMAL SPORTS
FIVE ELEMENTS ENERGY BALANCE
INFIGHTING
INTRODUCTION TO QI GONG FOR BEGINNERS
JOINT LOCKS
KNIFE DEFENSE
KUNG FU BODY CONDITIONING 1 & 2
KUNG FU FOR KIDS AND TEENS SERIES
LOGIC OF VIOLENCE
MERIDIAN QIGONG
NEIGONG FOR MARTIAL ARTS
NORTHERN SHAOLIN SWORD
QI GONG 30-DAY CHALLENGE
QI GONG FOR ANXIETY
QI GONG FOR ARMS, WRISTS, AND HANDS
QIGONG FOR BEGINNERS: FRAGRANCE
QI GONG FOR BETTER BALANCE
QI GONG FOR BETTER BREATHING
QI GONG FOR CANCER
QI GONG FOR DEPRESSION
QI GONG FOR ENERGY AND VITALITY
QI GONG FOR HEADACHES
QI GONG FOR THE HEALTHY HEART
QI GONG FOR HEALTHY JOINTS
QI GONG FOR HIGH BLOOD PRESSURE
QIGONG FOR LONGEVITY
QI GONG FOR STRONG BONES
QI GONG FOR THE UPPER BACK AND NECK
QIGONG FOR WOMEN WITH DAISY LEE
QIGONG FLOW FOR STRESS & ANXIETY RELIEF
QIGONG MASSAGE
QIGONG MINDFULNESS IN MOTION
QI GONG—THE SEATED WORKOUT
QIGONG: 15 MINUTES TO HEALTH
SABER FUNDAMENTAL TRAINING
SAI TRAINING AND SEQUENCES
SANCHIN KATA: TRADITIONAL TRAINING FOR KARATE POWER
SCALING FORCE
SEARCHING FOR SUPERHUMANS
SHAOLIN KUNG FU FUNDAMENTAL TRAINING 1 & 2
SHAOLIN LONG FIST KUNG FU BEGINNER—INTERMEDIATE—ADVANCED SERIES
SHAOLIN SABER: BASIC SEQUENCES
SHAOLIN STAFF: BASIC SEQUENCES
SHAOLIN WHITE CRANE GONG FU BASIC TRAINING SERIES
SHUAI JIAO: KUNG FU WRESTLING
SIMPLE QIGONG EXERCISES FOR HEALTH
SIMPLE QIGONG EXERCISES FOR ARTHRITIS RELIEF
SIMPLE QIGONG EXERCISES FOR BACK PAIN RELIEF
SIMPLIFIED TAI CHI CHUAN: 24 & 48 POSTURES
SIMPLIFIED TAI CHI FOR BEGINNERS 48
SIX HEALING SOUNDS
SUN TAI CHI
SWORD: FUNDAMENTAL TRAINING
TAEKWONDO KORYO POOMSAE
TAI CHI BALL QIGONG SERIES
TAI CHI BALL WORKOUT FOR BEGINNERS
TAI CHI CHUAN CLASSICAL YANG STYLE
TAI CHI FIGHTING SET
TAI CHI FIT: 24 FORM
TAI CHI FIT: ALZHEIMER'S PREVENTION
TAI CHI FIT: CANCER PREVENTION
TAI CHI FIT FOR VETERANS
TAI CHI FIT: FOR WOMEN
TAI CHI FIT: FLOW
TAI CHI FIT: FUSION BAMBOO
TAI CHI FIT: FUSION FIRE
TAI CHI FIT: FUSION IRON
TAI CHI FIT: HEALTHY BACK SEATED WORKOUT
TAI CHI FIT: HEALTHY HEART WORKOUT
TAI CHI FIT IN PARADISE
TAI CHI FIT: OVER 50
TAI CHI FIT OVER 50: BALANCE EXERCISES
TAI CHI FIT OVER 50: SEATED WORKOUT
TAI CHI FIT OVER 60: GENTLE EXERCISES
TAI CHI FIT OVER 60: HEALTHY JOINTS
TAI CHI FIT OVER 60: LIVE LONGER
TAI CHI FIT: STRENGTH
TAI CHI FIT: TO GO
TAI CHI FOR WOMEN
TAI CHI FUSION: FIRE
TAI CHI QIGONG
TAI CHI PUSHING HANDS SERIES
TAI CHI SWORD: CLASSICAL YANG STYLE
TAI CHI SWORD FOR BEGINNERS
TAI CHI SYMBOL: YIN YANG STICKING HANDS
TAIJI & SHAOLIN STAFF: FUNDAMENTAL TRAINING
TAIJI CHIN NA IN-DEPTH
TAIJI 37 POSTURES MARTIAL APPLICATIONS
TAIJI SABER CLASSICAL YANG STYLE
TAIJI WRESTLING
TRAINING FOR SUDDEN VIOLENCE
UNDERSTANDING QIGONG SERIES
WATER STYLE FOR BEGINNERS
WHITE CRANE HARD & SOFT QIGONG
YANG TAI CHI FOR BEGINNERS
YOQI: MICROCOSMIC ORBIT QIGONG
YOQI QIGONG FOR A HAPPY HEART
YOQI:QIGONG FLOW FOR HAPPY MIND
YOQI:QIGONG FLOW FOR INTERNAL ALCHEMY
YOQI QIGONG FOR HAPPY SPLEEN & STOMACH
YOQI QIGONG FOR HAPPY KIDNEYS
YOQI QIGONG FLOW FOR HAPPY LUNGS
YOQI QIGONG FLOW FOR STRESS RELIEF
YOQI: QIGONG FLOW TO BOOST IMMUNE SYSTEM
YOQI SIX HEALING SOUNDS
YOQI: YIN YOGA 1
WU TAI CHI FOR BEGINNERS
WUDANG KUNG FU: FUNDAMENTAL TRAINING
WUDANG SWORD
WUDANG TAIJIQUAN
XINGYIQUAN
YANG TAI CHI FOR BEGINNERS

AND MANY MORE . . .

Printed in the USA
CPSIA information can be obtained
at www.ICGtesting.com
JSHW022324140824
68134JS00019B/1282